Partnership and Transformation

Over the last 30 years, partnership has received growing attention across a range of sectors and disciplines. Widely used to describe a relationship in which different actors pool their resources, knowledge and skills to address common problems, partnership is currently presented as central to the achievement of more inclusive and sustainable development. Rejecting "one size fits all" approaches, and mindful of different understandings of the term, *Partnership and Transformation: The Promise of Multi-stakeholder Collaboration in Context*, which is designed to appeal to both academics and practitioners alike, argues that partnership must be understood in relation to specific contexts and the added value it may offer for individuals, organisations and wider society. It is further suggested that the transformational potential of partnership rests critically upon a move away from purely instrumental considerations of its worth to a deeper appreciation of its intrinsic value as a process based on interpersonal relationships. A stronger balance between pragmatic and reflective dimensions of partnership can, the author claims, enhance opportunities for meaningful deliberation and productive conflict and contribute to the systems change needed for a global citizenship that embraces human well-being and stewardship of the planet.

Leda Stott is a specialist in multi-stakeholder collaboration, a partnership expert for the European Commission and an associate of the Innovation and Technology for Development Centre at the *Universidad Politécnica de Madrid*, Spain.

Citizenship and Sustainability in Organizations
Series Editors: David F. Murphy and Alison Marshall

Exploring how organizations and citizens respond to and influence current and future global transformations, this book series publishes excellent, innovative and critical scholarship in the fields of citizenship, social responsibility, sustainability, innovation, and place leadership in diverse organizational contexts. These contexts include commercial businesses, social enterprises, public service organizations, international organizations, faith-based organizations (FBOs), non-governmental organizations (NGOs), community groups, hybrids and cross-sector partnerships. The role of the individual as citizen may also be explored in relation to one or more of these contexts, as could formal or informal networks, clusters and organizational ecosystems.

The Intelligent Nation: How to Organise a Country
John Beckford

Knowledge Management and Sustainability
A Human-Centered Perspective on Research and Practice
Edited by David Israel Contreras-Medina, Julia Pérez Bravo and Elia Socorro Díaz Nieto

Corporate Citizenship and Family Business
Edited by Claire Seaman

Citizenship and Sustainability in Organizations
Exploring and Spanning the Boundaries
Edited by David F. Murphy and Alison Marshall

Partnership and Transformation
The Promise of Multi-stakeholder Collaboration in Context
Leda Stott

For more information about this series, please visit: www.routledge.com/Citizenship-and-Sustainability-in-Organizations/book-series/CSO

Partnership and Transformation

The Promise of Multi-stakeholder Collaboration in Context

Leda Stott

Routledge
Taylor & Francis Group
NEW YORK AND LONDON

First published 2023
by Routledge
605 Third Avenue, New York, NY 10158

and by Routledge
4 Park Square, Milton Park, Abingdon, Oxon, OX14 4RN

Routledge is an imprint of the Taylor & Francis Group, an informa business

British Library Cataloguing-in-Publication Data:
A catalogue record for this book is available from the British Library

Library of Congress Cataloging-in-Publication Data
Names: Stott, Leda, author.
Title: Partnership and transformation : the promise of multi-stakeholder collaboration in context / Leda Stott.
Description: New York, NY : Routledge, 2023. | Series: Citizenship and sustainability in organizations | Includes bibliographical references and index.
Identifiers: LCCN 2022025249 | ISBN 9781032058337 (hardback) | ISBN 9781032058344 (library binding) | ISBN 9781003199434 (ebook)
Subjects: LCSH: Strategic alliances (Business) | Partnership—Social aspects. | Public-private sector cooperation. | Organizational sociology.
Classification: LCC HD69.S8 S76 2023 | DDC 658/.044—dc23/eng/20220622
LC record available at https://lccn.loc.gov/2022025249

ISBN: 978-1-032-05833-7 (hbk)
ISBN: 978-1-032-05834-4 (pbk)
ISBN: 978-1-003-19943-4 (ebk)

DOI: 10.4324/9781003199434

For Manolo and Itayi

Contents

Author biography

Leda Stott is an international specialist in multi-stakeholder collaboration and sustainable development. Over the last 25 years, she has managed and conducted partnership research, training and evaluation activities with intergovernmental bodies, bilateral development agencies and a wide range of foundations, businesses and non-governmental organisations in different countries and regions. She has a PhD on the topic of partnership from the University of Edinburgh and has taught on this theme at universities in the UK, Spain, Norway and South Africa. She works as a partnership expert for the European Commission and is an associate of the Innovation and Technology for Development Centre at the *Universidad Politécnica de Madrid* in Spain and the Partnership Brokers Association.

Figures

Tables

Foreword

Everyone has their own experience with partnership. My first encounter with the language of partners and partnership came in the late 1980s when I was a field director for the Canadian international development NGO Cuso in West Africa. As part of Cuso's strategic planning process, I was asked by senior colleagues at the head office in Ottawa: *Who are your partners?* I remember being uncertain about how to respond. We didn't work with partners. We worked with people, communities, and local organizations. The rallying cry for our work around the world at the time was: *Our strength is people working together.* For me, this ethos continues to be the essence of partnership working and is congruent with the diversity of ideas, understandings, stories, and approaches explored in the following pages of this timely book *Partnership and Transformation* by Leda Stott, someone who I have known, admired, and worked closely with for almost 20 years.

Leda and I share roots in development cooperation in Africa, with Leda's initial experience being in Eastern and Southern Africa. This means that we were both introduced to African literature early on and gained insights and learning about other cultures, including the concepts of Ubuntu and African humanism. In my case, I first encountered Nigerian writers such as the novelist Chinua Achebe and the poet Gabriel Okara, who both helped me to understand the historical linkages between the British colonial system, postcolonial modernity, and Nigerian traditions, customs, and values. Later, the Senegalese poet, politician, and cultural theorist Léopold Sédar Senghor enabled me to appreciate the central importance of human relationships in African societies and how they can transform technical transactions in fields such as commerce and productive labour into more meaningful interactions based on cooperation, happiness, and respect.[1]

I first met Leda in 2005 at a partnership workshop in Slovakia for UN private sector program officers from across Central and Eastern Europe. Our subsequent extensive joint partnering capacity-building efforts with the UN

1. Senghor, L.S. (1976) *Prose and Poetry*, edited and translated by J. Reed and C. Wake, London, UK: Heinemann.

system and its partners enabled us to work with people and organizations engaged in different forms of multi-stakeholder collaboration around the world. We also were tutors together on the pioneering Postgraduate Certificate in Cross-sector Partnership at the University of Cambridge. More recently, we have collaborated on education and research activities via our respective current university affiliations in Cumbria and Madrid. Our shared development and partnering experiences have enabled us to become trusted and valued partners equally as practitioners and academics.

Part of the Routledge series "Citizenship and Sustainability in Organizations," *Partnership and Transformation* is a book that explores valuable ideas and perspectives about the meaning, potential, and transformative power of partnership in diverse contexts. Leda Stott offers a hopeful present-day story with a more optimistic lens on the future than many other contemporary writers. For example, while social psychologist Jonathan Haight notes that effective democracies are shaped by "social capital (extensive social networks with high levels of trust), strong institutions, and shared stories,"[2] his current view of America is a "story about the fragmentation of everything . . . the shattering of all that had seemed solid, the scattering of people who had been a community. It's a metaphor for what is happening not only *between* red and blue, but within the left and within the right, as well as within universities, companies, professional associations, museums, and even families."[3] Haight identifies social media platforms, primarily Facebook and Twitter, as the culprits that are driving and enabling these divisions, and while he sees some hope with the emergence of "groups and organizations dedicated to building trust and friendship across the political divide,"[4] his overriding conclusion is largely pessimistic. Haight's prognosis is bleak: "there is little evidence to suggest that America will return to some semblance of normalcy and stability in the next five or 10 years."[5] In a related vein, British journalist Johann Hari's book *Stolen Focus: Why you can't pay attention* shares the author's struggles with managing his use of social media and technology which he acknowledges is undermining his ability to focus – as (like many other social media users) Hari finds himself "on a treadmill of continuous checking."[6] While recognizing that virtual connections are increasingly useful for multi-stakeholder collaboration, Stott also implies that the proximity of face-to-face interaction is central to more positive partnership futures. The wise words of writers old and new on the importance of meaningful

2. Haight, J. (2022) After Babel: How social media dissolved the mortar of society and made America stupid. *The Atlantic*, May, 329 (4): 54–66 (pp. 56–57). www.theatlantic.com/magazine/archive/2022/05/social-media-democracy-trust-babel/629369/
3. Ibid., p. 56.
4. Ibid., p. 66.
5. Ibid.
6. Hari, J. (2022) *Stolen Focus: Why You Can't Pay Attention*, Kindle Edition, London, UK: Bloomsbury Publishing (p. 130).

human exchange are used to reinforce her call to collaborative action and the associated possibilities of socio-ecological transformation.

Returning to my opening story about encountering partnership for the first time, I was curious about where the idea of partnership currently fits in Cuso's external messaging. So, I had a look at my former employer's website to see what I might find more than 35 years after my initial discovery of partnership language in a development context. I learned that partnership is one of the core values that drive the organization's work and is elaborated as follows: "We believe in the power of people. We employ a people-centred approach to development and the challenge of overcoming poverty and inequality."[7] Cuso then and now was and is about relationships between people: staff, volunteers, counterparts, community workers, and indeed representatives of a wide variety of organizational partners. This is what Leda Stott's book *Partnership and Transformation* is ultimately about – how mutually beneficial human relationships can unleash the power of engaged citizens, enable positive change in people's lives, and ultimately "achieve a better and more sustainable future for all."[8]

David F. Murphy
Series Editor, Citizenship and Sustainability in Organizations
Associate Professor of Sustainability and Collaborative Leadership
Academic Lead, Initiative for Leadership and Sustainability (IFLAS)
Institute of Business, Industry and Leadership
University of Cumbria, United Kingdom

7. See https://cusointernational.org/about-us/ (Accessed May 1, 2022).
8. See www.un.org/sustainabledevelopment/sustainable-development-goals/ (Accessed May 1, 2022).

Acknowledgements

This book would not have been possible without the generosity of those who have shared their partnership stories with me over the years. I am grateful to them and to the various research and practitioner teams with whom I have worked to compile and present these accounts in a manner that is conducive to learning.

I owe a huge debt to David F. Murphy for his support in the writing of this book and to Neil Thin, who supervised the PhD thesis upon which it is based and encouraged me to think about partnership from fresh perspectives. I am also grateful to my wonderful friends, Ken Caplan and Anette Scoppetta, whose insights have been invaluable to my work.

Among other colleagues and friends who have influenced my thinking on partnership and collaboration, I would particularly like to thank Paloma Andrés, Bulbul Baksi, Maria Bobenrieth, Herman Brouwer, Eva Curto, Gonzalo Delacámara, Oliver Escobar, Almaz Fiseha, Stan Hardman, Martin Kalungu-Banda, Tracey Keatman, Leonardo Martins, Carlos Mataix, Javier Mazorra, Caroline Meyers, Jaime Moreno, Maria Muenchenbach, Maria-Anna Paraskeva, Stella Pfisterer, Maria Prandi, Ruth Pritchard, Melanie Rein, Bettina Reuter, David Sanderson, Ros Tennyson, Helga van Kampen, Rob van Tulder, Marieke de Wal, Benedict Wauters and Kavwanga Yambayamba.

As well as those aforementioned, additional thanks go to the associates, staff and students I have worked with over the years at Building Partnerships for Development in Water and Sanitation; the Cambridge Programme for Industry; the *Escuela de Organización Industrial*; the European Commission and European Social Fund networks on partnership; the Innovation and Technology for Development Centre at the *Universidad Politécnica de Madrid*; Oxford Brookes University; The Partnering Initiative; the Partnership Brokers Association; Partnership Learning Loop; Partnerships in Practice and the Partnerships Resource Centre at the Rotterdam School of Management.

Last but not least, a huge thank you to Manolo and Itayi for their unending support.

The author and publishers are grateful to the following organisations for permission to use their materials in this book: Building Partnerships for Development in Water and Sanitation; the Innovation and Technology for Development Centre at the *Universidad Politécnica de Madrid*; The Partnering Initiative and the European Commission.

Acronyms and abbreviations

AECID	*Agencia Española de Cooperación Internacional para el Desarrollo* (Spanish Agency for International Cooperation and Development)
AMP	*Acciona Microenergía Perú*
BEE	Black Economic Empowerment (South Africa)
BPD	Building Partnerships for Development in Water and Sanitation
CLLD	Community-led local development
CN	Collaborative network
CNO	Collaborative networked organisation
CoP	Community of practice
CPI	Cambridge Programme for Industry
CSO	Civil society organisation
CSR	Corporate Social Responsibility
CU	Copperbelt University (Zambia)
DANIDA	Danish International Development Agency
DFID	Department for International Development (UK)
EC	European Commission
ECCP	European Code of Conduct on Partnership
EC-PREP	European Community Poverty Reduction Effectiveness Programme
EDD	*El Día Después* (The Day After) Initiative
ERDF	European Regional and Development Fund
ESF	European Social Fund
ESIF	European Structural and Investment Funds
EU	European Union
EWS	eThekwini Water and Sanitation (South Africa)
FAO	Food and Agriculture Organisation
FUNDAME	*Fundación Acciona Microenergía* (Acciona Microenergy Foundation)
gFSC	global Food Security Cluster
GIZ	*Deutsche Gesellschaft für Internationale Zusammenarbeit* (German Society for International Cooperation)

GPEDC	Global Partnership for Effective Development Cooperation
gsub	*Gesellschaft für soziale Unternehmensberatung mbH* (Society for Social Management Consulting)
IBLF	International Business Leaders Forum
ICT	Information and communications technology
INGO	International non-governmental organisation
INR	Institute of Natural Resources (South Africa)
itdUPM	Innovation and Technology for Development Centre, *Universidad Politécnica de Madrid* (Spain)
LDC	Local Development Company (Ireland)
MDG	Millennium Development Goal
MIF-IDB	Multilateral Investment Fund/Inter-American Development Bank
MSD	Multi-stakeholder dialogue
MSP	Multi-stakeholder platform
NEPAD	New Partnership for Africa's Development
NGO	Non-governmental organisation
NPM	New Public Management
ODA	Overseas Development Assistance
PBA	Partnership Brokers Association
PLL	Partnership Learning Loop
PPP	Public-private partnership
PrC	Partnerships Resource Centre
PTN	Thematic Network on Partnership (ESF)
SASA	South African Sugar Association
SDG	Sustainable Development Goal
SFP	Structural Fund Partnership
SHS	Solar Home System
SMME	Small, medium and micro enterprise
SPDC	Shell Petroleum Development Company (Nigeria)
TEP	Territorial Employment Pact
TPI	The Partnering Initiative
UKZN	University of KwaZulu-Natal
UN	United Nations
UNAIDS	Joint United Nations Programme on HIV/AIDS
UN DESA	United Nations Department of Economic and Social Affairs
UNDP	United Nations Development Programme
UNZA	University of Zambia
VSO	Voluntary Service Overseas
WASH	Water, sanitation and hygiene
WFP	World Food Programme
WSSD	World Summit on Sustainable Development
ZBCA	Zambia Business Coalition on HIV/AIDS

Introduction

Some years ago, on the way to a conference, a taxi driver asked me about the focus of the event. "It's about partnership," I replied, rummaging through a folder with the joining instructions. "Ah," he said, knowingly, "so you work in marriage guidance." Amused at the time, I now recall this anecdote as a useful reminder that people have very different views on what partnership is or might be. My PhD supervisor warned me about this when I submitted my first research proposal on the topic. Urging caution in my assumptions about how people use the label of partnership, he reminded me of the many concepts and evaluative stances related to it, and the effects of different usages. Mindful of his advice, this book, which is based on my doctoral thesis, is centred upon the premise that partnership must be understood in relation to practice and the particular context in which it is being applied.

Because the concept of partnership encompasses such a diverse range of perspectives and transcends so many different domains and settings, contextualising it is not an easy task. Most dictionary definitions of partnership relate to a state of being married or living together, or to a joint business venture. However, the term is now widely used to describe collaborative relationships that pool the resources of different societal actors in order to address an issue or a challenge that would be difficult to tackle alone. Such arrangements may take place between countries and regions, sectors and disciplines, organisations and their representatives, and between citizens themselves.[1] The aims of these connections are equally broad, ranging from tasks with technical purposes such as the building of infrastructure or the provision of a service to loftier goals such as poverty eradication, improved environmental governance and, perhaps more controversially, economic growth.[2] More recently, partnership has been posited as an important way of addressing complex, global or "wicked" problems such as climate disruption

1. United Nations (2012) The future we want, *Outcome document of the Rio+20 UN Conference on Sustainable Development, A/CONF.216/L.1*, Rio de Janeiro, Brazil: United Nations.
2. Rein, M. and Stott, L. (2009) "Working together": Critical perspectives on six cross-sector partnerships in Southern Africa. *Journal of Business Ethics*, 90: 79–89. doi.org/10.1007/s10551-008-9915-9

DOI: 10.4324/9781003199434-1

and social inequality, and central to the transformation necessary for the achievement of inclusive and sustainable development.[3]

In her book, *Mission Economy, A Moonshot Guide to Changing Capitalism*, the economist Mariana Mazzucato argues that attaining a more inclusive and sustainable future will necessarily involve substituting "the fashionable, bland terminology of 'partnership' with clearer metrics as to what a symbiotic and mutualistic ecosystem looks like."[4] While this demand is to be applauded, defining partnership more succinctly is not as straightforward as it sounds. Although the conceptualisation of partnership as an instrument for tackling a common problem has become prevalent, it can also be understood in other ways. As well as a structure or entity, for example, partnership is regarded by many as a process of "working together"[5] in which attention is paid to the manner in which different parties connect and build relationships. Another perspective is offered by those who see partnership as a manifestation of the human longing for "togetherness and interaction";[6] a vision that builds upon notions of an innate capacity for cooperation that incorporates values such as mutuality and reciprocity.[7] This mix of collaborative structures, processes and values indicates that partnership may be construed as a form of multi-stakeholder collaboration which embraces traits that are both pragmatic and reflective in nature. Indeed, at the level of practice, a growing body of research work suggests that though clearly not a magic bullet, partnership arrangements that balance these different dimensions can offer important, and sometimes unique, avenues for developing solutions to local, national and regional challenges.

Though the facility of partnership to embrace varied perspectives is problematic for those seeking a precise definition of the term, this ambiguity has usefully served its incorporation into diverse policy frameworks and political discourses.[8] While partnership has been lauded by some as a new and

3. See Tulder, R. van (2018) *Business and the Sustainable Development Goals: A Framework for Effective Corporate Involvement*, Rotterdam, the Netherlands: Rotterdam School of Management, Erasmus University; Tulder, R. van and van Mil, E. (2018) *Part II: The SDGs as 'Wicked Problems': Who Should Address What?* Rotterdam, the Netherlands: Rotterdam School of Management, Erasmus University and see also: United Nations (2015) *Transforming Our World: The 2030 Agenda for Sustainable Development*; Resolution 70/1 Adopted by the United Nations General Assembly on 25 September 2015; New York, NY, USA: United Nations.
4. Mazzucato, M. (2021) *Mission Economy: A Moonshot Guide to Changing Capitalism*, London, UK: Allen Lane (p. 8).
5. Rein, M., Stott, L., Yambayamba, E., Hardman, S. and Reid, S. (2005) *Working Together: A Critical Analysis of Cross-Sector Partnerships in Southern Africa*, Cambridge, UK: University of Cambridge Programme for Industry.
6. Bregman, R. (2020) *Humankind: A Hopeful History*, London, UK: Bloomsbury Publishing (p. 72).
7. See: Sennett, R. (2013) *Together: The Rituals, Pleasures and Politics of Cooperation*, London, UK: Penguin Books and Eisler, R. (2015) Human possibilities: The interaction of biology and culture. *Interdisciplinary Journal of Partnership Studies*, 1: 1–39. doi:10.24926/ijps.v1i1.88
8. Cornwall, A. and Eade, D. eds. (2010) *Deconstructing Development Discourse, Buzzwords and Fuzzwords*, Rugby, UK: Oxfam GB and Practical Action Publishing Ltd.

innovative type of governance and "one of our greatest hopes for meeting, together, the challenges of the twenty-first century,"[9] others have expressed concern about the positioning of partnership as a "development panacea."[10] For a number of critics, the loose nature of the concept masks dynamics of power in which "partners" such as multinational corporations, international development agencies and English-speaking "northern experts" engage on unequal terms with "southern" or local stakeholders.[11] The link between partnership and the corporate sector, and a perception that "neoliberal common sense is inscribed in the rules of the partnership game" have been highlighted as particularly problematic.[12]

Partnership, then, may be seen as a progressive force that promotes avenues for joint problem-solving and the integration of different interests in governance systems and, conversely, as undermining democracy by moving political decision-making away from elected to non-elected actors such as the private sector.[13] The coexistence of these contending stances is manifested starkly in the United Nations (UN) 2030 Sustainable Development Agenda in which partnership is positioned as vital to the systems change required for meeting the economic, social and environmental targets of its 17 Sustainable Development Goals (SDGs), as well as a more standard vehicle for "developed" countries to support "developing" countries using a combination of increased overseas aid and approaches that focus on the promotion of economic growth, recipes that can hardly be described as transformational.[14]

Given these differing viewpoints, and in the interests of probing the extent to which partnership may assist transformation towards a more sustainable and inclusive world, a deeper critical exploration of its ends and means is justified. Acknowledging Richard Sennett's maxim that "shedding context often means shedding sense,"[15] both the concept of partnership *and* its potential for transformation are examined here in relation to particular and changing contextual experiences. By exploring how partnership is understood and applied in situ, and with what hopes and intentions, the

9. Nelson, J. (2002) *Building Partnerships, Cooperation Between the United Nations System and the Private Sector*, New York, NY, USA: United Nations (p. 7).
10. See Rein et al. (2005) Op. cit. p. 11.
11. Eade, D. *Preface* in Cornwall, A. and Eade, D. eds. (2010) Op. cit. p. viii.
12. Davies, J.S. (2008) Against "partnership": Toward a local challenge to global neoliberalism. In: Gross. J. and Hambleton, R. eds. *Governing Cities in the Global Era*, Basingstoke, UK: Palgrave Macmillan, 199–210 (p. 201).
13. For more on these debates, see Davies (2008) Ibid.; Gold, M., Cressey, P. and Leonard, E. (2007) Whatever happened to social dialogue? From partnership to managerialism in the EU Employment Agenda. *European Journal of Industrial Relations*, 13 (1): 7–25 and Utting, P. and Zammit, A. (2009) United Nations-Business partnerships: Good intentions and contradictory agendas. *Journal of Business Ethics*, 90: 39–56. https://doi.org/10.1007/s10551-008-9917-7.
14. United Nations (2015) Op. cit.
15. Sennett (2013) Op. cit. p. 28.

transformational promise of partnership is considered with regard to how far it might add value for individuals, organisations and society in different contexts.

This inquiry suggests that to achieve "good change"[16] that embraces human development, well-being and environmental sustainability with notions of social justice and the promotion of equal rights and opportunities for all citizens, we need "deep shifts in the ways people and organisations behave and organise values and perceive their place in the world."[17] These shifts may be assisted by contextually embedded partnership arrangements that provide opportunities for critical reflection and meaningful or "dialogic" deliberation.[18] More crucially, they rest upon a renewed conceptualisation of partnership that transcends "conventional categories"[19] and a purely instrumental assessment of its worth in order to reconnect with the relational and reflective aspects that are at its heart.

Chapter 1 provides an overview of the evidence base used in this book. As well as drawing from a variety of academic and practitioner materials, the main findings are derived from three research programmes that critically explore diverse forms of partnership. Addressing a variety of themes, these studies were carried out at different points in time in countries in Africa, Europe and Latin America. The use of such a broad range of examples is intentional and designed to assist understandings of partnership in distinct contexts. More critically, as well as organisational and structural relationships, attention is paid to the individual, relational and process dimensions that these initiatives involve which are presented as integral to any investigation of the transformational potential of partnership.

The malleable conceptualisation of partnership and the difficulty in pinning it down is the subject of Chapter 2 of this book. Calls for greater precision on what partnership means and how it works are explored in relation to its use in different geographical, sectoral and organisational settings. Here, a distinction is made between notions of partnership as a structure and a process, as a means to an end and an end in itself, and as a relationship based on values. Recognising that partnership is not new and that cooperation is "written into who we are,"[20] a brief historical analysis examines how and why an instrumental view of partnership has become so prevalent, particularly in relation to a narrative that links partnership to private sector engagement and the culture and practice of managerialism. The chapter concludes

16. Chambers, R. (1995) Poverty and livelihoods: Whose reality counts? *Environment and Urbanization*, 7 (1): 173–204. doi:10.1177/095624789500700106 (p. 196).
17. Pelling, M. (2011) *Adaptation to Climate Change: From Resilience to Transformation*, London, UK, and New York, NY, USA: Routledge, Taylor and Francis.
18. Sennett (2013) Op. cit. p. 14.
19. Eisler, R. (2002) *The Power of Partnership: Seven Relationships That Will Change Your Life*, Novato, CA, USA: New World Library (p. xxi).
20. Leadbeater, C. (2012) *It's Co-Operation, Stupid, Why Richard Dawkins, Thomas Hobbes and Milton Friedman Got It Wrong*, London, UK: Institute for Public Policy Research (p. 9).

by exploring some of the different reasons given by partnership practitioners for choosing to work in partnership. Eschewing narrow interpretations of the term, these motivations for engaging in multi-stakeholder collaboration suggest a rich blend of instrumental, intrinsic and relational elements.

Chapter 3 of the book examines the meaning and value of partnership by engaging with the "chemistry" of frontline perspectives.[21] This chemistry is derived from the historical, geographical, political and social circumstances of the particular settings in which partnership initiatives operate; the nature of the stakeholders involved and the organisational and individual relationships that inform them. The drivers for working in partnership and the interaction between these levels are explored using examples from different partnership arrangements. The chapter concludes with a proposal for combining instrumental and extrinsic drivers for partnership with drivers that are integrative and intrinsic. Grouped under the banners of "pragmatic" and "reflective," the assumption is that a balance between these two sets of drivers is needed to maximise the impact of collaborative initiatives and their ability to promote systemic change.

As well as exploring how partnership is understood and applied in different contexts, attention is paid in this book to how far it is delivering on its promises of change. In view of the increasingly ambitious aspirations for partnership, closer scrutiny of whether it is meeting expectations is essential. However, to do this, more clarity is required on what the desired ends of different partnership arrangements are. Indeed, the elusiveness of partnership is compounded by the fuzzy nature of many of the goals that it is ostensibly working towards, including the target of "transformation" that is central to much recent discussion on partnership and highlighted in the UN's 2030 Sustainable Development agenda.[22]

The growing interest in the role that partnership might play in promoting transformation and systems change has led a number of writers to differentiate between "transactional partnership," in which partners exchange limited resources for specific activities, and "transformational partnership" which uses distinctive partner contributions to co-create sustainable societal, organisational and individual value.[23] It is these latter relationships that are

21. El Ansari, W., Phillips, C.J. and Hammick, M. (2001) Collaboration and partnerships: Developing the evidence base. *Health and Social Care in the Community*, 9 (4): 215–227. doi.org/10.1046/j.0966-0410.2001.00299.x (p. 218).

22. See, for example, Sachs, J.D., Schmidt-Traub, G., Mazzucato, M., Messner, D., Nakicenovic, N. and Rockström, J. (2019) Six transformations to achieve the sustainable development goals. *Nature Sustainability*, 2: 805–814 and Temper, L., Walter, M., Rodriguez, I., Kothari, A. and Turhan, E. (2018) A perspective on radical transformations to sustainability: Resistances, movements and alternatives. *Sustainability Science*, 13: 747–764. doi.org/10.1007/s11625-018-0543-8

23. See, for example, Austin, J. and Seitanidi, M.M. (2012) Collaborative value creation: A review of partnering between nonprofits and businesses: Part I. Value creation spectrum and collaboration stages. *Nonprofit and Voluntary Sector Quarterly*, 41 (5): 726–758. https://doi.org/10.1177%2F0899764012450777 and Gray, B. and Stites, J.P. (2013) *Sustainability Through Partnerships: Capitalizing on Collaboration*, Canada: Network for Business Sustainability.

seen as having the greatest possibility for achieving the targets of the SDGs. A deeper exploration of the attributes of transformational partnership and how it may be distinguished from other forms of partnership thus seems warranted. Chapter 4 begins with a short analysis of what transformation means in a partnership context with consideration of the depth of change that it seeks. The potential of partnership to transform is then examined in relation to how and where it might generate added value for individuals, organisations and society as a whole. The attributes of transformational partnership arrangements, the extent to which they combine both pragmatic and reflective elements, and how they compare with other collaborative connections are examined using a framework that builds upon existing transactional–transformational partnership continuums.

Chapter 5 explores how far meaningful change may be achieved through transformative participation in partnership arrangements in particular contexts. Here, in line with Amartya Sen's contention that, as well as needs, people "also have values, and, in particular, they cherish their ability to reason, appraise, act and participate,"[24] emphasis is placed on studying different kinds of stakeholder participation and related power dynamics. Findings from a selection of practices suggest that partnership can both promote and embody transformation when participation is embedded in particular contexts, carefully facilitated by partnership brokers or conveners, and based upon open-ended dialogue processes that seek to comprehend and work with different points of view.

In order to provide an overview of the evolving collaborative landscape in which partnership is situated and insights into how far it is likely to pursue a transformational direction going forwards, some examples of new and emerging multi-stakeholder approaches and constructs are shared in Chapter 6. These collaborative forms, which include dialogues, consortia, platforms and networks as well as processes such as co-creation and co-production, are examined in relation to their attention to systemic issues and the nature of stakeholder participation and facilitation processes.

As this book sits within a series on sustainability and citizenship, these terms and their link to partnership also deserve some scrutiny. The final chapter thus reflects on how attributes of transformational partnership may be linked to a "global citizenship" that embraces human well-being and stewardship of the planet. The advancement of this kind of citizenship rests upon forms of multi-stakeholder collaboration that better balance its pragmatic and reflective elements by promoting nexus approaches for sustainability that cut across different domains and levels; encouraging an overarching partnership "metagovernance" that facilitates as well as steers, and making use of deliberative decision-making processes that embrace diversity.

24. Sen, A. (2004) Why we should preserve the spotted owl. *London Review of Books*, 26 (3) (p. 5).

Because partnership is built upon the interaction between people and organisations from different situations and backgrounds, an acceptance of diversity is at its heart. In his writing on *The Other*, the Polish journalist, Ryszard Kapuściński, suggests that while humans may elect to fight or to isolate themselves when confronted with those who are different from themselves, they also have another choice: cooperation. Kapuściński positions cooperation at the heart of human experience and manifested in historical connections of teaching, travelling and trading in which people "exchanged thoughts, ideas and goods, traded and did business, made alliances and unions, found common aims and values."[25] This deep-seated relational connection underscores the dynamic interplay between people, process and place that sits at the core of transformational partnership arrangements. Through meaningful exchange and "productive conflict"[26] between individuals and organisations with diverse backgrounds, perspectives, beliefs and attitudes, multi-stakeholder collaboration can provide opportunities for "hot-housing social change."[27] It is here, in the generation of ideas and approaches that are brave, innovative and even revolutionary, that the promise of partnership may be fulfilled.

25. Kapuściński, R. (2018) *The Other*, London, UK: Verso (pp. 81–82).
26. Poncelet, E.C. (2001) A kiss here and a kiss there: Conflict and collaboration in environmental partnerships. *Environmental Management*, 27 (1): 13–25. http://dx.doi.org/10.1007/s002670010130 (p. 23).
27. Hastings, A. (1999) Analysing power relations in partnerships: Is there a role for discourse analysis? *Urban Studies*, 36 (1): 91–106. http://dx.doi.org/10.1080/0042098993754 (p. 93).

1 Setting the scene

In an article that explores the challenges involved in assessing the evidence for effective collaboration, Walid El-Ansari and his colleagues note that an appreciation of context is crucial.[1] Drawing upon their experience of evaluating community partnerships in the healthcare field in South Africa, and with a focus on ensuring that the evidence gathered is of practical use, they emphasise the importance of understanding how a collaborative initiative works in a *specific situation* so that its "chemistry" can be revealed.[2]

This observation resonates with the central argument of this book: that partnership and its potential for transformation must be understood in relation to particular and changing contexts. This is not an academic exercise. In view of the hopes invested in collaborative solutions to address pressing economic, social and environmental challenges, the evidence derived from assessments of partnership must be suitable for real-life application. To do this, honest appraisals of partnership in situ are required, the lessons from which can be shared with others.

Rather than seeking to rigidly define and classify partnership, the underlying premise here is that a broader understanding of the concept can be obtained by exploring "multiple realities" through different viewpoints and forms of knowledge.[3] This "discourse analysis" approach focuses on understanding partnership in relation to specific historical, social and cultural contexts.[4] The use of such a methodology can enable inquiries into why, how and where partnership is used by individuals and organisations to solve problems, what other concepts may be linked to it and how this influences relationships, strategies and activities.

1. El Ansari, W., Phillips, C.J. and Hammick, M. (2001) Collaboration and partnerships: Developing the evidence base. *Health and Social Care in the Community*, 9 (4): 215–227. doi.org/10.1046/j.0966–0410.2001.00299.x (p. 218).
2. Ibid.
3. Jørgensen, M. and Phillips, L. (2002) *Discourse Analysis as Theory and Method*, London, UK: Sage Publications (p. 4) and Wiggins, S. (2009) Discourse analysis. In: Reis, H.T. and Sprecher, S. eds. *Encyclopedia of Human Relationships*, London, UK: Sage, pp. 427–430 (p. 428).
4. Phillips, N. and Hardy, C. (2002) *Discourse Analysis: Investigating Processes of Social Construction*, London, UK: Sage (p. 4).

DOI: 10.4324/9781003199434-2

To assist a deeper understanding of partnership in context, this book draws upon findings from a selection of research programmes with which I have been involved as well as wider literature relating to multi-stakeholder collaboration. In order to enhance analysis and to draw more fully upon the untapped reservoir of materials relating to partnership in specific subject areas, a combination of both academic and practitioner sources has been used. It should be noted, however, that gathering and collating relevant information is complicated by the fragmented nature of partnership literature. In the academic arena, for example, resources on partnership straddle a vast range of disciplines and fields,[5] while "grey literature" on partnership covers an overwhelming variety of materials produced by partnership practitioners including reports, newsletters and presentations. As a result, although every effort has been made to draw from as wide a reference base as possible, many valuable sources are likely to have been missed.

The bulk of the illustrative material used here comes from three research studies that explored partnership arrangements in different countries in Africa, Europe and Latin America. These investigations, which aimed to critically examine collaborative processes and activities through diverse stakeholder perspectives,[6] are outlined in detail in a Case Study Map (Table 1.1). They include the following:

- Six case studies from Southern Africa which formed part of the research study *A Critical Analysis of Cross Sector Partnerships in Southern Africa – Do they work and are there identifiable patterns of good practice?* The study, which explored partnership arrangements in South Africa and Zambia in the fields of agriculture, education and health, was undertaken between 2003 and 2005 as part of the European Community's Poverty Reduction Effectiveness Programme (EC-PREP), a partnership between the European Commission and the UK Department for International Development (DFID).[7]

5. See: Dorado, S., Giles Jr., D.E. and Welch, T.C. (2009) Delegation of coordination and outcomes in cross-sector partnerships: The case of service learning partnerships. *Nonprofit and Voluntary Sector Quarterly*, 38: 368–391. doi.org/10.1177%2F0899764008316055 (p. 370); El Ansari, W., Phillips, C. J. and Hammick, M. (2001) Collaboration and partnerships: Developing the evidence base. *Health and Social Care in the Community*, 9 (4): 215–227. doi.org/10.1046/j.0966-0410.2001.00299.x (p. 217) and Lotia, N. and Hardy, C. (2008) Critical perspectives on collaboration. In: Cropper, S., Huxham, C., Ebers, M. and Smith Ring, P. eds. *The Oxford Handbook of Inter-Organizational Relations*, Oxford, UK: Oxford University Press. [Online] 1–28 (p. 3). www.oxfordhandbooks.com (accessed August 9, 2021).
6. Stott, L. (2006) Partnership case studies in context. *Research Paper*, London, UK: The Partnering Initiative (p. 3).
7. See Rein, M., Stott, L., Yambayamba, E., Hardman, S. and Reid, S. (2005) *Working Together: A Critical Analysis of Cross-Sector Partnerships in Southern Africa*, Cambridge, UK: University of Cambridge Programme for Industry and Rein, M. and Stott, L. (2009) Working together: Critical perspectives on six cross-sector partnerships in Southern Africa. *Journal of Business Ethics*, 90 (1): 79–89 https://doi.org/10.1007/s10551-008-9915-9

- Lessons from partnership practices and peer reviews in different European Union (EU) Member States as part of the work of the European Social Fund (ESF) Community of Practice on Partnership (2007–11) and the ESF Transnational Platform's Thematic Network on Partnership (2015–19).[8]
- Five case studies from a research initiative conducted between 2013 and 2014 for the Multilateral Investment Fund, a member of the Inter-American Development Bank (MIF-IDB), and the Innovation for Technology and Development Centre at the *Universidad Politécnica de Madrid* (itdUPM), which looked at innovative partnership arrangements for delivering basic services to marginalised populations in Bolivia, Guatemala and Peru, alongside a comparative study from South Africa.[9]

In contrast to much existing literature which has tended to explore the concept of partnership in relation to a specific theme, sector or academic discipline, partnership is here examined across different domains and settings. While presenting a more multidimensional view of partnership, a major challenge of this approach is that it is difficult to circumscribe such a diverse set of examples. The cases selected involve a variety of sectors, organisations and individuals from different geographical and spatial levels. They include partnership arrangements that focus on access and improvements to basic services such as education, health, energy, water and sanitation, initiatives that seek to strengthen organisational skills and capacity and others that focus on high-level policy changes relating to employment, social inclusion and sustainable development. They also encompass conceptions of partnership as a structural form, as a process of working together and as a relationship based on collaborative values.

8. See: Stott, L. (2008) *How European Social Fund Managing Authorities and Intermediate Bodies Support Partnership*, Brussels, Belgium: European Commission; Stott, L. (2012) *Partnership Learning Manual*, Vienna, Austria: Federal Ministry of Labour, Social Affairs and Consumer Protection (BMASK) and Centre for Social Innovation (ZSI); Stott, L. (2019) *How European Social Fund Managing Authorities and Intermediate Bodies Support Partnership*, Revised edition, Brussels, Belgium: European Commission and Stott, L. and Scoppetta A. (2013) Promoting local economic development through partnerships in Europe. *Skills@Work: Theory and Practice Journal*, 6: 2–12.
9. See Stott, L. (2014) *Partnerships for Innovation in Access to Basic Services*, Washington, DC, USA: Multilateral Investment Fund/Inter-American Development Bank (MIF/IDB) and Madrid, Spain: Innovation and Technology Centre for Human Development/*Universidad Politécnica de Madrid* (itdUPM); Egido, M.A. (2014) *Luz en Casa*: Access to sustainable energy in rural communities in Peru; Keatman, T. (2014) Innovative partnerships in access to water and sanitation: Equitable services in the Municipality of eThekwini, South Africa; Lumbreras, J. and Fernández, L. (2014) Comprehensive solid waste management: The *Ciudad Saludable* model in Peru; Martínez, A. (2014) eHealth in rural areas: Access to medical care, training and prevention in Guatemala, and: Sánchez, E. and Moreno, J. (2014) Inclusive sanitation markets: Sustainable solutions in peri-urban areas of Bolivia. In: *Partnerships for Innovation in Access to Basic Services Case Study*, Washington, DC, USA: Multilateral Investment Fund/Inter-American Development Bank (MIF/IDB) and Madrid, Spain: Innovation and Technology for Development Centre/*Universidad Politécnica de Madrid* (itdUPM).

While it would clearly be helpful to categorise these different arrangements in some way, because of the enormous range of forms that partnership may take, the quest to develop a comprehensive partnership typology is a challenging one.[10] Some of the classifications proposed for partnership include those based on the actors or sectors involved;[11] levels of operation;[12] partnership objectives and themes,[13] and governance structures.[14] Although these groupings provide interesting avenues for exploring partnership, the dynamic and constantly evolving nature of collaborative arrangements in different contexts makes them impossible to contain within static categories. As well as addressing diverse themes in different geographic locations, the case studies used here are spread chronologically and, as such, represent specific moments in partnership life cycles that are, in turn, subject to external and internal changes. Here, in addition to particular sociohistorical factors, organisational and individual relational and process dimensions influence the development of collaborative initiatives. These interconnecting variables also play an important role in determining the extent to which partnership initiatives might promote changes to systems, structures and ways of working.

Both case study and peer review methodologies were used in the three research programmes mentioned earlier. These approaches involved the use of qualitative research methods such as direct observation, semi-structured interviews, focus group discussions and stakeholder workshops in order to examine factors such as:

- The operational context in which the partnership initiative was situated
- The institutional and regulatory framework of the particular theme/s addressed
- The history and rationale for the partnership arrangement
- Key actors and stakeholders and their incentives for engagement
- The nature of different partner resource contributions
- Governance structures and processes, including administration, financial, communication, review and mediation arrangements
- The evolution and development of the initiative, including innovative aspects, efforts to ensure accountability and participation as well as responses to changing internal and external circumstances

10. Stott, L. and Murphy, D.F. (2020) An inclusive approach to partnerships for the SDGs: Using a relationship lens to explore the potential for transformational collaboration. *Special Issue: Partnerships for the SDGs, Sustainability*, 12 (19): 7905. https://doi.org/10.3390/su12197905
11. Selsky, J.W. and Parker, B. (2005) Cross-sector partnerships to address social issues: Challenges to theory and practice. *Journal of Management,* 31: 849–873, doi: 10.1177/0149206305279601
12. Murphy, D.F. and Bendell, J. (1997) *In the Company of Partners: Business, Environmental Groups and Sustainable Development Post-Rio*, Bristol, UK: The Policy Press.
13. Kelly, L. and Roche, C. (2014) *Partnerships for Effective Development*, Canberra, Australia: Australian Council for International Development (ACFID).
14. Tennyson, R. (2012) Emerging models of development partnerships, what do partnership brokers need to know? *Thinking in Progress Paper*, London, UK: Partnership Brokers Association.

- Results and impact of working in partnership with consideration of its added value for partners, other stakeholders and wider society
- Provisions for learning and sharing from the experience of working together

These data were triangulated by drawing upon partnership documents, contextual reviews and academic sources. To further facilitate a rounded examination of partnership and enhance opportunities for mutual learning, the studies also involved lengthy participatory review processes in which research conclusions were deliberated upon by stakeholders in various iterations before completion.

Although, as noted earlier, there is no uniformity in the focus and location of the studies outlined, an action research methodology was used to explore them all. This form of research has been described as "research conducted *with* rather than *on* people" (my italics).[15] Here, the researcher assumes the role of a facilitator or "critical friend" who seeks to explore relationships by asking questions that encourage reflection and ongoing dialogue.[16] The expectation is that the learning derived from this process will promote a deeper understanding of the factors that contribute to the "chemistry" of partnership and generate pointers for action that can improve the quality of relationships, activities and impact.

15. Reason, P. and Heron, J. (2001) The practice of co-operative inquiry: Research with rather than on people. In: Reason, P. and Bradbury, H. eds. *Handbook of Action Research: Participative Inquiry and Practice*, London, UK: Sage Publications (p. 179).
16. Rossman, G. and Rallis, S. F. (2000) Dialogue for learning: Evaluator as a critical friend. *New Direction in Program Evaluation*, 31. https://scholarworks.umass.edu/cie_faculty_pubs/31; Bambino, D. (2002) Critical friends. *Educational Leadership*, 59 (6): 25–27. www.ascd.org/publications/educational-leadership/mar02/vol59/num06/Critical-Friends.aspx Costa, A.L. and Kallick, B. (1993) Through the lens of a critical friend. *Educational Leadership*, 51 (10): 49–51.

Table 1.1 Case Study Map

European Community's Poverty Reduction Effectiveness Programme (EC-PREP) – Southern Africa (2003–5)				
Name	***Aim***	***Initiator***	***Partners***	***How partnership was understood and promoted***
Agriculture (promoting small-scale farming)				
Chamba Valley Partnership Zambia	To increase the income of small-scale farmers by providing them with support from government and non-governmental organisations (NGOs) to cultivate quality local produce to supply a supermarket chain	Zambia Partnership Forum (NGO intermediary)	- Chamba Valley Cooperative Society - Shoprite Zambia (supermarket chain) - Freshmark (supplier to Shoprite) - Zambia Seed Company (Zamseed) - Ministry of Agriculture and Cooperatives	A mutually beneficial relationship to generate income for partners and create employment
Small-scale Sugarcane Farming Communities Partnership South Africa	To develop local livelihoods among small-scale sugarcane growers through engagement with government agencies and the sugar industry	South African Sugar Association (SASA)	- SASA - Large-scale cane growers - Small-scale cane growers cooperatives - Department of Agriculture and Environmental Affairs - District municipalities - Traditional leaders	- Way of promoting rural development and improvement in quality of life in areas growing sugarcane - Response to calls for business to address inequalities inherited from the apartheid era, e.g. in response to Black Economic Empowerment (BEE) regulations,[17] as well as national and international Corporate Social Responsibility (CSR) trends

(Continued)

17. Ponte, S., Roberts, S. and van Sittert, L. (2007) 'Black Economic Empowerment' (BEE), business and the state in South Africa. *Development and Change*, 38 (5): 933–955. doi: 10.1111/j.1467-7660.2007.00440.x

Table 1.1 (Continued)

Name	*Aim*	*Initiator*	*Partners*	*How partnership was understood and promoted*
Health (addressing HIV/AIDS)				
Amangwe Village South Africa	To promote a holistic healthcare centre to work with and for people living with HIV/AIDS	Zululand Chamber of Business Foundation	- Mondi - BHP Billiton Aluminium - Richards Bay Coal Terminal - Richards Bay Minerals - Departments of Welfare, Education and Health - Zululand Lifeline - Empangeni Justice Centre - Richards Bay Rotary Club	- Way of identifying new, innovative and coordinated opportunities for the business sector to address challenges relating to HIV/AIDS. - Lower productivity and loss of profits due to increased cases of HIV/AIDS among workforce encouraged businesses to work with government bodies and NGOs to share approaches for managing HIV/AIDS
Zambia Business Coalition on HIV/AIDS (ZBCA) Zambia	To link the private sector with NGOs and government agencies to tackle the HIV/AIDS pandemic	- BP Zambia Plc - Barclays Bank - Standard Chartered Bank - Zambia National Commercial Bank	54 companies and local NGOs such as Africare, Network of Zambian People living with HIV/AIDS and others	Response to push by UNAIDS to increase capacity to respond effectively to HIV/AIDS epidemic through partnership arrangements between government, civil society and the private sector
Education (improving higher education)				
Mthashana Further Education and Training College Partnership Programme South Africa	To develop partnership connections for learning and skills development in KwaZulu Natal	South African Government	- Mthashana Further Education and Training College - National Business Initiative (NBI) - Danish International Development Agency (DANIDA) - ZENEX Foundation	- Policy shift designed to improve development planning at municipal level and provide educational opportunities that integrated entrepreneurial thinking with skills as the basis for work competency, equity and growth - Partnership promoted by college staff as means of working more effectively with employers and wider community (learnerships)

Sharing Responsibility for Higher Education Partnership Zambia	To engage businesses in improving educational infrastructure and teaching conditions	Zambia Partnership Forum (NGO intermediary)	- University of Zambia - Copperbelt University - Barclays Bank of Zambia - BP Zambia Plc - Chilanga Cement Plc - NCC Phønix Contractors International - Nkumba Farms - Unilever SEA - ZESCO Ltd. - Zambia National Broadcasting Corporation - Ministry of Education	Way of working with partners, especially business, to address lack of resources needed for quality teaching and research
European Social Fund/European Commission (2007–19)				
European Social Fund (ESF)/ European Commission (EC)	To generate smart, sustainable and inclusive growth in the EU by creating more and better jobs, and a socially inclusive society	ESF Managing Authorities/ Intermediate Bodies in EU Member States	- Public authorities - Social partners (employer organisations and trade unions) - NGOs - Umbrella organisations - Academic institutions	The EU "partnership principle" is a **process** of multi-stakeholder engagement in decision-making which promotes broad collective commitment and ownership of quality programmes. Partnership is also used to describe **mechanisms** in which representatives of different sectors of society work together to address issues relating to unemployment and social exclusion. In these cases, partnerships are structures with specific aims, objectives and governance procedures, e.g. territorial pacts and local partnerships.
Examples of partnership structures				
Territorial Employment Pacts (TEPs) Austria (1999–2014)	To better link employment policy with other policies and improve employment at regional and local levels	Federal Ministry of Economics and Labour	- Labour Market Service - Federal Office of State Affairs - Chambers of Agriculture, Economy and Labour - Local NGOs - Gender mainstreaming experts - Provincial government - Federation of Industry - Federation of Trade Unions - Provincial school boards - Educational institutions - Municipalities	

(*Continued*)

Table 1.1 (Continued)

Name	***Aim***	***Initiator***	***Partners***	***How partnership was understood and promoted***
Local Development Companies (LDCs) Ireland	To work with communities in order to promote local economic development, equality and social inclusion	Department of Environment, Community and Local Government	Community, statutory and social partners	The partnership principle is positioned as a vehicle both for promoting democracy and for assisting policy coherence through alignment of objectives between different levels of governance. These elements were central to the Europe 2020 Growth Strategy[18] for achieving smart, sustainable and inclusive growth, to the European Semester coordination framework[19] and, later, to the European Pillar of Social Rights.[20]
Structural Fund Partnerships and cooperation projects Sweden	To link regional growth with labour market policies in the eight regions of Sweden and support cooperation projects addressing access to employment and social exclusion at national, regional and local levels	Swedish ESF and European Regional and Development Fund (ERDF) Councils	Politicians and other stakeholders at national, regional and local levels	

18. European Commission (2010) *Europe 2020: A Strategy for Smart, Sustainable and Inclusive Growth*, Brussels. http://ec.europa.eu/eu2020/pdf/COMPLET%20EN%20BARROSO%20%20%20007%20-%20Europe%202020%20-%20EN%20version.pdf (accessed March 19, 2022).
19. The European Semester: https://ec.europa.eu/info/business-economy-euro/economic-and-fiscal-policy-coordination/eu-economic-governance-monitoring-prevention-correction/european-semester/framework/europe-2020-strategy_en (accessed March 19, 2022).
20. The European Pillar of Social Rights: https://ec.europa.eu/info/strategy/priorities-2019-2024/economy-works-people/jobs-growth-and-investment/european-pillar-social-rights_en (accessed March 19, 2022).

T model partnerships Germany	To establish horizontal partnerships at federal level to ensure joint planning and delivery, as well as vertical multi-level partnerships (initiated at federal level but addressing regional and local issues)	Federal ministries	- Social partners - Voluntary welfare organisations - NGOs	Recognition of the importance of the partnership principle for the European Social Fund was manifested in the Council Regulation (EC) No. 1083/2006[21] and the Common Provisions Regulation for European Structural and Investment Funds (ESIF), including the ESF (EU Regulation No. 1303/2013).[22] In 2014, the European Code of Conduct on Partnership (ECCP)[23] further provided common standards for partner involvement in Partnership Agreements and Operational Programmes supported by ESIF.

(*Continued*)

21. Regulation (EC) No. 1083/2006 of the European Parliament and of the Council of 11 July 2006 on the European Social Fund and repealing Regulation (EC) No. 1260/1999, *Official Journal of the European Union*, L 210, 49, July 31, 2006. https://eur-lex.europa.eu/legal-content/EN/ALL/?uri=CELEX:32006R1083 (accessed March 19, 2022).
22. EU Regulation (EU) No 1303/2013 of the European Parliament and of the Council of 17 December 2013 laying down common provisions on the European Regional Development Fund, the European Social Fund, the Cohesion Fund, the European Agricultural Fund for Rural Development and the European Maritime and Fisheries Fund and laying down general provisions on the European Regional Development Fund, the European Social Fund, the Cohesion Fund and the European Maritime and Fisheries Fund and repealing Council Regulation (EC) No 1083/2006, *Official Journal of the European Union*, December 20, 2013. https://eur-lex.europa.eu/legal-content/EN/TXT/?uri=celex%3A32013R1303 (accessed March 19, 2022).
23. European Commission (2014a) Commission Delegated Regulation (EU) No 240/2014 of 7 January 2 EU Regulation (EU) No 1303/2013 014 on the European code of conduct on partnership in the framework of the European Structural and Investment Funds Official. *Journal of the European Union, Brussels*, L 74 (7), March 14. http://eur-lex.europa.eu/legal-content/EN/TXT/PDF/?uri=CELEX:32014R0240andfrom=EN (accessed March 19, 2022).

Table 1.1 (Continued)

Name	*Aim*	*Initiator*	*Partners*	*How partnership was understood and promoted*
Partnerships for access to basic services in Latin America (and South Africa) (2013–14)				
Luz en Casa (Light at Home) **Cajamarca** **Peru**	To supply electricity to isolated rural inhabitants through Solar Home Systems (SHS)	*Acciona Microenergía Perú* (Social enterprise)	- *Fundación Acciona Microenergía* (Acciona Microenergy Foundation) - National and local public administration bodies - Micro-businesses - Photovoltaic Electrification Committees - Rural communities	Collaborative arrangements to pool expertise, resources and knowledge of different actors in the public, private and civil sectors, and incentivise vulnerable or marginalised populations to assume active roles in service provision. Partnership viewed as a way of promoting innovation by: • Repositioning the end user as an active agent in service provision • Ensuring close and ongoing cooperation with the public sector • Generating new business models for covering service costs and related activities
Inclusive Sanitation Markets **Cochabamba** **Bolivia**	To find new ways for small enterprises to generate income from the sanitation value chain	Water for People (International NGO)	- University of San Simón - Micro-businesses - Grassroots organisations - Families - Public administration bodies - International development agencies	
eHealth in rural areas **Alta Verapaz** **Guatemala**	To address high maternal and infant mortality rates among Indigenous communities in remote rural areas using information and communications technology (ICT)	TulaSalud (NGO)	- Health Department of Alta Verapaz - Ministry of Public Health and Social Assistance - Cobán National School of Nursing - Cobán Hospital - Tula Foundation	

Ciudad Saludable **Lima** **Peru**	To establish an integrated model for waste management	*Ciudad Saludable* (NGO)	- Peru Waste Innovation - Healthy Cities International - Central and municipal governments - Recyclers - Donors - Communities - Businesses - Educational institutions - Media - Social organisations
Innovative partnerships in access to water and sanitation Durban South Africa	To extend water and sanitation service coverage and meet the needs of different community groups	eThekwini Water and Sanitation Services (Department of Municipality)	- University of Kwazulu-Natal - Water Research Commission - Water and sanitation firms - Community representatives - International donors

2 Naming and framing partnership

"Developmentspeak," according to Andrea Cornwall and Deborah Eade in a book published in 2010, is a language composed of ambiguous buzzwords and positive sounding "fuzzwords" particular to the international development sector.[1] Describing this language as an eclectic mix of upbeat slogans, catchphrases and viewpoints, the authors note that its elasticity has impeded possibilities for critical analysis. As a widely used feel-good expression that is singularly difficult to pin down, both in the development world and beyond, it is no surprise that partnership is included in this lexicon of problematic idioms.

Strictly speaking, the classification of partnership as a buzzword, a new or existing expression that becomes fashionable for a period of time in a particular field or in popular culture, may be a misnomer.[2] The short-term nature of the buzz that makes a word topical is belied by the widespread use of the term partnership since the late 1980s.[3] The fuzz, however, remains, and it is, ironically, this very ambiguity that appears to have assisted partnership to transcend the status of a passing fad.

What is partnership?

The difficulty of arriving at a precise definition of partnership has been widely commented on in the literature relating to collaboration and development.[4]

1. Cornwall, A. and Eade, D. eds. (2010) *Deconstructing Development Discourse, Buzzwords and Fuzzwords*, Rugby, UK: Oxfam GB and Practical Action Publishing Ltd.
2. See www.collinsdictionary.com/dictionary/english/buzzword (accessed March 3, 2022).
3. Malyuga, E.N. and Rimmer, W. (2021) Making sense of "buzzword" as a term through co-occurrences analysis. *Helyion*, 7. https://doi.org/10.1016/j.heliyon.2021.e07208 (p. 10).
4. See, for example, Googins, B.K. and Rochlin, S. A. (2000) Creating the partnership society: Understanding the rhetoric and reality of cross-sectoral partnerships. *Business and Society Review*, 105 (1): 127–144. https://doi.org/10.1111/0045-3609.00068 (p. 131); Harrison, E. (2002) "The problem with the locals": Partnership and participation in Ethiopia. *Development and Change*, 33 (4): 587–610. https://doi.org/10.1111/1467-7660.00271 (p. 589); Tomlinson, F. (2005) Idealistic and pragmatic versions of the discourse of partnership. *Organization Studies*, 26 (8): 1169–1171. https://doi.org/10.1177%2F0170840605055338 (p. 1169) and Pattberg, P. and Widerberg, O. (2016) Transnational multistakeholder partnerships for sustainable development: Conditions for success. *Ambio*, 45: 42–51. https://doi.org/10.1007/s13280-015-0684-2 (p. 43).

DOI: 10.4324/9781003199434-3

As well as encompassing a diverse spectrum of relationships, the looseness of the term partnership is compounded by its positive nature and the fact that "it has a nice cuddly sound to it."[5] This sense of harmony has further assisted a widespread view that working in partnership is a panacea for solving all manner of societal concerns.[6] However, as Frances Tomlinson observes, "the presentation of partnership as 'good,' but unclear in its meaning, invites consideration of the question 'good' in what way, and for whom?"[7]

For some, the slipperiness of the term partnership conceals power dynamics that advance a particular set of perspectives and worldviews.[8] Cornwall, for example, includes partnership among a number of "loan-words" from an "Anglo-dominated development discourse" made mandatory by external agencies which masks important issues of influence and funding, power and control.[9] Partnership we are warned is not a value-free term. As a result, beyond questions of good or bad, it is useful to complement Tomlinson's questions by asking *who* is promoting partnership and *why*?[10] This is all the more necessary if we are to better understand why the term partnership has become so ubiquitous in the last 30 years or so.

Box 2.1 Origins of the term partnership

The word "partner" comes from the Latin word "partitio" or partition which relates to the act of dividing, sharing or parting. Following the Norman conquest of England in 1066, both Anglo-Norman French and Middle English used the word "parcener" to describe a joint heir with shared inheritance rights to an undivided estate. The word partner in English eventually came to be understood as someone associated with another in a common activity or interest. Linkage to the term "ship," meanwhile, denotes the state of being associated with a partner.[11]

5. Standing, G. (2010) Social protection. In: Cornwall, A. and Eade, D. eds. Op. cit. (p. 64).
6. As noted by De Souza Briggs, X. (2003) Perfect fit or shotgun marriage? Understanding the power and pitfalls in partnerships. *Strategy Tool No. 1*, Cambridge, USA: The Community Problem-Solving Project MIT. "First of all, who would want to be against 'working in partnership,' at least in principle? And second, is there any problem-solving that partnership doesn't somehow describe or can't be made to describe?" (p. 3).
7. Tomlinson (2005) Op. cit. p. 1170.
8. Harrison (2002) Op. cit. p. 590.
9. Cornwall, A. Introductory overview: Buzzwords and fuzzwords: Deconstructing development discourse. In Cornwall and Eade. eds. Op. cit. p. 2.
10. Hodge, G.A. and Greve, C. (2007) Public-private partnerships: An international performance review. *Public Administration Review*, May/June: 545–558. https://doi.org/10.1111/j.1540-6210.2007.00736.x (p. 553).
11. Online Etymology Dictionary. www.etymonline.com/;https://en.wiktionary.org/wiki/partner#English (accessed March 3, 2022) and see also Stott, L. and Murphy, D.F. (2020) An inclusive approach to partnerships for the SDGs: Using a relationship lens to explore the potential for transformational collaboration. *Special Issue: Partnerships for the SDGs, Sustainability*, 12 (19): 7905. https://doi.org/10.3390/su12197905

The etymological roots of the term partnership link it to the sharing and dividing of land or property (see Box 2.1). Most dictionary definitions, meanwhile, present partnership as a relational state such as marriage or living together, or a contractual arrangement in which two or more parties engage in a joint business venture in which risks and profits are shared.[12] More recently, partnership has been presented as a relationship in which different actors of society pool their diverse resources, capitalise on synergies and share risks and benefits in order to accomplish something that they could not do alone (see Box 2.2).[13] This broad definition has been used to position partnership as a remedy for addressing challenges in a vast range of fields, from business, management and organisational studies to social and political science, environmental studies, economics and psychology. To these may be added the sector (private, public or civil society) and thematic foci (education, health, etc.) of different initiatives, and their geographic and administrative levels of operation (local, regional, national and global as well as rural and urban location).[14]

Box 2.2 Partnership: some common definitions

Partnership is an arrangement whereby two or more organisations join some of their forces to accomplish a specific task. The arrangement falls well short of a joint venture, but the principle of complementary assets is the same.

Macdonald and Chrisp[15]

A cross-sector partnership is a collaborative effort in which parties from different societal sectors pool resources to provide solutions to (perceived) common problems.

The Partnerships Resource Centre (PrC)[16]

Partnerships are voluntary and collaborative relationships between various parties, both public and non-public, in which all participants agree to work together to achieve a common purpose or undertake a

12. See, for example: https://dictionary.cambridge.org/dictionary/english/partnership or www.oxfordlearnersdictionaries.com/definition/english/partnership?q=partnership (accessed January 3, 2021).
13. See, for example: Nelson, J. and Zadek, S. (2000) *Partnership Alchemy, New Social Partnerships in Europe*, Copenhagen, Denmark: The Copenhagen Centre (p. 14); UN General Assembly (2006) *Resolution Adopted by the General Assembly 60/215: Towards Global Partnerships*, Sixtieth session, Agenda item 5929, New York, NY: United Nations.
14. Stott and Murphy (2020) Op. cit.
15. Macdonald, S. and Chrisp, T. (2005) Acknowledging the purpose of partnership. *Journal of Business Ethics*, 59: 307–317. https://doi.org/10.1007/s10551-004-3235-5 (p. 308).
16. Partnerships Resource Centre (2012) Cross sector partnership formation, what to consider before you start, Rotterdam, the Netherlands: PrC. cross-sector_partnership_formation.pdf (rsm.nl) (accessed September 30, 2021).

specific task and, as mutually agreed, to share risks and responsibilities, resources and benefits.

United Nations, General Assembly[17]

The reductive descriptions of partnership in Box 2.2 give little insight into the kinds of issues that partnership seeks to address, the diversity of the actors that may be involved, the nature of the resources that are pooled and how they are combined. They also give no indication as to how these relationships are built and maintained or to the enormous challenges that working in partnership involves. These difficulties may relate to the impact of contextual factors, the alignment of different organisational missions, cultures and ways of working, the joint management of relationships and power dynamics linked to the influence and resources of the different players involved.[18] More significantly, such characterisations focus primarily on organisational and structural relationships that see partnership as a vehicle for achieving a goal and pay limited attention to the relational and process dimensions that it involves.

Different dimensions of partnership

In the English language, the term partnership incorporates two key concepts: the idea of a structure or entity (a partnership or partnerships) and that of a process (working in partnership or partnering). In exploring partnership, it is therefore useful to understand whether the term is being used as a structure or a process or both.

Structure or process?

The most widespread conceptualisation of partnership is as that of a structure.[19] This notion is exemplified in the terms used for different types of partnerships (see Figure 2.1).

The nomenclatures in Figure 2.1 categorise partnership as a construct in which two or more actors work towards a common goal through some kind of structure. Their end goals, which can overlap, may range from the fulfilment of a concrete task to longer-term goals such as capacity-building,

17. United Nations (2019) *Towards Global Partnerships: A Principle-Based Approach to Enhanced Cooperation Between the United Nations and All Relevant Partners*. Resolution A/Res/73/254; adopted by the General Assembly on 20 December 2018, New York, NY, USA: United Nations General Assembly.
18. Caplan, K. and Stott, L. (2008) Defining our terms and clarifying our language. In: Svensson, L. and Nilsson, B. eds. *Partnership: As a Strategy for Social Innovation and Sustainable Change*, Stockholm, Sweden: Santérus Academic Press (pp. 23–35).
19. The UN, for example, states that "partnerships will be critical to the achievement of the Sustainable Development Goals, *as an effective instrument* for mobilizing additional human and financial resources, expertise, technology and knowledge." See United Nations (2019) Op. cit. para. 5.

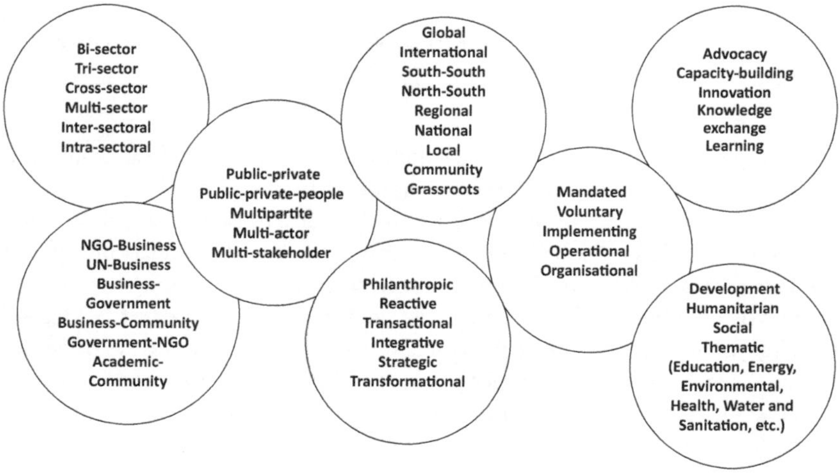

Figure 2.1 Different types of partnerships

behavioural or policy change[20] which are, as noted earlier, also overlaid by diverse geographical, disciplinary, sectoral and thematic foci.[21]

In order to further understand the nature of these partnership constructs, it is worth taking a look at how they differ from other formations in which actors collaborate such as dialogues, networks and joint ventures. To do this, Figure 2.2 positions partnership on a continuum between networks and joint ventures or new institutions.

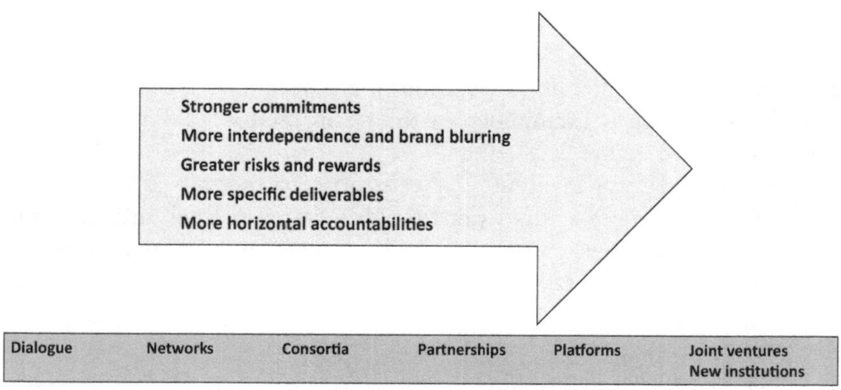

Figure 2.2 Different forms of collaboration

Source: Adapted from Caplan (2013)[22]

Credit: Building Partnerships for Development in Water and Sanitation (BPD)

20. Caplan and Stott (2008) Op. cit. pp. 24–25.
21. See Stott and Murphy (2020) Op. cit. pp. 7–8 for relevant examples.
22. Caplan, K. (2013) *Taking the Mythology Out of Partnerships: A View From the Ground Up*, BPD Classic Hits Series, London, UK: Building Partnerships for Development (BPD) (p. 3).

In this schema, the connections between the parties involved are likely to be more robust on the right-hand side of the spectrum. Here, actors will usually have stronger commitments to one another and may even use some form of joint branding or shared logo; both the risks and benefits of working together are likely to be greater and the expected results generally clearer. In addition, horizontal (as opposed to hierarchical or vertical) decision-making processes and accountabilities will reinforce shared ownership.

It is also helpful to distinguish a partnership arrangement from a project. While partnership may encompass project activities, the core differential between these two forms relates to the notion of horizontal accountability. A partnership initiative will rest upon collective responsibility and decision-making by all its members as opposed to a more top-down project hierarchy where responsibility for activities is likely to be assumed by a project manager or supervising team.

To prompt further discussion around these differences, the organisation Building Partnerships for Development in Water and Sanitation (BPD) proposed a definition of partnership structures that incorporates three key attributes:

> Partnerships involve two or more organisations that enter into a collaborative arrangement based on the following:
>
> 1. Synergistic goals and opportunities that address particular issues or deliver specified tasks that single organisations cannot accomplish on their own
> 2. Situations where individual organisations cannot purchase the appropriate resources or competencies purely through a market transaction
> 3. An understanding that the context will change and thereby constructs created will need to evolve and eventually morph into institutionalised mechanisms and practices[23]

This definition introduces two interesting elements to our thinking about partnership entities. First, the idea that this kind of formation may be unnecessary if a challenge or task can be resolved through the purchase of a product or service, and second, that partnerships can be construed as non-permanent transitional mechanisms that will necessarily disappear as the practices they advance become institutionalised or available via a commercial transaction.

While partnership is most often depicted as a structural form or construct, it can also be construed as "working in partnership" or "partnering." In the EU, for instance, as well as a structure for project delivery, partnership is also understood as an ongoing process of collaboration.[24] The EU's "partnership prin-

23. Ibid., p. 1.
24. Stott, L. (2019) *How European Social Fund Managing Authorities and Intermediate Bodies Support Partnership*, Revised edition, Brussels, Belgium: European Commission; Stott, L. and Scoppetta,

ciple" captures this idea in its depiction of partnership as close and continuous engagement between different social actors and levels of government, including regional and local authorities, socio-economic partners and civil society to support the effective delivery of European Structural and Investment Funds (ESIF).[25] Here, as well as an ongoing connection with stakeholders, partnership is central to a form of "multilevel governance" which ostensibly enhances democracy by offering different administrative levels, organisations and citizens the possibility of influencing political decision-making.[26] A view of partnership as an enduring form of "social" or "collaborative governance" in which diverse actors work together to address societal problems has also been promoted in the field of international development cooperation (see Box 2.4).[27]

Box 2.4 Partnering and international non-governmental organisations (INGOs)

Many INGOs rely on ongoing connections with organisations in different countries to support their missions. Oxfam, for example, outlines the importance of working with local partners such as grassroots NGOs, producer groups, cooperatives and small businesses in order to build local skills, experience and ownership. The organisation also engages with environmental and humanitarian NGOs, unions, faith groups and celebrities for their campaigns; with corporate partners that support projects through donations or staff engagement; with intergovernmental bodies such as the European Union and the United Nations and with suppliers who deliver goods and services for their emergency, development and campaigning work.[28] In a similar manner, CARE also partners with a wide number of individuals, corporations, trusts, foundations, governments, institutions and community

A. (2013) Promoting local economic development through partnerships in Europe. *Skills@ Work: Theory and Practice Journal*, 6: 2–12.

25. Bauer, M. W. (2002) The EU "Partnership Principle" Revisited: Still a Sustainable Governance Device Across Multiple Administrative Arenas? *Public Administration*, 80 (4): 769–789. http://dx.doi.org/10.1111/1467-9299.00328
26. Van den Brande, L. (2014) Multilevel governance and partnership. *The Van den Brande Report*. Prepared for Commissioner for Regional and Urban Policy Johannes Hahn, Brussels, Belgium: European Commission (p. 9).
27. Brinkerhoff, D.W. and Brinkerhoff, J.M. (2004) Partnerships between international donors and non-governmental development organizations: Opportunities and constraints. *International Review of Administrative Sciences*, 70: 253. https://doi.org/10.1177%2F0020852304044254; Zadek, S. (2007) Collaborative governance: The new multilateralism for the 21st century. *Global Development 2.0*, Washington, DC, USA: Brookings Institute and Crane, A. (2010) From governance to governance: On blurring boundaries. *Journal of Business Ethics*, 94: 17–19. https://doi.org/10.1007/s10551-011-0788-y
28. See www.oxfam.org.uk/about-us/how-we-work/about-our-partners/ (accessed January 3, 2022).

groups, including local grassroots organisations, cooperatives and small businesses; government officials who can provide local knowledge and expertise; advocacy allies such as humanitarian and development NGOs, national and regional alliances and celebrities; research institutions that can share relevant academic knowledge and technical advances, and suppliers who deliver essential goods and services for emergency and development work.[29]

Although there is a tendency to promote partnership as a structure *or* a process, many partnership arrangements combine understandings of both. Table 2.1 provides information on how these different perceptions of partnership were employed by those involved in the case studies that inform this book.

Table 2.1 Examples of partnership structures and processes

Structure	***Process***
Southern Africa studies	
Chamba Valley Partnership (Zambia) Relationship between a supermarket chain and local farmers to generate income and create employment	Small-scale Sugarcane Farming Communities Partnership (South Africa) Way of promoting development, empowerment and poverty alleviation in rural areas
Zambia Business Coalition on HIV/AIDS Multi-stakeholder mechanism to increase capacity for effective response to HIV/AIDS epidemic	Amangwe Village Partnership (South Africa) Way of identifying innovative and coordinated opportunities for business to work on HIV/AIDS
Sharing Responsibility for Higher Education Partnership (Zambia) Alliance between business and universities in Zambia to provide resources for quality teaching and research	Mthashana Further Education and Training College Partnership Programme (South Africa) Means of integrating entrepreneurial thinking with skills training as the basis for work competency, equity and growth
European Social Fund studies	
Different social actors work together to address access to employment and social exclusion through structures with specific aims, objectives and governance procedures	Multi-stakeholder engagement in decision-making to promote collective commitment and ownership of quality programmes

29. See www.care-international.org/who-we-are/partners (accessed January 3, 2022).

Structure	*Process*
Latin American (and South Africa) studies	
Collaborative arrangements to pool different resources from public, private and civil sectors and incentivise marginalised populations to assume active roles in provision of basic services	

Source: Stott (2017)[30]

Means to an end or end in itself?

Conceptualisation of partnership, as both a structure and a process, has largely centred upon its potential for the achievement of goals. However, the use of the term as a way of promoting ongoing participation in political and social processes suggests that less instrumental views of partnership are worth examining. These perspectives are focused on the interdependence between people and a belief that humans have an innate capacity for cooperation and partnership.[31] Anne-Marie Slaughter describes this as a life-sustaining connection that "is an end in itself, not just a means to an end."[32] In contrast to instrumental views of partnership, such views endorse the idea that partnership may also have intrinsic value (see Table 2.2).

This thinking resonates with worldviews based on the ethics of reciprocity and the premise that all humans are part of a collective. These understandings have informed a number of different national and regional understandings of partnership. In partnership research in Southern Africa, for example, elements of the philosophy of Ubuntu were often mentioned as defining and assisting collaboration (see Box 2.5).[33] In a similar manner, Michelle Evans notes

30. Stott, L. (2017) *Partnership and Social Progress: Multi-Stakeholder Collaboration in Context*. Ph.D. Thesis, University of Edinburgh, UK (p. 22).
31. See Eisler, R. (1987) *The Chalice and the Blade, Our History, Our Future*, San Francisco, CA, USA: Harper and Row; Eisler, R. (2008) Our great creative challenge: Rethinking human nature: And recreating society. In: Richards, R. ed. *Everyday Creativity and New Views of Human Nature: Psychological, Social, and Spiritual Perspectives*, Washington, DC, USA: American Psychological Association, pp. xiii: 261–285. http://rianeeisler.com/wp-content/uploads/2014/06/riane-eisler.pdf (accessed January 6, 2017); Eisler, R. (2015) Human possibilities: The interaction of biology and culture. *Interdisciplinary Journal of Partnership Studies*, 1 (1): 1–39; Korten, D.F. (2006) *The Great Turning, From Empire to Earth Community*, San Francisco, CA, USA: Berrett-Koehler Publishers; Korten, D.F. (2015) *Change the Story, Change the Future: A Living Economy for a Living Earth*, Oakland, CA, USA: Berrett-Koehler Publishers; Leadbeater, C. (2012) *It's Co-Operation, Stupid, Why Richard Dawkins, Thomas Hobbes and Milton Friedman Got It Wrong*, London, UK: Institute for Public Policy Research; Sennett, R. (2013) *Together: The Rituals, Pleasures and Politics of Cooperation* London, UK: Penguin Books; and Bregman, R. (2020) *Humankind: A Hopeful History*, London, UK: Bloomsbury Publishing.
32. Slaughter, A.M. (2017) *The Chessboard and the Web, Strategies of Connection in a Networked World*, New Haven, CT, USA: Yale University Press.
33. Rein et al. (2005) Op. cit. pp. 28–30.

Table 2.2 The instrumental and intrinsic value of partnership

Instrumental value	***Intrinsic value***
Means to an end	End in itself
Relationships between organisations	Relationships between people
Partners seek common ground	Partners are able to live with disagreement
Horizontal decision-making arrangements	Constant renegotiations of power in decision-making arrangements
Transitional in nature	Ongoing
Emphasis on impact and results	Emphasis on processes that facilitate achievement of impact and results

Source: Stott (2017)[34]

that in Australia, notions of partnership can be found in the idea of Dadirri which she describes as "a profound non-judgemental watching and listening" which "asks us to receive people individually as well as collectively, to be compassionate and to be committed to hearing beyond the words that are spoken."[35]

Box 2.5 Ubuntu

Commonly expressed as the idea that "a person is a person through other people," Ubuntu has been defined as a social philosophy that rests upon communal values of "compassion, reciprocity, dignity, harmony and humanity"[36] and shared understandings that are built through listening to and affirming others.[37] Although the concept is widely associated with South Africa, its precepts are found in many African countries and cultures where it is related to aspects of individual, family, community, societal, environmental and spiritual life.[38] While some have critiqued Ubuntu as a catch-all term that has been used politically to promote acceptance of particular policies

34. Stott (2017) Op. cit. p. 24.
35. Evans, M. cited in Evans, M. and Stott, L. (2008) Partnership inclusivity: Whose are the unheard voices? In: McManus, S. and Tennyson, R. eds. *Talking the Walk: A Communication Manual for Partnership Practitioners*, London, UK: International Business Leaders Forum (pp. 15–16).
36. Nussbaum, B. (2003) African culture and ubuntu reflections of a South African in America. *Perspectives, World Business Academy*, 17 (1) and see also: Mbiti, J.S. (1969) *African Religions and Philosophy*, Nairobi, Kenya: East African Educational Publishers (pp. 108–109).
37. Nussbaum (2003) Op. cit.
38. Mugumbate, R.J. (2021) Ubuntu philosophy, nuances and application in selected areas and disciplines, *Presentation at the Ubuntu Conference: A Comparative Study of an African Concept of Justice*, Boulder: University of Colorado, 27 August and see also: Mugumbate, J. and Nyanguru, A. (2013) Exploring African philosophy: The value of ubuntu in social work. *African Journal of Social Work*, 3 (1): 82–100.

and ideas,[39] others view it as an important belief system whose core features are central to the achievement of a more just, equitable and sustainable future for all.[40]

These belief systems suggest that partnership may be interpreted as a dynamic process of cooperation that has value in and of itself. In this sense, beyond a simple transactional relationship, partnering offers the possibility of a transformational bond that is developed over time. The intrinsic value of partnership is reflected in the ideas of thinkers such as Amartya Sen whose notion of agency acknowledges "people's desire, ability and capacity to engage in collective action and affect change."[41] The sociologist Richard Sennett believes that meaningful cooperation relies upon "dialogic deliberation" which seeks to comprehend difference through open-ended conversations, careful listening and responsiveness to others.[42] These ideas are complemented by those of Riane Eisler who contends that, rather than hierarchies of domination, partnership depends upon "hierarchies of actualization" in which those with power empower others.[43]

Partnership as a relationship based on values

The intrinsic value of working in partnership and its links to worldviews such as Ubuntu and Dadirri implies the possibility of a further understanding of partnership, that of a relationship based on shared values such as fairness, reciprocity and mutual benefit. This view is endorsed by Willem Elbers and Lau Schulpen, who believe that "partnerships differ from other types of institutional relationships due to their value-based nature and qualities such as shared goals, mutual influence, trust, and mutual respect," attributes that have been highlighted as essential for the building of effective partnership initiatives.[44]

39. Nussbaum (2003) Op. cit. and see also: Matolino, B. and Kwindingwi, W. (2013) The end of ubuntu. *South African Journal of Philosophy*, 32 (2): 197–205. https://doi.org/10.1080/02580136.2013.817637 on the use of *ubuntu* in South Africa, and Sekwat, A. (2000) Beyond African humanism: Economic reform in post-independent Zambia. *International Journal of Organizational Theory and Behavior*, 3 (3 and 4): 521–546. https://doi.org/10.1108/IJOTB-03-03-04-2000-B013
40. Nussbaum (2003) Op. cit. and see also, Lutz, D.W. African *Ubuntu* Philosophy and Global Management. *Journal of Business Ethics*, 84: 313 (2009). https://doi.org/10.1007/s10551-009-0204-z
41. Sen, A. (2004) Why we should preserve the spotted owl. *London Review of Books*, 26 (3) (p. 5) and West, S., Haider, J., Masterson, V., Enqvist, J.P., Sevdin, U. and Tengö, M. (2018) Stewardship, care and relational values. *Current Opinion in Environmental Sustainability*, 35: 1–9. https://doi.org/10.1016/j.cosust.2018.10.008
42. Sennett (2013) Op. cit. p. 14.
43. Eisler (2015) Op. cit. p. 6.
44. Elbers, W. and Schulpen, L. (2010) Decision making in partnerships for development: Explaining the influence of local partners. *Nonprofit and Voluntary Sector Quarterly*, 2011;40 (5): 795–812.

Strong partnership principles can also be found in the development field where calls for aid relationships based on greater respect and solidarity have been central to demands for more equitable development cooperation between "North and South."[45] The development agency Oxfam has, for example, presented a formulation of "partnerships as mutually empowering relationships, cognisant of power imbalances, focused on impact, mutual growth, organisational development and institutional strengthening and achieving impact."[46] This conceptualisation of partnership resonates with Ros Tennyson's allusion to a set of core partnership principles: equity, which implies that all partners have an equal right to be at the table, thus validating different resource contributions; transparency and the promotion of openness and honesty in working relationships so that trust-building is enhanced, and mutual benefit, whereby each partner is able to achieve specific benefits over and above those common to all partners.[47] Tennyson's principles have been built upon by the Partnership Brokers Association (PBA) to include diversity and recognition of the need to bring together actors with both complementary and diverse strengths, experiences and approaches, and courage, which embraces the ability to challenge and take and manage risks.[48]

The promotion of partnering values and principles, and expectations of ethical behaviour, ultimately rely upon how individuals work together in partnership arrangements. As it is representatives of organisations that join collaborative initiatives, the emotional connections and dynamics encountered in interpersonal relationships thus demand close attention.[49]

---

doi: 10.1177/0899764010366304 (p. 796) and see also Sloan, P. and Oliver, D. (2013) Building trust in multi-stakeholder partnerships: Critical emotional incidents and practices of engagement. *Organization Studies*, 34 (12): 1835–1868. https://doi.org/10.1177%2F0170840613495018 (pp. 1856–1857).

45. See Pearson, L. (1969) *Partners in Development: Report of the Commission on International Development*. London, UK: Pall Mall Press and Brandt, W. (1980) *North-South: A Programme for Survival* ("Brandt Report") Independent Commission on International Development Issues, London, UK: Pan Books, as well as: Fowler, A (2000) Introduction: Beyond partnership: Getting real about NGO relationships in the aid system. In: Fowler, A. ed. *Questioning Partnership: The Reality of Aid and NGO Relations, IDS Bulletin*, 31 (3): 1–13; Hewitt, W.E. (2002) Partnership as process: Municipal co-operation for international development. *Canadian Journal of Development Studies*, 23 (2): 25–247. http://dx.doi.org/10.1080/02255189.2002.9668864 and Bailey, F. and Dolan, A. (2011) The meaning of partnership in development: Lessons in development education. *Policy and Practice: A Development Education Review*, 13: 30–48. http://hdl.handle.net/10395/1916 (p. 34).
46. Oxfam International (2012) *Working Together, Oxfam's Partnership Principles*, Oxford, UK: Oxfam GB (p. 5).
47. Tennyson, R. (2011) *The Partnering Toolbook*, London, UK: The Partnering Initiative (IBLF) (p.9).
48. Mundy, J. (2018) Embedding ethical and principled partnering approaches. In: Stott, L. ed. *Shaping Sustainable Change: The Role of Partnership Brokering in Optimising Collaborative Action*, London, UK: Greenleaf Publishing, Routledge.
49. Battisti, M. (2009) Below the surface, The challenges of cross-sector partnerships. *Journal of Corporate Citizenship*, 35: 95–108. www.jstor.org/stable/jcorpciti.35.95 (p. 96).

In a collaborative context, "relational intelligence" will rest upon skills for navigating relationships that involve awareness and understanding of people's emotions, principles, interests and positions.[50] A sensitive and reflective approach to working with others is further encapsulated in the notion of "relational values" which comprise connections between people and the natural world.[51] These "place-based" values are both collective and individual, embracing cultural identities, social cohesion and civic responsibility, as well as personal ties to land and nature. Such bonds are manifested in the idea of stewardship and respect and care for the natural environment as a moral duty. E.F. Schumacher captures a sense of what relational values might mean in practice in the conclusion to his celebrated book *Small is Beautiful; A Study of Economics as if People Mattered* by invoking humankind's traditional wisdom as central to the individual and collective transformations needed to address resource consumption and depletion, and to minimise gaps between those with wealth and power and those without.[52]

The diverse interpretations outlined earlier suggest that partnership encompasses multiple dimensions and levels and, while clearly dynamic and evolving, may best be understood as an umbrella term for an assortment of collaborative structures, processes and values (see Figure 2.3).

A view of partnership as the blending of collaborative structures and processes with relational elements is somewhat different from more commonplace representations of partnership which are, as noted earlier, largely instrumental and focused primarily on its use as a means to an end. However, while a more multifaceted understanding of partnership may better assist in positioning it as a way of moving towards a fairer and more sustainable human future,[54] there is still a strong perception that it is little more than "a mobilizing term,"[55] the essence of which has been usurped by a

50. Pless, N.M. and Maak, T. (2005) Relational intelligence for leading responsibly in a connected world. *Academy of Management Annual Meeting Proceedings*, 1–16. https://doi.org/10.5465/ambpp.2005.18783524 (p. 2).
51. Chan, K.M.A., Gould, R.K. and Pascual, U. (2018) Editorial overview: Relational values: What are they, and what's the fuss about? *Current Opinion in Environmental Sustainability*, 35: 1–7. https://doi.org/10.1016/j.cosust.2018.11.003
52. Schumacher, E.F. (1974) *Small Is Beautiful: A Study of Economics as If People Mattered*. London, UK: Abacus Books (pp. 247–249).
53. Stott (2017) Op. cit. p. 25.
54. See for example: Eisler, R. (2008) *The Real Wealth of Nations, Creating a Caring Economics*, Oakland, CA, USA: Berrett-Koehler Publications, Inc.
55. Utting, P. and Zammit, A. (2009) United Nations-business partnerships: Good intentions and contradictory agendas. *Journal of Business Ethics*, 90: 39–56. https://doi.org/10.1007/s10551-008-9917-7 (p. 40).

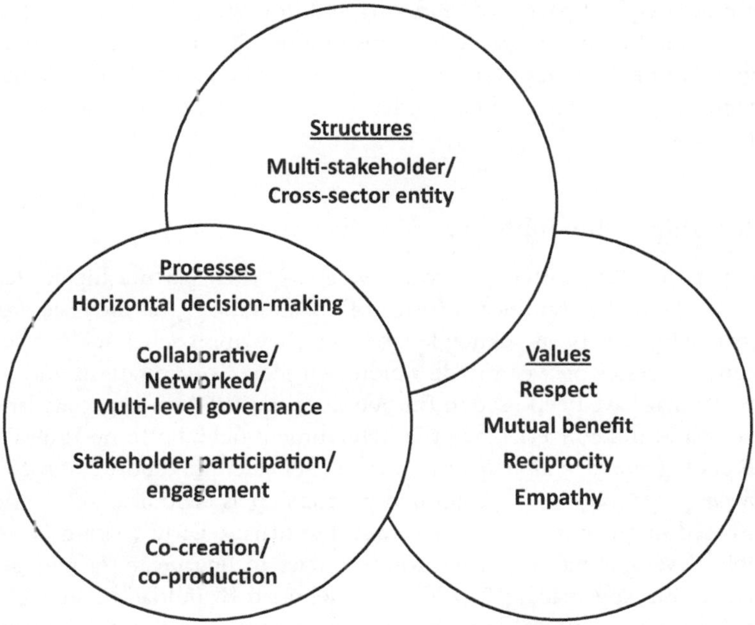

Figure 2.3 Different components of partnership

Source: Stott (2017)[53]

"managerialist and technocratic approach" which privileges organisations over individuals and limits "democratic deliberation."[56] This latter view is reinforced in a narrative that positions engagement with business as central to partnership. Two contending views of partnership thus need to be explored: one that promotes democracy through joint problem-solving and the integration of different interests in governance systems and, conversely, one that undermines democracy by moving political decision-making away from elected to non-elected actors, particularly the private sector.[57] These

56. Davies, J.S. (2008) Against "partnership": Toward a local challenge to global neoliberalism. In: Gross, J. and Hambleton, R. eds. *Governing Cities in the Global Era*, Basingstoke, UK: Palgrave Macmillan, pp. 199–210 (p. 202); Miraftab, F. (2004) Public-private partnerships: The Trojan horse of neoliberal development? *Journal of Planning Education and Research*, 24: 89–101. https://doi.org/10.1177%2F0739456X04267173 (p. 97) and Gold, M., Cressey, P., and Leonard, E. (2007) Whatever happened to social dialogue? From partnership to managerialism in the EU Employment Agenda. *European Journal of Industrial Relations*, 13 (1): 7–25. https://doi.org/10.1177%2F0959680107073963

57. Rein et al. (2005) Op. cit. p. 7. For more on these debates, see Slaughter, A.M. (2005) *A New World Order*, Princeton, NJ, USA: Princeton University Press; Bäckstrand, K. (2006) Multi-stakeholder partnerships for sustainable development: Rethinking legitimacy, accountability and

divergent opinions raise important questions about how partnership has been presented and packaged, and why and how such different interpretations are able to coexist. To explore this in more detail, and to assist deeper comprehension of its application in practice, it is helpful to look at some of the ideological currents and trends that have informed the recent history of partnership.

Partnership – the contemporary discourse

If cooperation "is written into who we are,"[58] then partnership is clearly not new. As well as traditional forms of collaboration, the intrinsic worth of partnership has been acknowledged in policy approaches such as social dialogue processes between trade unions, employer organisations and governments that have been used in Europe since the 1960s to negotiate labour market issues and concerns.[59] In the development field, both the 1969 Pearson Report *Partners in Development* and the 1980 Brandt Report *North-South: A Programme for Survival*,[60] positioned partnership as central to aid relationships based on greater respect, quality and solidarity. Early writings on sustainable development also called for countries to engage in "a new sense of partnership and sharing"[61] with the celebrated Brundtland Report noting the need for partnership between different actors in the public, private and civil society spheres to ensure a shift towards sustainable development.[62] While clearly embracing instrumental elements, such as the centrality of the state in overseeing collaborative solutions to address development challenges, these appeals for partnership have a strong moral undercurrent that resonates deeply with the notion of shared values and ongoing collaborative connections. In the late 1980s, however, this discourse changed to one

---

effectiveness. *European Environment*, 16: 290–306 https://doi.org/10.1002/eet.425; Schäferhoff, M., Campe, S. and Kaan, C. (2007) Transnational public-private partnerships in international relations: Making sense of concepts, research frameworks, and results. *SFB-Governance Working Paper Series*, No. 6, Berlin, Germany: DFG Research Center; Steets, J. (2010) *Accountability in Public Policy Partnerships*, Basingstoke, UK: Palgrave Macmillan; and Andonova, L. (2014) Boomerangs to partnerships? Explaining state participation in transnational partnerships for sustainability. *Comparative Political Studies* 47 (3): 481–515. https://doi.org/10.1177%2F0010414013509579

58. See Sennett (2013) Op. cit. p. 5 and Leadbeater (2012) Op. cit. p. 26.
59. Nelson and Zadek (2000) Op. cit. p. 11 and Andersen, S.K. and Mailand, M. (2002) *The Role of Employers and Trade Unions in Multipartite Social Partnerships*, Copenhagen, Denmark: The Copenhagen Centre.
60. Maxwell. S. and Riddell, R. (1998) Conditionality or contract: Perspectives on partnership for development. *Journal of International Development*, 10: 257–268. https://doi.org/10.1002/(SICI)1099-1328(199803/04)10:2%3C257::AID-JID527%3E3.0.CO;2-S (pp. 258–259).
61. Jackson, B. (Ward) and Dubos, R.J. (1972) *Only One Earth: The Care and Maintenance of a Small Planet*, Stockholm, Sweden: United Nations Conference on the Human Environment (p. 215).
62. Brundtland, G. (1987) *Report of the World Commission on Environment and Development: Our Common Future*, New York, NY, USA: United Nations.

which centred primarily on the presentation of partnership as a mechanism or vehicle for achieving private sector-based objectives. This reinterpretation of partnership, and the fanfare around it, can be linked directly to the profound economic and political changes that took place during the latter part of the twentieth century.

Figure 2.4 offers a rough overview of how globalisation has led to the evolution of a set of paradigms that have influenced the naming and framing of partnership in contemporary discourse.

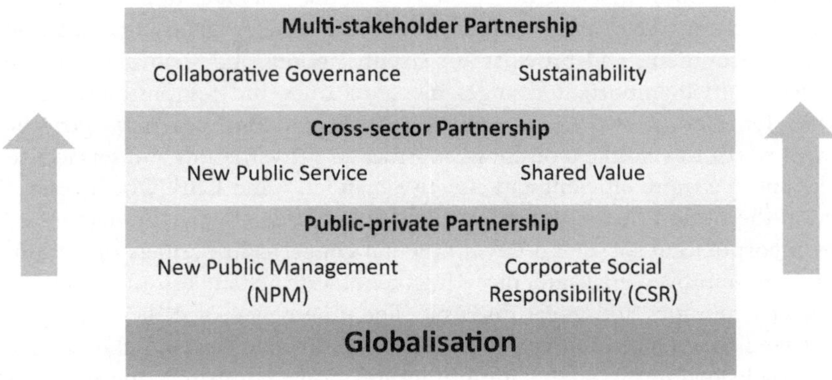

Figure 2.4 Shifting global paradigms: The evolution of multi-stakeholder partnership

The following section looks briefly at how some of the trends linked to globalisation have informed and shaped a widespread view of partnership as being integrally linked to private sector involvement in development and governance. These developments include New Public Management (NPM) and Corporate Social Responsibility (CSR). Although there has been a movement away from NPM and CSR in recent years towards new paradigms such as Collaborative Governance and Sustainability, the continued influence of these tendencies has inhibited a return to a more rounded view of partnership, one that centres on equity and inclusiveness and repositions intrinsic perspectives as central to multi-stakeholder collaboration.

New public management and corporate social responsibility

While debates continue to rage about the definition, meaning and repercussions of globalisation,[63] the advent of this phenomenon at the end of the 1980s can be correlated with the emergence of a new partnership

63. See, for example, Stiglitz, J.E. (2002) *Globalization and Its Discontents*, London, UK: Penguin Books and Stiglitz, J.E. (2006) *Making Globalization Work*, London, UK: Penguin Books.

narrative that has had an important influence on views of both sustainable development and governance.[64] Most understandings of globalisation include acceptance of the world as a unified economy in which markets, standards and ideas are shared. In its most recent guise this has been manifested in increased international trade and investment flows; the subsuming of national economies within an international financial system in which capital crosses national borders; the dispersion of production, service and management functions across different countries;[65] rapid technological and digital change, and a widespread perception of "state failure." Peter Utting and Ann Zammit describe this latter view as the "inability of governments, particularly in developing countries, to be effective agents of regulation and development, and providers of essential goods and services."[66] These shifts signified important changes in sector roles and responsibilities that were reflected in two key tendencies: NPM and the idea that "government needs to run like a business" in order to deliver goods and services to citizens in a more efficient and effective manner,[67] and CSR which centres upon the notion that shareholder value and confidence may be maximised by incorporating social and environmental concerns in business operations through improved engagement with stakeholders such as customers, suppliers, communities and governments.[68] The emergence of NPM and CSR reflected acceptance of increased private sector involvement in public affairs, acknowledged in the presentation of multinational companies and multilateral financial institutions as "development partners," and the management of social and economic challenges through joint mechanisms for project delivery such as public-private partnerships (PPPs).

A strong focus on public engagement with the private sector was apparent in the launch of the UN's Global Compact in 2000, a voluntary initiative in which businesses were invited to sign up to ten principles relating to human rights, labour, the environment and anti-corruption by working together with UN agencies and NGOs.[69] In the same year, partnership was also positioned as central to the eight Millennium Development Goals (MDGs) which governments across the world aimed to achieve by 2015. With a particular focus on engagement with the business community, one of the goals,

64. In this sense, Utting and Zammit (2009) Op. cit. (p. 42) are correct in their assumption that much of the current focus on partnership emerged as *"a logical* response to structural changes in state-market-society relations that have occurred since the 1980s."
65. Leslie, P. (2002) Regionalization, multi-level governance, and globalization, *Paper presented at the Conference Globalization, Multilevel Governance, and Democracy*, Kingston, Canada: Institute of Intergovernmental Relations School of Policy Studies, 3–4 May.
66. Utting and Zammit (2009) Op. cit. (p. 42).
67. Mazzucato, M. (2021) *Mission Economy: A Moonshot Guide to Changing Capitalism*, London, UK: Allen Lane (p. 35).
68. Nelson, J. (1998) *Building Competitiveness and Communities: How World Class Companies Are Creating Shareholder Value and Societal Value*, London, UK: The Prince of Wales Business Leaders Forum.
69. See www.unglobalcompact.org/ (accessed January 3, 2022).

MDG8, called for *A Global Partnership for Development* that included targets for addressing the needs of "developing nations" with a fairer trading and economic system, ensuring the availability and affordability of essential drugs in the developing world through alliances with pharmaceutical companies, and access to new technologies in collaboration with the private sector.[70]

Two years later, at the World Summit on Sustainable Development (WSSD) in Johannesburg, emphasis was placed on the positive role that business could play in poverty eradication and the promotion of human development. As well as Type I partnerships involving legally binding commitments to development targets by governments, the Summit endorsed a complementary category of voluntary transnational Type II partnerships involving public, private and civil society actors working together to address specific goals.[71] This move was lauded as advancing a new era of networked environmental governance characterised by collaborative decision-making and shared responsibility between different sectors for the management of transnational public issues.[72] In the field of aid and humanitarian action, meanwhile, so-called "North-South" partnerships were promoted between development agencies and NGOs. These relationships responded to the call for decentralisation, one of the core precepts of NPM, and the idea that aid delivery would be more efficient and effective if administered through locally owned country development strategies.[73]

These developments were viewed with disquiet by those who perceived them to be part of a generalised movement to roll back the state. Simon Heap, for example, observed that the welfare state appeared to be "giving way to business welfare."[74] A view that corporate interests dominated social and political life was expressed in concerns about "regulatory capture" and the ability of corporations to advocate voluntary, self-regulated codes capable of neutralising international provisions.[75] Meanwhile, protests against global forums such as the World Trade Organisation in Seattle in 1999 and the G8 Summit in Genoa in 2001 heralded a growing backlash against globalisation

70. MDG8 www.mdgmonitor.org/mdg-8-develop-a-global-partnership-for-development/ (accessed September 30, 2021).
71. Witte, J.M., Streck, C. and Benner, T. eds. (2003) *Progress or Peril? Partnerships in Global Environmental Governance: The Post-Johannesburg Agenda*, Washington, DC, USA: Global Public Policy Institute.
72. Ibid.
73. Abrahamsen, R. (2004) The power of partnerships in global governance. *Third World Quarterly*, 25 (8): 1453–1467. https://doi.org/10.1080/0143659042000308465 (p. 1455) and Crawford, G. (2003) Partnership or power? Deconstructing the "partnership for governance reform" in Indonesia. *Third World Quarterly*, 24 (1): 139–159. https://doi.org/10.1080/713701365 (p. 140).
74. Heap, S. (2006) NGO-business partnerships, research-in-progress. *Public Management*, 2 (4): 555–563. https://doi.org/10.1080/14719030000000033 (p. 556).
75. Rundall, P. (2000) Partnerships with TNCs: An attempt to compartmentalise ethics? *Buy in or Sell Out? Understanding Business-NGO Partnerships, Discussion Papers* 10: 10–15, London, UK: World Vision (p. 12).

and what was seen as the unregulated power of multinationals. A spate of corporate scandals such as those involving Enron, Arthur Andersen and WorldCom, further transmitted a sense that CSR principles were not integrated into core business activities and could be dismissed as little more than marketing tools.[76]

Sensitivities about the negative impact of the private sector's intrusion into public and social life were, predictably, manifested in criticisms of partnership arrangements involving business organisations. Type II voluntary partnership arrangements were, for example, described as opportunities for the private sector to position itself as a partner in the implementation of development solutions and, more worryingly, as a way of frustrating government efforts to address global problems.[77] Partnership was also presented as a mechanism for "institutional capture" that, through increased access to policymakers, enabled corporations to influence public decision-making processes[78] and enter the realm of social service provision.[79] In his book *The Corporation: The Pathological Pursuit of Profit and Power*, Joel Bakan went so far as to assert that because partnerships between the public and private sectors were built upon the notion of equality between partners, democracy, which rests upon the sovereignty of government, was at risk.[80]

Questions about the ideological underpinning of partnership were compounded by a view of PPPs as "the Trojan Horse of neoliberal development."[81] These arrangements were accused of allowing businesses to "greenwash" their image by engaging with government and NGOs to address environmental concerns and the fight against poverty while simultaneously expanding their markets,[82] and participating in "bluewashing," a practice that enabled the corporate sector, using frameworks such as the Global Compact, to enhance its reputation and access international decision-making processes through relationships with the UN.[83] In response to these accusations,

76. Bakan, J. (2004) *The Corporation: The Pathological Pursuit of Profit and Power*, London, UK: Constable and Robinson Ltd (pp. 58–59).
77. Doran, P. (2002) World summit on sustainable development (Johannesburg): An assessment for IISD, *Briefing Paper*, 3 October, Geneva, Switzerland: International Institute for Sustainable Development.
78. Richter, J. (2000) "Partnerships" between UN agencies and transnational companies: A critical perspective, *Public-Private "Partnerships" Addressing Public Health Needs or Corporate Agendas?* Report on the HAI Europe/BUKO Pharma-Kampagne Seminar, 3 November 2000, HAI *Europe* and Utting, P. (2001) UN-business partnerships: Whose agenda counts? *Third World Network*, 24 July (p. 7).
79. Standing, G. (2010) Social protection. In: Cornwall, A. and Eade, D. eds. Op. cit. p. 64.
80. Bakan (2004) Op. cit. p. 5.
81. Miraftab (2004) Op. cit. and see also Davies (2008) Op. cit. p. 201.
82. CorpWatch (2001) *Greenwash 101 Fact Sheet*. www.corpwatch.org/article/greenwash-101-fact-sheet (accessed February 8, 2022).
83. Bruno, K. and Karliner, J. (2000) *Tangled Up in Blue, Corporate Partnerships at the United Nations*, San Francisco, CA, USA: The Transnational Resource and Action Center and see also Bruno,

a rethink about partnerships with the private sector was called for with demands for stronger public sector control of these arrangements. Writers such as Judith Richter, for example, suggested that while public-private connecting points could be explored, more effort should first be invested in establishing stronger regulation and licensing regimes to ensure corporate accountability.[84]

Towards collaborative governance and sustainability

The popularity of NPM has waned of late with growing interest in alternatives such as New Public Service,[85] which promotes a view of public service centred upon public interest and the building of collaborative relationships with citizens, and New Public Governance,[86] in which diverse actors contribute to public service delivery and policymaking. These notions are integral to the concept of collaborative governance, a mode of governance that replaces adversarial and managerial modes of policy making with more cooperative relationships in which multiple stakeholders come together in common forums with public agencies to engage in consensus-oriented decision-making.[87]

In a similar manner, and most obviously since the financial and social crisis of 2007–8, alongside calls for greater corporate regulation[88] and adherence to stronger codes of business conduct,[89] the concept of CSR has also been modified and even replaced by paradigms such as "shared value" and "business sustainability." These trends represent a move away from a short-term view of CSR to more comprehensive business management approaches that seek to maximise long-term economic, social and environmental value.[90]

K. and Karliner, J. (2002) *Earthsummit. Biz: The Corporate Takeover of Sustainable Development*, Oakland, CA, USA: Food First Books.

84. Richter, J. (2004) Public-private partnerships for health: A trend with no alternatives? *Development*, 47 (2): 43–48. https://doi.org/10.1057/palgrave.development.1100043 (p. 47).
85. Denhardt, R. and Denhardt, J. (2000) The new public service: Serving rather than steering. *Public Administration Review*, 60: 549–559. doi: 10.1111/0033-3352.00117 and Denhardt, J. and Denhardt, R. (2015) *The New Public Service: Serving, Not Steering*. doi: 10.4324/9781315699356
86. Dickinson, H. (2016) From new public management to new public governance: The implications for a 'new public service'. doi: 10.22459/TSS.07.2016.03
87. Ansell, C. and Gash, A. (2007) Collaborative governance in theory and practice. *Journal of Public Administration Research and Theory*, 18 (4): 543–571. doi: 10.1093/jopart/mum032 (p. 543).
88. See Stiglitz, J. (2008) A crisis of confidence. *The Guardian*, 22 October. www.theguardian.com/commentisfree/cifamerica/2008/oct/22/economy-financial-crisis-regulation (accessed January 3, 2022).
89. Jacob, C.K. (2012) The impact of financial crisis on corporate social responsibility and its implications for reputation risk management. *Journal of Management and Sustainability*, 2 (2).
90. See www2.deloitte.com/ru/en/pages/risk/solutions/sustainability-and-csr.html (accessed January 3, 2022) and Porter, M.E. and Kramer, M.R. (2011) The big idea: Creating shared value. *Harvard Business Review*, 89: 2–17 and Murray, A., Haynes, K. and Hudson, L.J. (2010) Collaborating to achieve corporate social responsibility and sustainability? Possibilities and

Shared value, a term coined by Michael E. Porter and Mark R. Kramer in 2011, refers to policies and operating practices that enhance the competitiveness of a company while simultaneously advancing the economic and social conditions in the communities in which it operates.[91] Multi-stakeholder collaboration is presented as one of the strategies that can enable companies to generate shared value by, for example, assisting the development of industry clusters among private companies and other actors.[92] Business sustainability, which is sometimes expressed simply as "sustainability," is linked explicitly to the idea of sustainable development, the broader relationship between business and society and the private sector's long-term environmental, social and economic impact.[93] As well as a greater focus on systemic issues,[94] collaboration is positioned at the core of sustainability which, rather than being viewed solely as a management issue, gives special attention to its relational aspects.[95]

From public-private partnership to multi-stakeholder partnership

Although NPM and CSR still have traction, the concepts of collaborative governance and sustainability have clearly had an impact on how partnership is currently named and framed. This is manifested most obviously in a shift away from interest in PPPs and bi-lateral relationships with the corporate sector to broader forms of stakeholder collaboration (see Figure 2.5).

The adoption of terms such as "multi-stakeholder" or "multi-actor" collaboration and partnership has much to do with pressure from civil society and a growing non-profit sector to address the downside of globalisation with more effective solutions to issues such as environmental degradation, poverty and social exclusion. In the 1990s, recognition of this role appears to have contributed to the emergence of references to trisector (public, private and civil society) and later cross-sector partnership, both of which were helpful in transmitting a sense that, as well as partners from government and business, partnership could also embrace a broader spectrum of actors,

---

problems. *Sustainability Accounting, Management and Policy Journal*, 1 (2): 161–177. https://doi.org/10.1108/20408021011089220

91. See www.sharedvalue.org/about/what-is-shared-value/
92. Porter and Kramer (2011) Op. cit.
93. Murray et al. (2010) Op. cit. p. 162.
94. Interestingly, this perception is noted by John Elkington, who coined the term "the triple bottom line" (TBL or 3BL), a framework to encourage businesses to consider its social, environmental and financial impacts. In an article in 2018, Elkington states that, rather than the CSR accounting tool that this has become, the original term was generated with a focus on systemic change and transformation of capitalism and should be revisited using this lens. See Elkington, J. (2018) 25 years ago I coined the phrase "triple bottom line": Here's why it's time to rethink it. *Harvard Business Review*. https://hbr.org/2018/06/25-years-ago-i-coined-the-phrase-triple-bottom-line-heres-why-im-giving-up-on-it?msclkid=e2737cb8b10411ecbffa3ef623a31b1d (accessed March 30, 2022).
95. Ibid., p. 174.

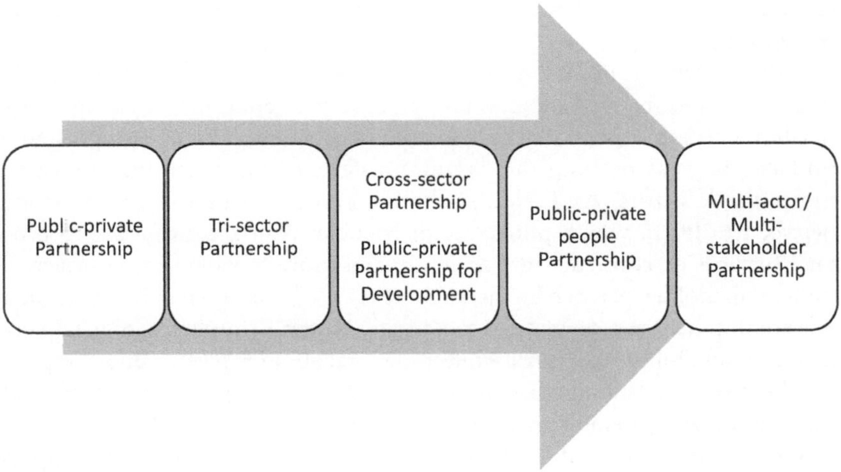

Figure 2.5 From public-private partnership to multi-stakeholder partnership

including NGOs, civil society organisations (CSOs), academic institutions and research bodies, among others. It was also noted that private sector involvement in partnership initiatives was not a prerequisite.[96] Surveys of the transnational partnership arrangements developed after the 2002 WSSD in Johannesburg, for example, noted particularly the absence of the business sector in Type II partnerships.[97] Nonetheless, in spite of notable efforts to adopt broader denominations in the early 2000s,[98] partnership connections with business, albeit of a broader nature, continued to dominate the field and were apparent in the use of terms such as PPPs for Development;[99] Development Partnerships with the private sector;[100] and Public-private-people Partnerships (P4).[101] Since 2015, however, and largely due to the

96. Mandell, M. and Steelman, T. (2003) Understanding what can be accomplished through inter-organizational innovations: The importance of typologies, context and management strategies. *Public Management Review*, 5 (2): 197–224. https://doi.org/10.1080/1461667032000066417 (p. 198) and Selsky and Parker (2005) Op. cit. p. 854.
97. Pattberg and Widerberg (2016) Op. cit. p. 44.
98. See, for example, the use of Cross-sector Social Interactions (CSSI). CSSI Community: www.cssicommunity.org/ (accessed March 30, 2022).
99. The term *Alianzas Publico Privadas para el Desarrollo* (Public-private Partnerships for Development) has been used extensively in the development sector in Spain and Latin America with an explicit understanding that such forms do not correspond to traditional public-private partnerships; see AECID (2021) *Guía AECID para las alianzas multiactor*, Madrid, Spain: AECID (p. 12).
100. See www.giz.de/en/worldwide/61034.html?msclkid=01b311c4b10311ec844fd2eeb12c4fed (accessed March 30, 2022).
101. Ng, S.T., Wong, J.M.W. and Wong, K.K.W. (2013) A public private people partnerships (P4) process framework for infrastructure development in Hong Kong. *Cities*, 31: 370–381 https://

language adopted in the UN 2030 Sustainable Development Agenda, the terminology of multi-stakeholder or multi-actor partnership has become predominant.

Although the term PPP is still used in a confusing and interchangeable manner,[102] and many academics and practitioners continue to equate partnership with some form of private sector engagement, it is increasingly being understood as something that is quite different from partnership involving multiple actors. As Table 2.3 shows, a clear distinction can be made between PPPs, in which public sector agencies contract businesses to provide services or construct infrastructure and more flexible non-contractual multi-stakeholder partnership arrangements. PPPs are generally based on a relationship between signatories to a legally binding contract with clear vertical accountability structures while multi-stakeholder partnerships emphasise horizontal accountability, have more flexible targets, deliverables and timeframes, are generally unregulated and may not have a legal identity.[103]

The nomenclature of multi-stakeholder or multi-actor partnership is important because it embraces the inclusion of multiple players and levels in collaborative arrangements. As well as challenging the perception of private sector predominance and business as a "special partner," the term is

Table 2.3 Public-private partnership and multi-stakeholder partnership

Public-private partnership (PPP)	***Multi-stakeholder partnership***
Contract-based arrangement with clear vertical accountability structures	Generally less contractual with emphasis on horizontal accountability
Clear targets, deliverables and timeframes	More flexibility around targets and deliverables with less determined timeframes
Operates within legal and regulatory constructs	Partners operate within legal regulatory constructs but partnership itself is unregulated
Limited stakeholder engagement	More extensive stakeholder engagement

Source: Adapted from Caplan (2013)[104]
Credit: Building Partnerships for Development in Water and Sanitation (BPD)

doi.org/10.1016/j.cities.2012.12.002; and: Zhang, J., Zou, W. and Kumaraswamy, M. (2015) Developing public private people partnership (4P) for post disaster infrastructure procurement. *International Journal of Disaster Resilience in the Built Environment*, 6 (4): 468–484. https://doi.org/10.1108/IJDRBE-06-2014-0040

102. Bäckstrand, K. and Kylsäter, M. (2014) Old wine in new bottles? The legitimation and delegitimation of UN Public-Private Partnerships for sustainable development from the Johannesburg Summit to the Rio+20 Summit. *Globalizations*, 11 (3): 331–347. http://dx.doi.org/10.1080/14747731.2014.892398
103. Caplan and Stott (2008) Op. cit. p. 25.
104. Caplan (2013) Op. cit. p. 3.

also broad enough to include actors that do not fit neatly within rigid sector categories such as trade unions, academic institutions and media organisations.[105] The unpacking of umbrella categories such as "government," "civil society" and the "private sector" also invites consideration of the roles that more diverse organisations and groups might play in partnership initiatives. In the case of the private sector, for example, this has enabled a more nuanced view of business and recognition of "new" partnership players such as small, medium and micro enterprises (SMMEs), national businesses, parastatals, social enterprises, chambers of commerce and business coalitions, among others.

Reframing partnership

While it is important to explore the contemporary trends and narratives that have contributed to generalised understandings of partnership, such an exploration gives little insight into the wide variety of empirical reasons for choosing to work collaboratively and to the fact that, in many cases, alternatives to working in partnership may be limited. Table 2.4 summarises some of the overarching motivations for partnering cited by those involved in the

Table 2.4 Reasons for working in partnership

Access to resources	Diverse financial and in-kind resources that can be pooled to address an issue or challenge
Capacity-building	Opportunities to build strategic and operative capacity and skills and strengthen institutions
Coordination	Reach is improved and duplication avoided
Empowerment	Stronger voice for the disadvantaged and marginalised
Focus	Gaps, needs and priorities are more clearly identified and targeted
Innovation	More creative and dynamic approaches to societal challenges
Learning	Opportunities for learning and knowledge exchange
Legitimacy	Wider stakeholder mobilisation gives a more democratic mandate
Social capital	Connections and relationships that reinforce the social fabric of society
Stability	Inclusion of different stakeholders contributes to a more integrated and cohesive society
Sustainability	Joint ownership and action promote long-term, durable and positive change

Source: Adapted from Stott (2019)[106]

105. Stott, L. and Keatman, T. (2005) Tools for measuring community engagement in partnerships. *BPD Practitioner Note*, London, UK: Building Partnerships for Development (p. 4).
106. Stott, L. (2019) *How European Social Fund Managing Authorities and Intermediate Bodies Support Partnership*, Revised edition, Brussels, Belgium: European Commission (pp. 12–14).

research programmes that inform this book. These viewpoints suggest that, as well as instrumental reasons for collaboration, there is also interest in its intrinsic value.

The diverse motives for working in partnership in Table 2.4 are reflected in calls for more "innovative" and "inclusive" multi-stakeholder initiatives and collaborative solutions that address complex global challenges. These "wicked problems" include issues

> such as poverty, climate change, environmental degradation or food insecurity, have no closed-form definition, emerge from complex systems in which cause and effect relationships are either unknown or highly uncertain, and have multiple stakeholders with strongly held and conflicting values related to the problem.[107]

A focus on addressing "wicked" problems is central to the UN 2030 Sustainable Development Agenda which calls for stronger collective action and more varied resources to address global challenges such as climate change, poverty and rising inequality by engaging with diverse stakeholders to achieve its 17 SDGs.[108] However, although attention here is given to the implementation of "inclusive" and "transformative" partnerships "built upon principles and values, a shared vision, and shared goals: placing people and planet at the center,"[109] it is noteworthy that SDG17, *Partnerships for the Goals*, essentially promotes a much contested economic growth model that is likely to deepen rather than reduce social and environmental problems.[110] This dichotomy reflects the continued ambiguity of partnership and its straddling of contradictory viewpoints; one which seeks to maintain the status quo, often through the adaptation of "business as usual" models, and another that calls for the transformation of existing systems and structures in order to promote long-term change.[111] In this regard, it is worth asking how

107. Dentoni, D., Bitzer, V. and Pascucci, S. (2016) Cross-sector partnerships and the co-creation of dynamic capabilities for stakeholder orientation. *Journal of Business Ethics*, 135: 35–53. https://doi.org/10.1007/s10551-015-2728-8 (pp. 35–36).
108. United Nations (2015) *Transforming Our World: The 2030 Agenda for Sustainable Development*, Resolution 70/1 Adopted by the United Nations General Assembly on 25 September 2015, New York, NY, USA: United Nations.
109. United Nations (2014) The Road to Dignity by 2030: Ending poverty, transforming all lives and protecting the planet. *Synthesis report of the Secretary-General on the post-2015 sustainable development agenda*, New York, NY, USA: United Nations, a call is made for "inclusive" and "transformative" partnerships "built upon principles and values, a shared vision, and shared goals: placing people and planet at the center" (p. 24).
110. Stott, L. and Scoppetta, A. (2020) Partnerships for the Goals: Beyond SDG17, *Revista Diecisiete: Investigación interdisciplinar para los Objetivos de Desarrollo*, 2: 29–38 doi: 10.36852/2695-4427_2020_02.02
111. Richter, J. (2004b) *Public-Private Partnerships and International Health Policy-Making: How Can Public Interests Be Safeguarded?*, Helsinki, Finland: Ministry of Foreign Affairs of Finland, Development Policy Information Unit.

far partnership can realistically be expected to address pressing development issues on a large scale when systemic issues relating to global economic and political power relations remain unchallenged.[112]

Attention to the link between partnership and transformation appear to respond to a growing consensus that profound structural changes are required to achieve the targets of the SDGs. This, in turn, demands a "nexus approach" that joins up collaborative efforts at different spatial levels, across institutions, themes and sectors, and between policy and practice.[113] In this regard, beyond changes to how partnership is *named*, a further evolution in how partnership is *framed* seems imperative. In order to transmit its potential for generating "real" transformation, it is surely timely then to decouple partnership from a narrative that centres almost exclusively on the promotion of relationships with the private sector and, correspondingly, an ideological straitjacket that links it unequivocally to a capitalist growth model. More crucially, it involves a movement away from an understanding of partnership as a purely instrumental and managerial form of collaboration to one that more fully embraces its relational and intrinsic dimensions. These changes will, according to Eisler, necessitate attention to the principle of "linking rather than ranking" so that no actors are regarded as superior or inferior to others.[114]

The need for deeper acknowledgement of the real-life expectations of partnership for people who seek innovative and collective ways of supporting their own development is at the core of this reframing.[115] In order to comprehend partnership more fully, it is thus vital to consider the specific and dynamic locations in which multi-stakeholder collaboration evolves and how individual and organisation variables crosscut and connect with them in particular and changing circumstances. This "chemistry" determines the nature and scope of collaborative relationships, and the drivers for participation in them, and is essential to any genuine understanding of partnership.[116]

112. See Rein et al. (2005) Op. cit. pp. 122–123 and Stott, L. (2005) *Listening to the Critics: Can We Learn From Arguments Against Partnerships With Business?*, London, UK: Building Partnerships for Development. www.bpdws.org/web/d/doc_46.pdf?statsHandlerDone=1 (accessed January 5, 2022).
113. Boas, I., Biermann, F. and Kanie, N. (2016) Cross-sectoral strategies in global sustainability governance: Towards a nexus approach. *International Environmental Agreements*, 16: 449–464. https://doi.org/10.1007/s10784-016-9321-1 (p. 455).
114. Eisler (1987) Op. cit. p. xvii.
115. Rein and Stott (2009) Op. cit. p. 86.
116. El Ansari, W., Phillips, C.J. and Hammick, M. (2001) Collaboration and partnerships: Developing the evidence base. *Health and Social Care in the Community*, 9 (4): 215–227. https://doi.org/10.1046/j.0966-0410.2001.00299.x (p. 218).

3 Exploring contextual drivers for partnership

In 2000, an agricultural partnership was established in Luangeni, a small village in the Chipata District of Zambia's Eastern Province. The partnership began in response to protests by members of the local community against the opening of a branch of the South African supermarket chain, Shoprite, in the locality. The concern was that the supermarket would rob the community of their livelihoods as people would choose to shop there instead of buying from local farmers. The village leader went as far as to say that it would be good if the supermarket was set on fire so that "we can go on with our business of selling vegetables."[1]

Learning that Shoprite would not accept locally produced vegetables because of their "inferior quality," members of the Zambia Partnership Forum, a grouping of business, public and academic actors that had been established to promote corporate citizenship and sustainable development,[2] proposed a collaborative initiative with the Luangeni community that involved a seed company, the Ministry of Agriculture and NGOs working together to train local farmers to produce vegetables that could be marketed directly to Shoprite. An international donor also took an interest in the partnership and agreed to contribute funds to support its activities. Local farmers soon began producing high-quality vegetables that Shoprite could buy and sell. As a result, the average monthly income in Luangeni increased dramatically and community participants were better able to cover education and health expenses. The active involvement of women farmers was also perceived as having promoted gender equality.[3]

The success of the Luangeni Partnership generated enormous interest, and calls were made for its replication in other parts of Zambia where

1. Raworth, K. and Wren-Lewis, L. (2008) How change happens in the private sector. In *From Poverty to Power Case Study*, Oxford, UK: Oxfam International. http:/dx.doi.org/10.2139/ssrn.2659221 (p. 2).
2. The Forum for Business Leaders and Social Partners (Partnership Forum) was established in 1999 to promote corporate social responsibility and sustainable development in Zambia.
3. Yambayamba, K.E. (2006) "Do it for us?" The challenges of replicating a partnership. *Partnership Matters, Current Issues in Cross-Sector Collaboration*, 4: 69–72. London, UK: The Partnering Initiative (p. 69).

DOI: 10.4324/9781003199434-4

Shoprite operated, including Chamba Valley on the outskirts of the capital city, Lusaka.[4] In this location, however, the partnership failed to live up to expectations. In addition to funding constraints and a weaker case for business involvement due to more stringent quality demands for produce sold to urban customers, this lack of success also rested crucially on differences in the nature of the organisations and individuals involved, and the interactions between them (see Box 3.1).[5]

This story reinforces the importance of exploring partnership in relation to particular and changing contexts, and of the need to analyse the distinct and sometimes subtle external, organisational and individual variables that might affect them, even when, as in this case, a collaborative initiative is developed in the same country to address the same problem.

Box 3.1 The Chamba Valley Partnership in Zambia

The Chamba Valley Partnership was established in Lusaka, the capital city of Zambia in 2002. The aim of the partnership was to provide opportunities for the 98 farmers who made up the Chamba Valley Cooperative Society to increase their income from small-scale farming. The farmers, many of whom were retrenched civil servants, were supported by the Zambia Partnership Forum from whom they had learned about the Luangeni Partnership. The Forum assisted them to broker relationships with the Zambia Seed Company (Zamseed) and the Ministry of Agriculture and Cooperatives who provided them with seeds and extension services in order to supply Freshmark, a subsidiary of the Shoprite supermarket chain. For Shoprite, access to locally produced fruit and vegetables was viewed as a useful way of reducing the costs of importing produce from South Africa. Although the Partnership initially appeared to enhance community cohesion, two years after it began only ten farmers had been able to supply produce to Freshmark. Low output and inability to provide produce on a consistent basis were attributed to lack of resources, weak public sector support and Shoprite's scepticism about working with small-scale producers in a competitive urban setting. The Partnership itself also lacked joint governance structures and systems with a tendency for each partner to work through the Zambia Partnership Forum rather than with one another.

4. The Partnership was showcased at the 2002 World Summit on Sustainable Development (WSSD) (Yambayamba, 2006:72).
5. Rein, M. and Stott, L. (2009) Working together: Critical perspectives on six cross-sector partnerships in Southern Africa. *Journal of Business Ethics*, 90 (1): 79–89. https://doi.org/10.1007/s10551-008-9915-9 (p. 83).

The importance of context

As interest in partnership has grown and "wicked" problems such as climate change and social inequality have promoted a perception that single-sector approaches to address complex challenges are unviable, contextualising the experiences of working collaboratively has become more urgent. As well as assisting the development of tailor-made rather than "one size fits all" collaborative approaches, looking into specific contextual variables is also a useful way of assessing whether a partnership arrangement is in fact the most appropriate solution to a problem.[6] Thus, in addition to ascertaining whether there has been consideration of conventional project or contractual arrangements to address a *particular* problem, it is also necessary to ask how a partnership intervention might make a difference in a *particular* situation.[7]

The importance of paying attention to context when looking at social phenomena is not new. It is at the heart of the case study research approach and has been recognised by thinkers from the realms of sociology and anthropology as being essential to understanding "deeds and words."[8] Studying what Eric C. Poncelet describes as the "sociohistoric factors" that influence partnership can help us to understand how different partnership meanings and narratives have been shaped, sustained and changed in specific settings.[9] This approach involves much more than an examination of the overarching context in which a partnership approach develops; it also includes attention to the multiple levels that this embraces and the connections between them. The contextual interactions that affect partnership have been described as occurring, "not only at the macro level, e.g. from North to South, but also *within partnering organisations* (which can be located in several regions) and *by individuals* working for or affected by the organisations or the partnership (my italics)."[10] Analysis of this multi-layered landscape can provide insights into the complex and dynamic interactions that occur between the place, purpose and players involved in partnership.

6. Pattberg, P. and Widerberg, O. (2016) Transnational multistakeholder partnerships for sustainable development: Conditions for success. *Ambio*, 45: 42–51. https://doi.org/10.1007/s13280-015-0684-2 (p. 49).
7. El Ansari, W., Phillips, C. J. and Hammick, M. (2001) Collaboration and partnerships: Developing the evidence base. *Health and Social Care in the Community*, 9 (4): 215–227. https://doi.org/10.1046/j.0966-0410.2001.00299.x (p. 218).
8. See Murphy, D.F. and Stott, L. (2021) Partnerships for the Sustainable Development Goals (SDGs). In: Murphy, D.F. and Stott, L. eds. *Partnerships for the Sustainable Development Goals (SDGs)*, Basel, Switzerland: MDPI (p. 1).
9. Poncelet, E.C. (2001) A kiss here and a kiss there: Conflict and collaboration in environmental partnerships. *Environmental Management*, 27 (1): 13–25. https://doi.org/10.1007/s002670010130 (p. 15).
10. Kolk, A. (2013) Partnerships as a panacea for addressing global problems? On rationale, context, actors, impact and limitations. In: Seitanidi, M. and Crane, A. eds. *Social Partnerships and Responsible Business: A Research Handbook*, London, UK: Routledge, [Online] 1–30. https://papers.ssrn.com/sol3/papers.cfm?abstract_id=2089577 (accessed February 9, 2022) (p. 9).

Contextual drivers for partnership

The interactions between what has been described as macro (societal), meso (inter-organisational) and micro (individual) levels[11] can be correlated with external, organisational and individual drivers, the interplay between which will define a partnership arrangement's nature and purpose (see Figure 3.1).[12]

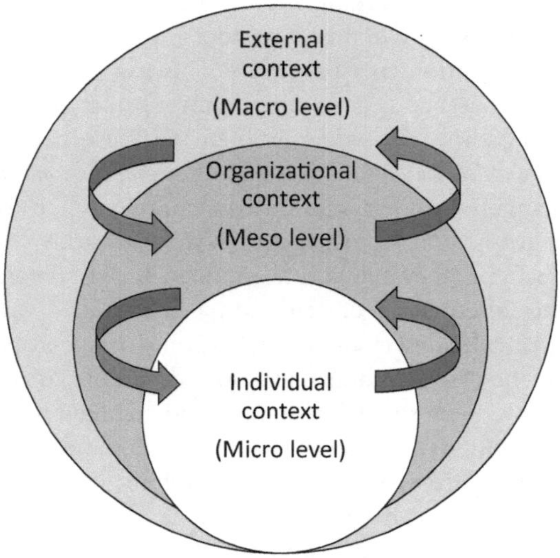

Figure 3.1 Contextual interactions in partnership

Source: Stott and Murphy (2020)[14]

The premise here is that choices about working in partnership respond to partnership drivers. These drivers include enabling factors that "push" actors to work together in partnership and partnership disablers that "pull" against working in this way.[13] Because partnership approaches are often mandated by international and national laws and organisational directives, obligations that promote partnership also need to be considered. Here, a further push–pull factor will relate to the nature of sanctions that may be imposed if this way of working is not adopted (see Table 3.1).

11. Kolk, A., Van Dolen, W. and Vock, M. (2010) Trickle effects of cross-sector social partnerships. *Journal of Business Ethics*, 94 (Supplement 1): 123–137. https://doi.org/10.1007/s10551-011-0783-3 (pp. 123–124).
12. Caplan, K., Gomme, J., Mugabi, J. and Stott, L. (2007) *Assessing Partnership Performance: Understanding the Drivers for Success*, London, UK: Building Partnerships for Development (pp. 9–10).
13. Ibid., p. 8.
14. Stott, L. and Murphy, D.F. (2020) An inclusive approach to partnerships for the SDGs: Using a relationship lens to explore the potential for transformational collaboration. *Special Issue: Partnerships for the SDGs, Sustainability*, 12 (19): 7905. https://doi.org/10.3390/su12197905

Table 3.1 Partnership drivers

Incentives Factors that motivate organisations and individuals to engage in partnership	**Disincentives** Factors that discourage organisational and individual engagement in partnership
Obligations Factors that oblige organisations and individuals to participate in partnership	**Sanctions** Penalties incurred by organisations and individuals for non-participation in partnership

Source: Adapted from Stott (2017)[15]

Research on contextual drivers for partnership indicates that a collaborative approach can be enhanced when there is an enabling environment in which a series of aspects is in place that encourage this way of working. These factors include supportive legal and regulatory frameworks for working in collaboration; awareness and knowledge about partnership and its potential; positive relationship histories between different sectors and organisations such as structures and traditions of social dialogue, previous partnership experiences, and the existence of organisations or individuals capable of bringing different actors, sectors and institutions together. Where these aspects are weak or absent, the general view is that it may be more difficult to work in partnership (see Figure 3.2).

Figure 3.2 Factors influencing an enabling environment for partnership

Source: Adapted from Stott (2019)[16]

15. Stott, L. (2017) *Partnership and Social Progress: Multi-Stakeholder Collaboration in Context*. Ph.D. Thesis, University of Edinburgh, UK (p. 38).
16. Stott, L. (2019) *How European Social Fund Managing Authorities and Intermediate Bodies Support Partnership*, Revised edition, Brussels, Belgium: European Commission (pp. 21–23).

While the factors presented in Figure 3.2 offer useful preliminary pointers for assessing a partnership landscape, their interaction and connection with other variables in specific contexts merit deeper examination. As well as considerations relating to time constraints and demands in specific contexts, such as programme, project, electoral and planning cycles, and the different schedules of partners and funding agencies, which impose deadlines for the achievement of individual and organisational targets,[17] external events such as economic, political and social crises or humanitarian emergencies in different contexts will also determine whether or not the timing for developing a partnership arrangement is appropriate. Partnership initiatives addressing HIV/AIDS in South Africa and Zambia, for example, show that the urgency of addressing a particular issue or challenge is an important trigger for different sector organisations to work together and find joint solutions to a problem.[18] This example further suggests that in some contexts, what may be conceived as a "pull" against working in partnership may sometimes be a "push" towards it and that, at times, the very absence of the "push" factors mentioned in Figure 3.2 may drive a partnership approach. Such a view is reinforced by the proliferation of partnership arrangements in the field of humanitarian action[19] and demands for more strategic and innovative collaborative arrangements to address the socio-economic consequences of the financial crisis of 2007–8 in Europe.[20]

Awareness about partnership and its potential, and the existence of guidance and skills that might support working in this way, also need to be carefully considered. In this regard, it is helpful to look at who is promoting partnership, why and in what ways. Partnership, as shown in Chapter 1, can embrace diverse and sometimes opposing paradigms and perspectives, so exploration of how it is understood by organisations and their representatives, and the reasons for its adoption in particular contexts, is useful. Analysis of contextual drivers will also necessitate examination of power dynamics and the nature of the influence wielded by different organisations and individuals in promoting partnership arrangements, including those who assume a role in bringing different partners together.

Attention to conveners, facilitators and partnership brokers who act as intermediaries that bring different sectors and organisations together in particular contexts, such as the Zambia Partnership Forum mentioned earlier,

17. Rein, M., Stott, L., Yambayamba, K., Hardman, S. and Reid, S. (2005) *Working Together: A Critical Analysis of Cross-Sector Partnerships in Southern Africa*, Cambridge, UK: University of Cambridge Programme for Industry (p. 11).
18. Rein and Stott (2009) Op. cit.
19. The 2016 World Disaster Report (WDR) reinforces the necessity of working in partnership due to the need for rapid, cross-sector and cohesive approaches to crisis situations, see IFRC (2016) *World Disasters Report, Resilience: Saving Lives Today, Investing for Tomorrow*, Geneva, Switzerland: International Federation of Red Cross and Red Crescent Societies (IFRC) (pp. 162–185).
20. Stott, L. and Scoppetta, A. (2013) Promoting local economic development through partnerships in Europe. *Skills@Work: Theory and Practice Journal*, 6: 2–12 (p. 5).

is essential to any consideration of partnership drivers.[21] The nature of the partnership intermediary role and how it works in practice will be explored more deeply in Chapter 5 of this book. Here, however, it is of importance for two reasons: first, because, as it may be assumed by both individuals and organisations, it reinforces the fact that drivers at these levels are crucial to understanding context; and, second, because it raises questions about the partnership "push" exerted by those assuming this function. Although growing evidence positions partnership brokers as critical in shaping and galvanising the development of effective partnership arrangements,[22] the traditional external intermediary role exercised by many donor or funding agencies invites caution about actors who are not partners but initiate or promote this way of working, often in response to mandated organisational norms. In advocating for and contributing funds to partnership arrangements, these agencies often exert enormous influence on collaborative relationships. Their motivations for engaging in partnership initiatives and how far they might distort possibilities for finding other ways of addressing issues or problems thus merit attention.

Box 3.2 Overcoming obstacles to partnership

In identifying different partnership drivers, emphasis in the literature has been placed on promoting greater awareness of how the factors that impede partnership might be addressed *before* a collaborative initiative is established.[23] Peter Newborne and Ken Caplan propose that this may be done by encouraging organisations to reflect on the wider context in which a partnership arrangement will be implemented, the internal organisational context of potential partners and relationships among them. Once these issues have been examined and enablers and disablers identified, decisions can be made about whether it is worthwhile pursuing a partnership option and what action might be taken to address challenges. This process involves carefully analysing obstacles to partnership and looking at how they might be:

- **Influenced or overcome** by addressing and changing the blockage directly, e.g. appealing to policy decision-makers to make legal changes that assist partnership promotion or working to address lack of skills, knowledge and expertise so that a partnership initiative is able to develop.

21. Stott, L. ed. (2018) *Shaping Sustainable Change: The Role of Partnership Brokering in Optimising Collaborative Action*, London, UK: Greenleaf Publishing, Routledge, Taylor and Francis Group.
22. Ibid.
23. Newborne, P. and Caplan, K. (2006) *Creating Space for Innovation, Understanding Enablers for Multi-Sector Partnerships in the Water and Sanitation Sector*, London, UK: Building Partnerships for Development.

- **Circumvented** by moving around the impediment in order to find innovative ways of addressing it, e.g. working around legal and regulatory impediments or enlisting the support of other organisations and individuals to support a partnership approach or initiative.
- **Redirected** by shifting the partnership focus, e.g. widening the thematic aim, using a different approach or location or involving new or different actors.

Research work on partnership in the European Social Fund (ESF) endorses this approach as a useful way of exploring what measures it may be necessary or realistic to undertake to support partnership approaches, and whether other avenues for addressing problems should be investigated.[24]

The factors listed in Figure 3.2 show that partnership drivers combine different external, organisational and individual enablers and disablers. Although these drivers overlap and are difficult to disentangle, in the interest of throwing greater light on how they are manifested in different contexts and the nature of their influence on the development of partnership initiatives, efforts have been made here to examine some of their key components in turn.

External drivers

In the literature on partnership, the study of particular historical, cultural, social and political contexts is recommended.[25] To this may be added financial, institutional, sectoral (public, private and civil society sectors) and thematic aspects (health, education, etc.) as well as particular conditions in different regional, national and local environments.[26] Additional variables, as noted earlier, might include crisis or conflict situations,[27] and settings where there are "weak governance and formal institutional voids, with a

24. Stott (2008) Op. cit. p. 33 and (2019) Op. cit. pp. 22–24.
25. Harrison, E. (2002) "The problem with the locals": Partnership and participation in Ethiopia. *Development and Change* 33 (4): 587–610. https://doi.org/10.1111/1467-7660.00271 (p. 607); Mandell, M. and Steelman, T. (2003) Understanding what can be accomplished through interorganizational innovations: The importance of typologies, context and management strategies. *Public Management Review*, 5 (2): 197–224. https://doi.org/10.1080/1461667032000066417 (pp. 212–213), and Seitanidi, M.M. and Ryan, A. (2007) A critical review of forms of corporate community involvement: From philanthropy to partnerships. *International Journal of Nonprofit and Voluntary Sector Marketing*, 12: 247–266. https://doi.org/10.1002/nvsm.306 (p. 255).
26. Rein and Stott (2009) Op. cit. p. 81.
27. Tennyson, R., Stott, L, Marhubi, A. and Wood, E. (2016) The necessity of transformation, emerging partnership lessons from diverse contexts. *Report for the Promoting Effective Partnering (PEP) Facility*, London, UK: Partnership Brokers Association. http://partnershipbrokers.org/w/wp-content/uploads/2010/08/Emerging-Partnership-Lessons-from-Diverse-Contexts-sm2.pdf (accessed February 9, 2022) (p. 15).

prevalence of informal institutions."[28] These "external" sociohistoric elements are essential for the organisations and individuals that develop and engage in partnership arrangements to consider as they will influence the way partners work together and how they develop their relationship. Figure 3.3 presents some of the external factors that are likely to play a critical role in the adoption of a partnership approach.

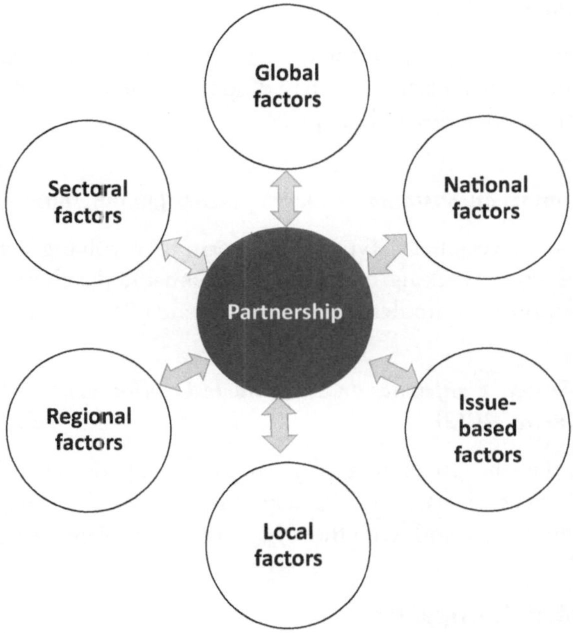

Figure 3.3 External partnership drivers
Source Stott (2017)[30]

Some of the external drivers that might promote or impede the uptake of partnership in specific country contexts and localities include global tendencies and goals.[29] As well as contemporary ideological trends and development paradigms, efforts to address climate change and respond to humanitarian and social equality concerns also play a role in promoting collaborative approaches in different environments. International frameworks that capture the focus of these movements have been identified as driving forces for partnership since the late 1980s (see Box 3.3). These overarching agendas may focus on topical development issues and concerns as well as specific sector issues and themes at particular points in time.

28. Kolk (2013) Op. cit. p. 8.
29. Pattberg and Widerberg (2016) Op. cit. p. 48.
30. Stott (2017) Op. cit. p. 42.

Box 3.3 Examples of global frameworks that have promoted partnership

Earth summits[31]

United Nations Conference on Environment and Development, Rio de Janeiro (1992)

The Agenda 21 action plan for sustainable development called for the creation of a global partnership based upon cooperation among states, key sectors of societies and people.

World Summit on Sustainable Development, Johannesburg (2002)

Promotion of voluntary Type II partnerships involving actors from different sectors working on different sustainable development focus areas to support the implementation of Agenda 21.

United Nations Conference on Sustainable Development, Rio de Janeiro (2012)

Called for the reinvigoration of the global partnership for sustainable development launched in Rio in 1992 with commitment from major groups and stakeholders to work with the UN to address implementation gaps.

UN Global Compact[32]

Promotion of partnerships among UN, business, government and civil society stakeholders through different business collaborations, e.g. within a value chain, across industries, with a local government or civil society organisation, or with the UN, to help create long-term value and positive impact on society, advance the sustainable development agenda and address key global challenges.

High-level Fora on Aid Effectiveness[33]

Seek to transform aid relationships between donors and partners in line with five partnership principles that encourage local ownership,

31. UN Conferences, Environment and Development. www.un.org/en/conferences/environment/rio1992
www.un.org/en/conferences/environment/rio1992 (accessed February 9, 2022).
32. UN Global Compact, Partnerships: www.unglobalcompact.org/take-action/partnerships/how-to-partner (accessed February 9, 2022).
33. OECD, Fourth High Level Forum on Aid Effectiveness. www.oecd.org/dac/effectiveness/fourthhighlevelforumonaideffectiveness.htm (accessed February 9, 2022).

align development programmes around country development strategies, harmonise practices to reduce transaction costs, avoid fragmented efforts and create results frameworks. The *Busan Partnership for Effective Development Cooperation* (2011) provided a framework for development cooperation between donors, country governments, civil society organisations and private funders.

United Nations Development Goals[34]

Millennium Development Goals (2000–15): Goal 8 of the eight international development goals that followed the adoption of the United Nations Millennium Declaration promoted a global partnership for development. The Declaration also committed countries to developing strong partnerships with the private sector and civil society organisations in pursuit of development goals such as poverty eradication.

Sustainable Development Goals (2015–30): Goal 17 of the 17 goals that make up the 2030 Agenda for Sustainable Development calls for revitalisation of the global partnership for sustainable development and development of multi-stakeholder partnerships to share knowledge, expertise, technology and financial support in order to achieve national development targets.

Global climate summits/COPs[35]

Collaborations between governments, businesses and civil society to support the achievement of climate goals such as the Paris Agreement which seeks to limit global warming.

Sendai Framework for Disaster Risk Reduction (2015–30)[36]

International cooperation and global partnership are positioned as central to disaster risk reduction through an effective and meaningful global partnership and development of partnerships at local, national, regional and global levels for the implementation of disaster risk reduction strategies and plans.

34. Sustainable Development Goals Fund, From MDGs to SDGs: www.sdgfund.org/mdgs-sdgs (accessed February 9, 2022).
35. United Nations Climate Change, Conference of the Parties (C=P). https://unfccc.int/process/bodies/supreme-bodies/conference-of-the-parties-cop (accessed February 9, 2022).
36. United Nations Office for Disaster Risk Reduction (UNDRR) Implementing the Sendai Framework. www.undrr.org/implementing-sendai-framework/what-sendai-framework (accessed February 9, 2022).

UN Habitat New Urban Agenda (2017)[37]

To implement the Agenda, national, subnational and local governments, as well as all relevant stakeholders are required to create, strengthen and revitalise partnerships and make systematic use of multi-stakeholder partnerships in urban development processes.[38]

Many of the case studies presented in Chapter 1 were developed in response to global pushes for partnership. In Southern Africa, for example, CSR trends, the UN Global Compact and promotion of engagement with the private sector by donor governments and aid agencies clearly encouraged partnership initiatives involving business.[39] A call by UNAIDS for partnership approaches to address the HIV/AIDS pandemic also led to the development of collaborative councils between business and other actors across Africa, including the Zambia Business Council on HIV/AIDS (ZBCA) (see Box 3.10).[40] In Latin America, meanwhile, accessing remote communities as part of a "last push" to meet the MDGs was an important driver for the development of innovative partnership arrangements to address basic service provision.[41] The case studies from Bolivia, Guatemala and Peru further suggest that much of the impetus for partnership came from donor agencies keen to promote and share new models for reaching the "poorest of the poor" in countries where the public sector faced challenges such as weak capacity, poor accountability and unstable financial provision.[42] More recently, a plethora of multi-stakeholder initiatives has been developed to support the achievement of the SDGs and respond to climate, humanitarian and health concerns including the COVID-19 pandemic.[43]

Regional frameworks have also stimulated the adoption of partnership approaches. In Southern Africa, for example, the New Partnership for Africa's Development (NEPAD) proposed by the African Union in 2001 to

37. UN-Habitat, New Urban Agenda: https://unhabitat.org/about-us/new-urban-agenda (accessed February 9, 2022).
38. UN-Habitat (2017) UN-Habitat Partnership Strategy, 2017–2022. https://mirror.unhabitat.org/downloads/docs/13579_1_596506.pdf (accessed February 9, 2022).
39. Rein et al. (2005) Op. cit. pp. 23–34.
40. Ibid., p. 77.
41. Stott, L. (2014) *Partnerships for Innovation in Access to Basic Services*, Washington, DC, USA: Multilateral Investment Fund/Inter-American Development Bank (MIF/IDB) and Madrid, Spain: Innovation and Technology for Development Centre/*Universidad Politécnica de Madrid* (itdUPM) (p. 6).
42. Ibid., p. 7.
43. See: Murphy and Stott (2021) Op. cit. and Moreno-Serna, J., Purcell, W.M., Sánchez-Chaparro, T., Soberón, M., Lumbreras, J., Mataix, C. (2020) Catalyzing transformational partnerships for the SDGs: Effectiveness and impact of the multi-stakeholder initiative *El día después*. *Sustainability*, 12: 7189. https://doi.org/10.3390/su12177189

promote socio-economic development across the continent was important in promoting partnership, particularly with regard to engagement with the private sector.[44] In the EU, meanwhile, a more multi-stakeholder vision of partnership was situated as central to the Europe 2020 Growth Strategy[45] for achieving smart, sustainable and inclusive growth and later integrated in the European Semester coordination framework[46] and the European Pillar of Social Rights.[47] The partnership principle was further endorsed by the 2014 European Code of Conduct on Partnership (ECCP) which established minimum partnership requirements for national authorities charged with disbursing ESIF.[48] This mandated partnership approach led to the development of initiatives such as the Austrian Territorial Employment Pacts (TEPs) which sought to integrate labour market and employment policies with other policy areas (see Box 4.3) and Swedish Structural Fund Partnerships (SFPs) (see Box 3.4).

Box 3.4 Structural Fund Partnerships (SFPs) in Sweden[49]

In Sweden, the European Social Fund (ESF) and the European Regional Development Fund (ERDF) collaborated together in Structural Fund Partnerships (SFPs) in the eight regions of the country. The SFPs were developed in 2007 in response to feedback indicating the need for a better balance of power between national and regional political levels and improved linkages between regional growth and labour market policies. Put forward as a mechanism for streamlining national-level policies with regional administration and decision-making, SFPs were supported by a law that regulated their tasks and membership. With about 17–21 members in total, the SFP chairperson, who was elected by Government, designated other representatives. As well as municipal and regional politicians, and representatives

44. Rein et al. (2005) Op. cit. p. 20.
45. European Commission (2010) *Europe 2020: A Strategy for Smart, Sustainable and Inclusive Growth*, Brussels: European Commission: http://ec.europa.eu/eu2020/pdf/COMPLET%20EN%20BARROSO%20%20%20007%20-%20Europe%202020%20-%20EN%20version.pdf (accessed February 9, 2022).
46. The European Semester: https://ec.europa.eu/info/business-economy-euro/economic-and-fiscal-policy-coordination/eu-economic-governance-monitoring-prevention-correction/european-semester/framework/europe-2020-strategy_en (accessed February 9, 2022).
47. The European Pillar of Social Rights: https://ec.europa.eu/info/strategy/priorities-2019-2024/economy-works-people/jobs-growth-and-investment/european-pillar-social-rights_en (accessed February 9, 2022).
48. Ibid., p. 5 and see also European Commission (2014) *European Code of Conduct on Partnership in the Framework of the European Structural and Investment Funds*, Brussels, Belgium: European Commission, Directorate-General for Employment, Social Affairs and Inclusion.
49. Stott, L. (2019) Synergies between the ESF and ERDF from a partnership perspective. In: *Lessons Learned from Transnational Cooperation*, Brussels, Belgium: DG Employment, Social Affairs and Inclusion, European Commission.

from the Sami Parliament in the sparsely inhabited northern parts of Sweden, members came from labour market organisations, the Swedish Employment Service, social partners, NGOs, universities, the private sector and public authorities such as county councils, county administrative boards and county labour boards. The work of SFPs included participation in the drawing up of ESF and ERDF plans and programmes based on analysis of regional conditions and responsibility for implementation of a joint selection process for cooperation projects recommended for ERDF and ESF funding. The prioritisation of projects carried out by SFPs aimed to reflect national and regional growth policy, labour market policy and the EU's cohesion policy.

These examples indicate that a deeper examination of how global and regional trends and policy drivers are played out in national and local contexts is warranted. Within such an inquiry, a specific area of interest relates to power dynamics that may exist with regard to the endorsement of particular policy and regulatory frameworks. The global push for collaboration with the private sector by both international development agencies and national governments in South Africa and Zambia is an example of this.[50] In the EU, meanwhile, Structural Fund directives stipulate the use of partnership mechanisms in order to receive funding.[51] The downside here is that, because this approach is mandated, many of the authorities that manage funds have engaged in what have been described as "tick box exercises" to meet regulations, thus making the partnership process dull and undemanding, and hardly conducive to vibrant delivery and transformation. Sometimes, as well, European regulations promoting partnership have conflicted with national law (see Box 3.5).

Box 3.5 Addressing legal impediments to partnership in the Czech Republic

In the Czech Republic, in line with EU legislative requirements, partnership has been promoted at both ESF programme and project levels. At the project level, legislative drawbacks were encountered in

50. Rein et al. (2005) Op. cit. pp. 27, 33.
51. Stott, L. (2008) *How European Social Fund Managing Authorities and Intermediate Bodies Support Partnership*, Brussels, Belgium: European Commission (pp. 17–18); Stott, L. (2019) *How European Social Fund Managing Authorities and Intermediate Bodies Support Partnership*, Brussels, Belgium: European Commission, Revised edition (pp. 11–12) and Stott, L. and Scoppetta, A. (2013) Promoting local economic development through partnerships in Europe. *Skills@Work: Theory and Practice Journal*, 6: 2–12 (pp. 3–4).

2004–6 when it was discovered that partnership, as understood by the EU, was not defined in relevant national legislation. As a result, existing public procurement regulations meant that partners were considered as "suppliers." This had a major impact at the programme level because it endangered the implementation of partnership projects. In order to address the situation, the ESF Managing Authority worked for an Amendment to the Act on Budgetary Rules which meant that although partnership was not legally defined, it could nonetheless be supported.

At the national level, the legal environment, institutional rules and norms, and private and civil society sector missions and mandates further induce the take-up of partnership. The case studies show that in South Africa, partnership was favoured by positive government policies, pressure from an active civil society and a "push" for the private sector to assume a role in post-apartheid reconstruction.[52] Black Economic Empowerment (BEE) regulations were, for example, a key driver for the partnership approach adopted by the South African Sugar Association (SASA) in developing the Small-scale Sugarcane Farming Communities Partnership (see Box 3.6).[53] In Zambia, while the prevalence of extreme poverty was a central driver, there was less interest from the government in promoting legal regulations and norms for partnership. Regulatory pressure, however, did appear to have pushed the business sector to contribute to development projects with other actors and national policy targets relating to education clearly assisted the development of the Sharing Responsibility for Higher Education Partnership.[54] A growing sense among CSOs that institutional strengthening rested on more robust engagement with other sectors of society also encouraged their involvement in the partnership initiatives proposed by the Zambia Partnership Forum.[55]

Box 3.6 The Small-scale Sugarcane Farming Communities Partnership in South Africa

The Small-scale Sugarcane Farming Communities Partnership was initiated in 2004. As well as responding to Black Economic Empowerment (BEE) regulations which stipulated that 30% of productive land should be in Black South African hands, the partnership responded to post-apartheid changes that encouraged small-scale

52. Rein and Stott (2009) Op. cit. p. 81.
53. Rein et al. (2005) Op. Cit. pp. 49–56.
54. Ibid., pp. 87–94.
55. Ibid., p. 33.

farmers to exercise their political rights and participate in entrepreneurially driven government-funded development initiatives. In this new landscape, the sugar industry committed itself to partnering with central and local government, small- and large-scale cane growers and stakeholders such as traditional leaders to support sustainable rural development and improvement in the quality of life of small-scale sugarcane farming communities.[56]

Spatial connections that promote partnership are often overlaid by particular public, private and civil society sector drivers. The Partnerships Resource Centre (PrC) explicitly mentions this sectoral level as a distinct contextual layer alongside the individual, organisational and external dimensions outlined in Figure 3.1.[57] Thematic factors are also important to consider here, particularly in relation to specific norms and regulations pertaining to issues such as agriculture, health and education, water and sanitation, etc. In both South Africa and Zambia, for example, although conditions varied, issue-based drivers such as the need to increase agricultural productivity, manage approaches to HIV/AIDS and improve higher educational opportunities were important catalysts for partnership.[58] In the Latin American case studies, and the South African study in eThekwini (see Box 3.7), government policies endorsing new forms of service delivery for energy, health, waste management and water and sanitation also led to the development of partnership initiatives that sought to provide basic services to marginalised populations.[59]

Box 3.7 Innovative partnerships in access to water and sanitation in the municipality of eThekwini, South Africa

In order to address the challenges of extending water and sanitation service coverage to a population that had increased by some 2.6 million people between 2001 and 2014, the municipality of eThekwini's Water and Sanitation Unit (EWS) developed a system of service provision based upon innovative multi-stakeholder partnerships. The aim of these partnership arrangements was to ensure that the diverse needs of different community groups, particularly those living in informal

56. Rein et al. (2005) Op. cit. p. 97.
57. Partnerships Resource Centre (2021) *MSP Impact Narrative and Visual Tool.* www.partnerschaften2030.de/wp-content/uploads/2021/02/Impact-Narrative-Visual-and-Tool.pdf (accessed February 11, 2022).
58. Rein et al. (2005) Op. cit.
59. Stott, L. (2014) Op. cit. p. 31.

settlements and rural areas, were adequately met. This approach was enabled by a positive national regulatory regime with clear frameworks for water and sanitation services and water resource management, including a Free Basic Water Policy which provided poorer customers with a minimum level of water and sewage disposal services at no cost. To further improve and extend water and sanitation services, the different skills, capacities and knowledge of academia, business, civil society, donors and government were drawn upon via a range of mutually reinforcing initiatives that developed appropriate facilities for those without services while also addressing social, health and environmental issues. The EWS model, which continues today, has centred upon understanding and meeting the right incentives for different partners to contribute to water and sanitation services. Academic partners include the Pollution Research Group at the University of KwaZulu-Natal (UKZN) which undertakes trans-disciplinary research on water and sanitation delivery. Here, researchers are able to test out their work in practice and at scale and are also afforded opportunities to work on research projects with international partners. Private sector partners, meanwhile, undertake service delivery activities such as the treatment of sewage and wastewater, and the emptying of pit latrines. As well as clarity around tender procedures, such relationships are beneficial for building positive connections with the community through job creation. Community engagement has been further promoted through user platforms that monitor water services and carry out conservation activities. Platform members have been provided with a short cross-disciplinary training course on basic legislation, water and sanitation policy, environmental conservation and hygiene issues. Community representatives have also participated in focus groups that address the specific needs of groups such as women and people with disabilities.

As well as institutional rules and norms, the influence of previous collaborative connections and histories on partnership approaches can influence the adoption of a partnership approach. In Latin America, the partnership models for access to basic services drew upon traditional organisational structures to engage with communities in the design of the *Luz en Casa* initiative in Peru and with Mayan cultural beliefs in the e-health partnership in Guatemala.[60] In South Africa and Zambia, local and political traditions of working

60. Ibid. and see also Egido, M.A. (2014) Luz en casa: Access to sustainable energy in rural communities in Peru Martínez, A. (2014) eHealth in rural areas: Access to medical care, training and prevention in Guatemala. *Partnerships for Innovation in Access to Basic Services Case Study*. Washington, DC, USA: Multilateral Investment Fund/Inter-American Development Bank (MIF/IDB)

together were also mentioned as catalysts for partnership.[61] More recent histories are also important to highlight. Cross-sectoral connections that were developed before the end of the apartheid regime in South Africa, for example, contributed to the widespread adoption of modes of working conducive to partnerships such as alternative forms of service delivery through public-private and public-community partnerships.[62] In Europe, meanwhile, traditions of social dialogue were drawn upon in Sweden to encourage different parties to accept joint responsibility for development, while in Ireland, partnership approaches for social inclusion have built upon historical connections of community collaboration.[63]

The Irish ESF approach to partnership reinforces the importance of local level drivers. Here, a partnership approach was adopted and implemented by the national government through the devolution of funding and service delivery to local partnership and community structures such as Local Development Companies (LDCs), thus underscoring strong grassroots links (see Box 3.8). The EU's use of community-led local development (CLLD) which encourages the formation of Local Action Group partnerships that design and implement an integrated development strategy for their area offers another example of how regional, national and local drivers can combine to support different grassroots initiatives.[64]

Box 3.8 Local partnership in Ireland

Ireland has a long history of working in partnership. As an approach underpinning urban and rural development, particularly in areas of economic and social disadvantage, partnership is often implemented through devolution of funding and service delivery to local partnership and community structures. Using Local Development Companies (LDCs), independent companies limited by guarantee without share capital, a clear framework has been provided for the development of collaborative activities. Following the 2014 Local Government Reform Act, Local Community Development Committees (LCDCs) were established in all administrative areas. These committees brought together local authority elected members and officials,

and Madrid, Spain: Innovation and Technology for Development Centre/Technical University of Madrid (itdUPM).

61. Rein et al. (2005) Op. cit. p. 28 and p. 33.
62. Ibid., p. 22.
63. Stott, L. (2019) Stott, L. *Guidebook: How ESF Managing Authorities and Intermediate Bodies Support Partnership*, Revised edition, Brussels, Belgium: DG Employment, Social Affairs and Inclusion, European Commission (pp. 23–24).
64. See Community-led local development (CLLD). https://ec.europa.eu/regional_policy/en/information/publications/brochures/2014/community-led-local-development (accessed February 10, 2022).

state and non-state development agencies, community and voluntary organisations and representatives of civil society, business and farming communities to engage in collective decision-making for their local area. Such local partnerships have been funded by the National Exchequer through the Department of Rural and Community Development and other sources.

The Ballyfermot Chapelizod Partnership is an example of a local partnership that was established as a company limited by guarantee without share capital. The partnership, which is located in a disadvantaged area outside Dublin, began its work in 1996 to address long-term unemployment and poverty and now implements nationally funded programmes for local socio-economic and community development across the Ballyfermot Chapelizod area. Working closely with the Public Employment Services, the principles of partnership have been used to leverage inter-agency working, foster community development approaches and promote employability and lifelong learning support to disadvantaged neighbourhoods and groups, including the long-term unemployed, one-parent families and young people who are not in employment, education or training. In 2014, the partnership became an implementer of the Social Inclusion and Community Activation Programme (SICAP), co-funded by the Irish Government and the ESF, which aimed to reduce poverty and promote social inclusion.

In Southern Africa, the Luangeni partnership in Zambia, which is mentioned at the start of this chapter, provides an example of how the introduction of a branch of a supermarket chain in a rural community precipitated a collaboration among different actors that became a model for the Chamba Valley Partnership as well as the rest of the country. These two initiatives were created and developed by a national intermediary organisation, the Zambia Partnership Forum, which drew its inspiration from international connections and trends relating to CSR and sustainable development. This catalytic combination of local, national and international drivers is further manifested in the role played by the eThekwini Metropolitan Municipality in promoting local water and sanitation partnerships in South Africa, and by national and international intermediaries such as *Ciudad Saludable*, *Acciona Microenergía Perú* (AMP) and the *Fundación Acciona Microenergía* (FUNDAME) in Peru, the NGO TulaSalud and the Canadian-based Tula Foundation in Guatemala and the American NGO Water for People (WFP) in Bolivia, which channelled and shaped local needs and demands into partnership arrangements.[65] In Europe too, intermediaries such as Pobal in Ireland, gsub in Germany and Kooo in Austria appear to have ensured that local

65. Stott (2014) Op. cit.

actors were clearly positioned in partnership activities by translating and making sense of European and national requirements at local levels.[66] The role played by these organisations in promoting and supporting partnership further points to the importance of understanding organisational drivers for working collaboratively.

Organisational drivers

While external drivers are critical to determining the viability of partnership arrangements, the different visions and missions of organisations that become partners also form part of the context for working in this way.[67] Their drivers are likely to relate to core business incentives; organisational mandates and directives; interorganisational relationships; relationships with other organisations and organisational capacities and skills (see Figure 3.4).

Mats Andersson and his colleagues observe that "the potential that partnerships offer . . . is encompassed by the drive, energy, and ability to take action that stems from the explicit commitment of each of the partners."[68]

Figure 3.4 Organisational partnership drivers

Source: Stott (2017)[69]

66. Stott, L. and Scoppetta A. (2013) Adding value: The broker role in partnerships for employment and social inclusion in Europe. *Betwixt and Between: The Journal of Partnership Brokering*, May (1).
67. Caplan et al. (2007) Op. Cit. p. 9.
68. Andersson, M., Svensson, L., Wistus, S. and Äberg, C. eds. (2006) *On the Art of Developing Partnerships*, Stockholm, Sweden: The National Institute for Working Life (p. 91).
69. Stott (2017) Op. cit. p. 45.

This commitment will derive from the fulfilment (or possible fulfilment) of both common *and* organisational interests. Potential partners thus need to be especially clear that the benefits of entering a partnership outweigh the risks.[70] Figure 3.5 lists some of the organisational risks and benefits of working in partnership.

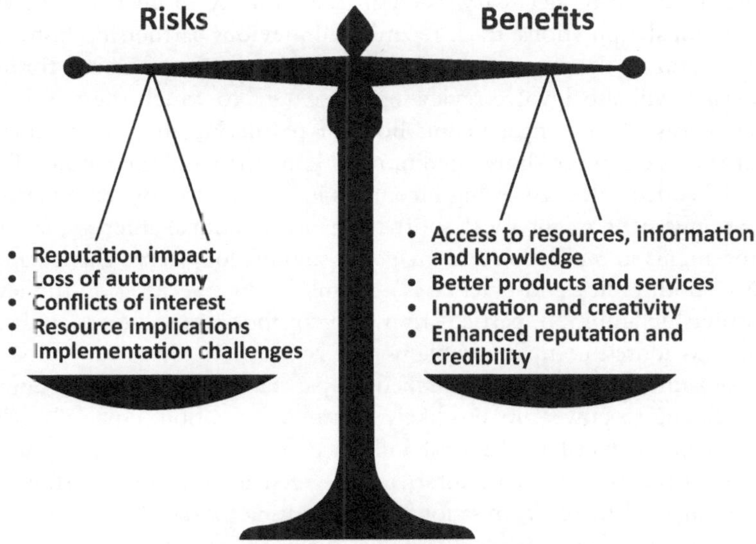

Figure 3.5 Risks and benefits of working in partnership

Source: Adapted from Tennyson (2011)[71]

Credit: The Partnering Initiative

The risks and benefits in Figure 3.5 are generic in nature and clearly need to be studied in relation to specific contexts and the complex sector systems within which organisations operate.[72] Attention also needs to be paid to "intra-organisational and inter-organisational contexts."[73] Newborne and Caplan indicate that consideration of these latter settings may include questions

70. Otiso, K.M. (2003) State, voluntary and private sector partnerships for slum upgrading and basic service delivery in Nairobi City, Kenya. *Cities*, 20 (4): 221–229. https://doi.org/10.1016/S0264-2751(03)00035-0 summarises this succinctly, "each sector is drawn to the partnership by specific benefits that must exceed the cost of participation" (p. 225).
71. Tennyson, R. (2011) *The Partnering Toolbook*, London, UK: The Partnering Initiative (IBLF) (p. 12).
72. Googins, B.K. and Rochlin, S. A. (2000) Creating the partnership society: Understanding the rhetoric and reality of cross-sectoral partnerships. *Business and Society Review*, 105 (1): 127–144. https://doi.org/10.1111/0045-3609.00068 (p. 137).
73. Seitanidi and Ryan (2007) Op. cit. p. 256.

relating to internal awareness about partnership arrangements and their potential; whether a legal mandate is required to work in partnership; the rapidity with which internal decisions are made; the degree of support from senior staff and, crucially, the availability of time and resources for partnering.[74] An examination of the state of relationships among potential partners and how far different organisations are comfortable about working with one another may also be necessary. Such analysis is likely to involve reviewing organisational reputations, track records and previous partnership histories.

Discussion of the organisational benefits that may be achieved through partnering will also involve reviewing the extent to which there is a core "business case"[75] for engagement; how far partnering may offer value to the organisation in the short, medium and long term and the nature of this potential added value. Assessing incentives in relation to how far a partnership arrangement might meet short-term organisational interests, such as improvements in reputation and image, or support long-term change at the levels of both policy and practice is a useful way of checking on the levels of partnership ambition, particularly when collaborative solutions are being adopted to address complex problems.

As organisational drivers are linked to particular missions and cultures, issues relating to power are also likely to require attention, especially when players with financial or political influence such as national government agencies, large businesses or international agencies initiate a partnership. The rationale of these organisations for promoting partnership is important to understand and may assist in gauging the depth of their motivations for working in this way and the ends that they seek in doing so. UN agencies, for example, have been criticised for ceding decision-making powers to transnational corporations in partnership relationships[76] while the EU's promotion of local partnerships has been accused of enshrining "elitist, neocorporatist or neopluralist principles."[77] Because these perceptions are intimately linked

74. Newborne, P. and Caplan, K. (2006) *Creating Space for Innovation, Understanding Enablers for Multi-Sector Partnerships in the Water and Sanitation Sector*, London, UK: Building Partnerships for Development (pp. 13–21).
75. Caplan, K. (2003) The purist's partnership: Debunking the terminology of partnerships, *BPD Practitioner Note Series*, London, UK: Building Partnerships for Development notes that core business can be defined in many ways though including unwritten "contracts" with shareholders, communities, the electorate or otherwise (p. 3).
76. Bruno, K. and Karliner, J. (2000) *Tangled up in Blue, Corporate Partnerships at the United Nations*, San Francisco, CA, USA: The Transnational Resource and Action Center: Zammit, A. (2003) *Development at Risk, Rethinking UN-Business Partnerships*, Geneva, Switzerland: South Centre/UNRISD and Utting, P. and Zammit, A. (2006) Running in the dark? The rise of United Nations-Business partnerships. *Paper for UNRISD*, Geneva, Switzerland: UNRISD.
77. Geddes, M. (2000) Tackling social exclusion in the European Union? The limits of the new orthodoxy of local partnership. *International Journal of Urban and Regional Research*, 24 (4): 782–800. https://doi.org/10.1111/1468-2427.00278 (p. 797).

to power differentials among the actors involved,[78] it is also useful to explore how far the partnership "push" exercised by these organisations relates to core institutional drivers such as a business licence to operate, election mandates or serving public interests, or whether their motives for engaging in partnership are more lightweight, such as "jumping on the bandwagon," interest in the "feel good" factor that may accrue from participating or curiosity as to what might be on offer. These drivers are important to identify because they have implications for how well a partnership might work, particularly in view of arguments suggesting that if the incentives for partners to participate are not sufficiently met partnership effectiveness will be limited.[79]

Box 3.9 The Sharing Responsibility for Higher Education Partnership in Zambia

The Sharing Responsibility for Higher Education Partnership was initiated in 2000 by the Zambia Partnership Forum. The aim of the partnership was to attract and channel resources into university education in response to deteriorating economic conditions and cutbacks in higher education which had led to dilapidation of the institution's infrastructure and made it difficult for universities in Zambia to retain the services of qualified local staff, resulting in a marked decline in academic quality. To address this situation, the Partnership Forum brought together stakeholders from the business sector to form a partnership with the University of Zambia and the Copperbelt University. The companies involved contributed financial resources, scholarships and products to improve infrastructure and support learning activities, in some cases with their staff engaging in teaching activities. While a core motivation for business engagement was the enhancement of their reputation and image, each company also had particular reasons for supporting the partnership. Barclays Bank of Zambia (BBZ), Unilever, Chilanga Cement Plc and the Zambia Electricity Supply Corporation (ZESCO Ltd.) saw their contributions as being directly linked to the need to attract qualified personnel from the universities' graduate pool. In the case of BBZ, employment of these graduates was viewed as central to the company's plans to develop a local workforce and reduce reliance on expatriate personnel. BP Zambia Plc saw involvement in the partnership as part of its CSR strategy while the Zambia National Broadcasting Corporation (ZNBC) perceived its media coverage of the Partnership as helpful in

78. Brinkerhoff, D.W. (1999) Exploring state-civil society collaboration: Policy partnerships in developing countries. *Nonprofit and Voluntary Sector Quarterly*, 28: 59–86. http://dx.doi.org/10.1177/089976499773746438 (p. 61).
79. Caplan et al. (2007) Op. cit. p. 5.

attracting local audiences. Meanwhile, Nkumba Farms, which made breeding pigs available to the Schools of Agricultural Sciences and Veterinary Medicine, viewed its participation as a way of supporting animal research that could provide them with important data.

The reasons for different business partners to engage in the Sharing Responsibility for Higher Education Partnership (Box 3.9) offer insights into how organisational drivers may vary in relation to particular interests. These drivers are explored further in Table 3.2 which looks at different partner incentives and disincentives in the Chamba Valley Partnership in Zambia.

Table 3.2 Organisational drivers in the Chamba Valley Partnership

Partners	***Organisational drivers***	
	Incentives	***Disincentives***
Chamba Valley Cooperative Society	• Market access for fruit and vegetables • Accessible seed and extension services • Guaranteed income • Capacity-building opportunities	• Scepticism about working with government agencies due to historical lack of extension services • Working through Freshmark rather than directly with Shoprite
Shoprite Zambia (South African supermarket chain)/ Freshmark (Subsidiary)	• Pressure from government to obtain produce locally • Access to a constant supply of produce • Reduction of costs on importation of produce from South Africa • Improvement of reputation and image	• Concerns about: – Quality and consistency of local supplies – Capacity for engaging with community – Lack of real difference to profit margins • No social investment push
Ministry of Agriculture and Cooperatives	• Model for community farming (replication of Luangeni Partnership) • Support from local farmers	• Financial constraints • Lack of legal/regulatory framework • Time and human resource demands
Zambia Seed Company (Zamseed)	• Guaranteed market for seed • Seedlings could be sold on to other customers	• Time and availability of staff to engage
All partners	• Existence of trusted intermediary (Partnership Forum) • Positive experience of Luangeni Partnership	• Lack of experience of working in partnership

Source: Stott (2017)[80]

80. Stott (2017) Op. cit. p. 46 and see also Rein et al. (2005) Op. cit. pp. 37–48.

It is important to note here that potential partners may not always be upfront about their motives for wishing to partner. The existence of "covert" motives for partnering such as "the pursuit of funding, credibility, or a licence to operate" is noted by Ruth Findlay Brooks, Wayne Visser and Thurstan Wright, who suggest that reluctance to share these interests is often due to the fact that they may be substantially different to jointly proposed partnership outcomes.[81] This raises ethical concerns about the true purpose of partnership and the time and resources invested in its promotion.[82]

Tension around motives for partnering is well illustrated in a UN-Business Partnership which was established to support primary education and gender equity.[83] Here, the *given* organisational incentives for working in partnership are set out in Table 3.3. However, research showed that these incentives were secondary to the *unstated* desire by the company to ensure long-term profit and effective brand reinforcement and the UN agency's

Table 3.3 Given organisational incentives for joining a UN-Business Partnership

UN Agency	***Business***
Fulfilment of the MDGs 2 and 3* – primary education for all and gender equity, especially in areas with competing resource priorities	Corporate commitment to donating a small percentage of pre-tax annual profits to communities around the world
Coverage of education programme infrastructure, training and equipment costs	CSR focus on making a strong stand against child labour
Involvement in a more integrated approach and a far wider range of activities	Community investment programme to support the MDG 2 objective of universal primary education by 2015
Promotion of gender equity through special interventions encouraging female enrolment in primary education	Commitment to developing strategic partnerships internationally

*MDG 2: Achieving universal primary education – Ensure that, by 2015, children everywhere will be able to complete a full course of primary schooling.

MDG 3: Promoting gender parity – Eliminate gender disparity in primary and secondary education, preferably by 2005, and to all levels of education no later than 2015.

Source: Adapted from Stott (2007)[84]

Credit: The Partnering Initiative

81. Findlay Brooks, R., Visser, W. and Wright, T. (2007) Cross-sector partnership as an approach to inclusive development. *University of Cambridge Programme for Industry Research Paper Series*, No. 4, Cambridge, UK: Cambridge Programme for Industry (p. 5).
82. Macdonald, S. and Chrisp, T. (2005) Acknowledging the purpose of partnership. *Journal of Business Ethics*, 59: 307–317. https://doi.org/10.1007/s10551-004-3235-5 (p. 315).
83. Stott, L. (2007) Conflicting cultures: Lessons from a UN-Business partnership. *Making a Difference, Exploring Issues in Partnering Practice Series*, London, UK: International Business Leaders Forum.
84. Stott (2007) Op. cit. p. 5.

desire to attract corporate funding for its wider work. The fact that these "real" incentives were never shared openly by the two partners was one of the reasons that the relationship failed.[85] In fact, the challenge of documenting these "hidden agendas," and other more negative aspects of partnership-building, meant that in order to prepare the case study, an agreement was made to disguise the location, theme and identity of the partners involved.[86]

A key task then is to find ways in which "hidden" agendas among different partners can be teased out, discussed and debated in order to appreciate the specific priorities of each partner and ensure understanding of what each partner expects from the partnership.[87] As Table 3.4 shows, transparency around the organisational expectations of different partners and their incentives (and challenges) for working in this way can enhance the process of partnering.

A recommendation in *Working Together* is that discussion of incentives should be carried out prior to the development of joint activities in order to avoid misunderstandings relating to "hidden agendas" over time.[88] However, while a concrete understanding of different organisational motives for partnering is clearly advantageous in providing a solid foundation for ongoing collaboration, the reality is that detailed discussion of organisational incentives in partnership arrangements is often problematic, particularly at the start of a relationship when partners may not know one another well. In the six partnership initiatives studied in South Africa and Zambia, for

Table 3.4 The advantages of sharing incentives for partnering

Accountability	• Ensures transparency and shared understanding of different constraints for individual partners
Clarity	• Provides a common understanding of benefits and risks for different partners • Creates a more open environment and promotes the building of trust • Minimises unwelcome surprises and potential damage regarding partnership risks
Improved performance	• Improves communication, decision-making and performance management • Allows greater chance of achieving common objectives through identification, discussion and management of risks • Enables a better basis for allocation of resources and delivery of activities
Sustainability	• Enhances achievement of objectives through ongoing review and management of barriers and opportunities • Creates durable connections that offer opportunities for innovative solutions to challenges

85. Ibid., p. 10.
86. Ibid., p. 4.
87. Tennyson, R. (2011) *The Partnering Toolbook*, London, UK: The Partnering Initiative (IBLF) (p. 12).
88. Rein et al. (2005) Op. cit. p. 126.

example, very few had jointly articulated or incorporated specific organisational incentives into the establishment of common partnership objectives.[89] While internal deliberations to decide whether organisations should enter a partnership initiative are recommended, it is also worth noting that in many contexts there is little room for choice. As well as limitations in finding the "right" partners, a decision to partner is often taken because there is simply no other realistic alternative to working in this way. In the Chamba Valley Partnership, for example, the absence of both government and donor funding to support small-scale peri-urban farmers was the main reason the collaboration was initiated.

A number of partnership practitioners have noted that clarity around organisational incentives for partnering is only likely to be achieved through the promotion of ongoing discussion that enables honest assessments of drivers, both within and between partner organisations as they develop their work together and begin to respect and trust one another.[90] As partnership arrangements are operated and maintained by organisational representatives, this should ideally entail an inquiry into personal drivers, particularly when organisational and individual incentives do not coincide. Bradley K. Googins and Steven A. Rochlin endorse this compellingly in their assertion that "If cross-sector partnerships are indeed appropriate for encouragement, each participant must have an understanding of how partnership will generate value for them."[91] An overarching partnership assessment process that is based upon regular exploration of both organisational *and* individual incentives for working in collaboration is thus likely to be useful.[92]

Individual drivers

Implicit in a multi-layered view of context is the assumption that connections between people will influence the manner in which partnership is undertaken. Although partnership arrangements are composed of organisations from different sectors, they are initiated and driven by individuals acting on their behalf. While some writers have acknowledged individual interests and their interplay with organisational incentives,[93] most scholarship on multi-stakeholder partnership has overlooked "micro-level interactions" relating to individual characteristics and interpersonal dynamics.[94] This absence is somewhat surprising and suggests that more effort is needed

89. Ibid., pp. 117–118.
90. Caplan (2003) Op. cit. pp. 2–3.
91. Googins and Rochlin (2000) Op. cit. p. 142.
92. Caplan et al. (2007) Op. cit.
93. See Gazley, B. (2010) Linking collaborative capacity to performance measurement in government-nonprofit partnerships. *Nonprofit and Voluntary Sector Quarterly*, 39 (4): 653–673. https://doi.org/10.1177%2F0899764009360823 and Kolk (2013) Op. cit. p. 13.
94. Kolk, van Dolen and Vock (2010) Op. cit. p. 128 and Sloan, P. and Oliver, D. (2013) Building trust in multi-stakeholder partnerships: Critical emotional incidents and practices of engagement. *Organizational Studies*, 34: 1835–1868. https://doi.org/10.1177%2F0170840613495018

to understand partnership from a personal perspective, not just an organisational one.[95]

David F. Murphy and I contend that acknowledgement of the centrality of interpersonal relationships and the connections between individual, organisational and external levels of context can assist better understanding of partnership.[96] We consider that personal and organisational relationships are integrally related to the wider geographic, socio-historic, cultural political and institutional settings in which they operate, and a complex and changing interplay will exist between these different contextual layers throughout the lifetime of a partnership (see Figure 3.6).

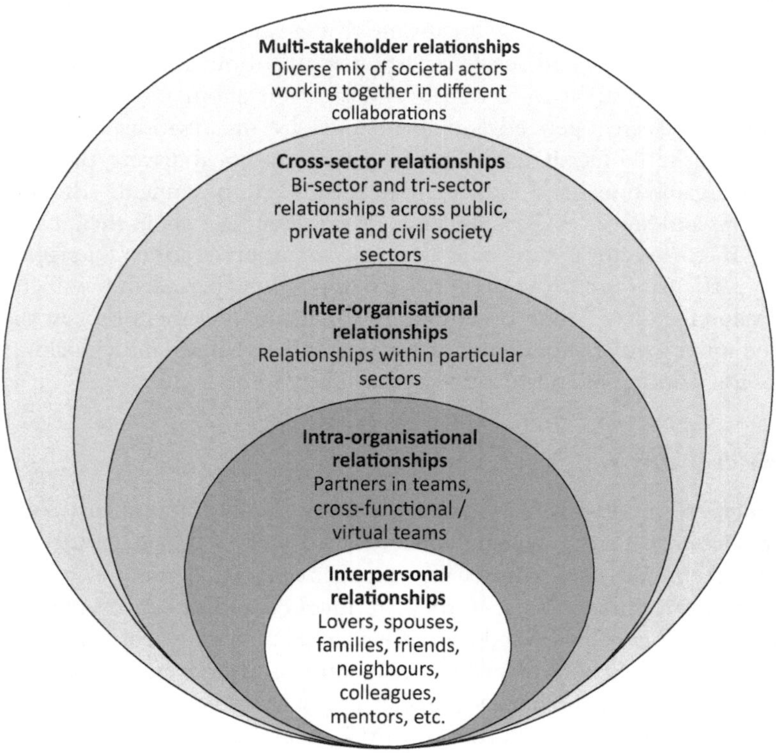

Figure 3.6 Linking personal and organisational relationships

Source: Adapted Stott and Murphy (2020)[97]

95. Battisti, M. (2009) Below the surface, The challenges of cross-sector partnerships. *Journal of Corporate Citizenship*, 35: 95–108. www.jstor.org/stable/jcorpciti.35.95 notes that "cross-sector partnerships are about collaboration and it is the individuals who work together and engage in partnerships rather than the organisations or the sectors" (p. 96).
96. Stott and Murphy (2020) Op. cit.
97. Ibid.

These connections, which are illustrated in the case of the Zambia Business Coalition on HIV/AIDS (Box 3.10), suggest that

> how a partnership actually functions – and thus, can have an impact – also depends on individual factors and the process of interactions, as these can yield not only organisational benefits but also more indirect (trickle) effects within and between the micro, meso and macro levels.[98]

Box 3.10 The Zambia Business Coalition on HIV/AIDS (ZBCA)[99]

The ZBCA was established in 2000 as a collaborative umbrella organisation involving business, NGOs and the public sector to advocate and promote activities concerned with the prevention and treatment of HIV/AIDS in the Zambian business sector. At the national level, the effects of the HIV/AIDS pandemic in the workplace meant the loss of trained and experienced personnel. Companies were also experiencing increasing absenteeism due to illness and attendance at funerals which resulted in lower productivity, reduced profits and increased health bills and funeral expenses. As a result, the Chief Executives of four leading companies, BP Zambia Plc, Barclays Bank, Standard Chartered Bank and Zambia National Commercial Bank, met in 1999 to discuss the health status of their workers and the effect of the pandemic on their business. At the instigation of the UN Resident Coordinator who had visited Thailand prior to coming to Zambia, and with the support of the United Nations AIDS Programme (UNAIDS) and Zambia's UN Country Team (UNCT), a delegation from Zambia consisting of representatives from the business community, young people and UN personnel went to Thailand to study the strategies of the Thailand Business Coalition on AIDS which involved the private sector in HIV/AIDS prevention control programmes. This visit led to the establishment of the ZBCA.

The "human element" in partnership can be explored by looking at how individual characteristics such as "personal . . . goals, informal group pressures, and professional backgrounds" shape collaborative decisions and activities.[100] Here, three overlapping identities are likely to play a role in

98. Kolk, A., van Tulder, R. and Kostwinder, E. (2008) Business and partnerships for development. *European Management Journal*, 26 (4): 262–273. https://doi.org/10.1016/j.emj.2008.01.007 (p. 13).
99. Rein et al. (2005) Op. cit. pp. 77–84.
100. Gazley (2010) Op. cit. p. 655.

the take-up and shaping of partnership; professional, position and personal identities (see Figure 3.7).

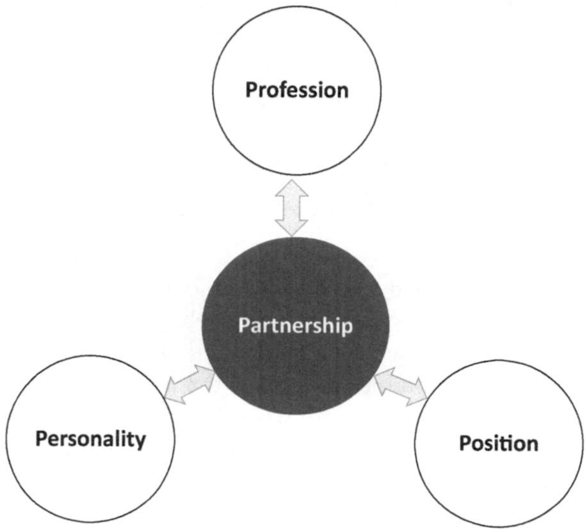

Figure 3.7 Individual partnership drivers
Source: Stott (2017)[101]

Professional identities may encourage individual involvement in partnership in order to improve working cultures and deepen knowledge and expertise; position identities may see opportunities to enhance status and career options, and personal identities to engage with others, expand networks and enhance knowledge and understanding.[102] The combination of these identities can play an important part in making or breaking partnership arrangements. Practitioners repeatedly allude to the role that the particular characters and behaviour of individuals play in both promoting and advancing partnership as well as stalling or impeding it.[103] This raises questions about the need for oversight of potential conflicts between individual and organisational drivers for partnership[104] and how far individuals adequately represent or act on behalf of organisational interests. Analysis of

101. Stott (2017) Op. Cit. p. 50.
102. Caplan et al. (2007) Op. cit. p. 10.
103. See Stott (2007) Op. cit.
104. Tomlinson, F. (2005) Idealistic and pragmatic versions of the discourse of partnership. *Organization Studies*, 26 (8): 1169–1171. https://doi.org/10.1177%2F0170840605055338 suggests, "power issues are inevitable because individual (organizational) self-interest and the pursuit of collaborative goals are not necessarily congruent" (p. 1174).

"lightweight" individual "whims" for partnering and how they interact with organisational incentives are also relevant here.

Box 3.11 Amangwe Village in South Africa

Amangwe Village was set up in 2002 as a holistic healthcare centre working with and for people suffering from HIV/AIDS. Initiated as a partnership mechanism by the Zululand Chamber of Business Foundation (ZCBF), Amangwe Village responded to a series of problems faced by large companies in relation to managing HIV/AIDS, including employees exhausting their medical aid benefits, provincial hospitals refusing to take HIV/AIDS patients because of lack of facilities and perceptions of risk in hospitals. Employees with HIV/AIDS were also reluctant to use occupational health clinics due to possible stigmatisation by colleagues. The Partnership began with a comprehensive strategic plan for creating a one-stop shop supported by three different services: a clinic, Orphans and Vulnerable Children Services and Community Outreach, Education and Training Services. The funding plan for this was drawn up by a Project Manager contracted by ZCBF who was able to incorporate interdisciplinary knowledge of integrated health systems from her studies in social work, business management and healthcare. Under her leadership, an integrated understanding of the systemic nature of HIV/AIDS was advocated for the local community which, in turn, was used to guide business investment. She also consulted with 35 stakeholder groups from NGOs and government departments, including the Department of Health, in order to ensure support for the strategy. The departure of the Project Manager in early 2003 led to a professional vacuum which the Village found it difficult to recover from.

All six of the partnership initiatives researched in Southern Africa were started by individuals, "who discerned or realised a need within a given environment and went on to devise a strategy in which contextual drivers and triggers were central to the establishment of the partnerships."[105] These individuals were usually highly respected figures who possessed good negotiation and communication skills. In addition, many of them also had prior experience of working in partnership, solid track records in the partnership theme that was being tackled and were used to working with diverse teams. This mix of individual qualities and attributes may be manifested in different ways at different times. Ros Tennyson captures this well in a description

105. Rein et al. (2005) Op. cit. p. 111.

of her attempts to decipher which "hat" partner representatives were wearing during a partnership consortium meeting:

> In chairing the Consortium meeting today – it felt as if I was actually managing 27 rather than 9 people. Whenever one person had a reaction to an important issue that was at odds with the rest of the group, I felt I had to "unpick" whether their objection was arising from a difference of professional judgement or whether it was evidence of potentially serious organisational divergence or whether it was simply a personality clash with one or more of the others. Only when I felt that I had clearly ascertained from which of these perspectives they were speaking could I properly assess (on behalf of the group) how much their views should be allowed to sway the decision-making process.[106]

While Tennyson's analysis is of interest, it is worth noting that disentangling individual motivations in the manner she describes is not straightforward, particularly as people are more complex than these categorisations imply and may wear more than one "hat" at the same time. In addition, some individuals are likely to view their involvement in partnership as an opportunity to reinforce and put into practice deeply held collaborative convictions and ideals that may crosscut their professional, position and personal identities. In the cases considered in this book, the majority of the individuals who initiated partnership arrangements had a deep commitment to transformation and "a better world," and manifested qualities that may be attributed to a relational intelligence that encompasses emotional and ethical capabilities. This notion takes us back to the views of authors such as Rutger Bregman, Riane Eisler, Charles Leadbeater and Richard Sennett who believe that humans have an innate capacity for cooperation and partnership and may seek to engage in a partnership arrangement because it has value in and of itself.[107] The idea that the "interior condition" of those working in part-

106. Tennyson, R. (2003) *Institutionalising Partnerships: Lessons from the Frontline*, London, UK: International Business Leaders Forum (p. 10).
107. See Eisler, R. (1987) *The Chalice and the Blade, Our History, Our Future*, San Francisco, CA, USA: Harper and Row; Eisler, R. (2008) Our great creative challenge: Rethinking human nature: And recreating society. In: Richards, R. ed. *Everyday Creativity and New Views of Human Nature: Psychological, Social, and Spiritual Perspectives*, Washington, DC, USA: American Psychological Association, pp. xiii: 261–285. http://rianeeisler.com/wp-content/uploads/2014/06/riane-eisler.pdf (accessed January 6, 2017); Eisler, R. (2015) Human possibilities: The interaction of biology and culture. *Interdisciplinary Journal of Partnership Studies*, 1 (1): 1–39; Leadbeater, C. (2012) *It's Co-Operation, Stupid, Why Richard Dawkins, Thomas Hobbes and Milton Friedman Got It Wrong*, London, UK: Institute for Public Policy Research; Sennett, R. (2013) *Together: The Rituals, Pleasures and Politics of Cooperation*, London, UK: Penguin Books; and Bregman, R. (2020) *Humankind: A Hopeful History*, London, UK: Bloomsbury Publishing.

Battisti (2009) Op. cit. p. 97.

nership has a significant impact on a partnership arrangement[108] is further explored by Sennett who suggests that the depth of cooperation will depend on the extent to which individuals have a genuine interest in others and are able to look outward.[109]

As well as endorsing the idea that partnership can offer opportunities for the expansion of human capabilities, the critical role played by individual drivers reinforces the centrality of people in partnership relationships. Although partnership is consistently portrayed as a form of organisational collaboration, it is individual representatives who ultimately determine the objectives of different partnership arrangements and their levels of ambition. This implies that we need to look more closely at how individual collaborative skills can be developed,[110] including the competencies required by partnership brokers to bring different actors together and assist the development of constructive relationships.[111] The importance of paying attention to individual "emotions and unconscious dynamics" and how they might have an influence on partnership relationships also needs to be highlighted.[112] Indeed, in work on partnership in different contexts, it has been noted that "it is the constant, on-going (and sometimes relentless) interplay between people and their contexts that can make or break collaborative efforts and, at their best, create the conditions for genuine transformation."[113] Within this contextual interplay, relational dimensions are crucial to examine further.

Pragmatic and reflective drivers for partnership

In an article on the challenges of working in collaboration, Chris Huxham and Siv Vangen note that collaborative leaders require a mix of pragmatism and idealism in order to develop adaptive and situation-driven approaches.[114] This perception, which reinforces the idea that both instrumental and relational elements are central to collaboration, offers a useful basis for exploring partnership drivers and the connections between the different levels of context examined in this chapter.

To bring together these different layers, two sets of contrasting motivations for second language learning have been applied to partnership.[115]

108. Tennyson et al. (2016) Op. cit. p. 5.
109. Sennett (2013) Op. cit. p. 278.
110. Googins and Rochlin (2000) Op. cit. p. 140.
111. Tennyson, R. (2005) *The Brokering Guidebook, Navigating Effective Sustainable Development Partnerships*, London, UK: The Partnering Initiative, International Business Leaders Forum (p. 9).
112. Battisti (2009) Op. cit. p. 97.
113. Tennyson et al. (2016) Op. cit. p. 28.
114. Huxham and Vangen. (2004) Op. cit.
115. See, for example, Gardner, R.C. (2001) Integrative motivation and second language acquisition. In Dörnyei, Z. and Schmidt, R. eds. *Motivation and Second Language Acquisition*, Honolulu, HI, USA: University of Hawaii Press; Legault, L. (2016) Intrinsic and extrinsic motivation. In:

These motivations suggest that incentives for engaging in a collaborative arrangement may correspond to:

- **Instrumental motivations** – doing something as a means to an end in order to achieve a result or practical goal
- **Integrative motivations** – relational connections and a desire to interact with, and become part, of a broader community.
- **Extrinsic motivations** – external mandates for doing something, including the promise of reward(s) or, conversely, the avoidance of some form of sanction
- **Intrinsic motivations** – interest in doing something because it is rewarding for its own sake

Table 3.5 combines these sets of incentives into *pragmatic* (instrumental and extrinsic) and *reflective* (integrative and intrinsic) motivations for partnering.

Table 3.5 Pragmatic and reflective motivations for partnering

Pragmatic ***Partnership as a means to an end*** ***(Instrumental and extrinsic motivations)***	***Reflective*** ***Partnership as an end in itself*** ***(Integrative and intrinsic motivations)***
Alignment Partners do not have to agree on everything, but they do need to align around a common goal	**Nexus approach** Partners develop cross-cutting connections with issues/concerns/themes/stakeholders that link to their focus area
Results focus Partners work towards the achievement of well-defined shared outcomes with monitoring and evaluation systems in place for this	**Process focus** Close attention is paid to the involvement of all partners in planning, implementation and evaluation of activities
Compliance Partners comply with policy, institutional rules and mandates as well as agreed partnership plans and norms	**Experimentation** Partners ensure space and opportunities for testing and learning from what works and what does not
Commitment Partners commit to provision of resources, delivery of activities, carrying out of responsibilities, etc.	**Ongoing assessment** There is constant revision of progress towards goals with attention to partner relationships and processes for working together

Zeigler-Hill, V. and Shackelford, T.K., eds. *Encyclopedia of Personality and Individual Differences*, Cham, Switzerland: Springer International Publishing; Matsuzaki Carreira, J. (2005) New framework of intrinsic/extrinsic and integrative/instrumental motivation in second language acquisition. *Keiai Journal of International Studies*, 16, 39–64. Kimberly, N.A., Clément, R. and Pelletier, L.G. (1999) Perceptions of teachers' communicative style and students' intrinsic and extrinsic motivation. *The Modern Language Journal*, 83: 23–34. https://doi.org/10.1111/0026-7902.00003 (pp. 155–159).

Pragmatic ***Partnership as a means to an end*** ***(Instrumental and extrinsic motivations)***	***Reflective*** ***Partnership as an end in itself*** ***(Integrative and intrinsic motivations)***
Recognition Partners seek clear and tangible benefits and rewards from their work together	**Learning, reflection and exchange** Partners capture experience of working together and proactively share lessons in order to improve partnership practice

Source: Adapted from Stott and Murphy (2020)[116]

Pragmatic motivations for partnering relate to rules-based compliance such as international and national norms, organisational mandates and institutional guidelines. Practical in nature, they are focused on the achievement of results and reaching agreed goals which may be obtained by partners committing the necessary resources and ensuring organisational alignment. Often short term, these connections may be driven by the promise of benefits such as improved reputation and status. Reflective motivations, on the other hand, embrace more holistic and joined-up approaches between the actors involved. Emphasis is placed on ensuring the active involvement of all partners and the provision of spaces for experimentation in the search for solutions to address problems or challenges which may be achieved in the longer term. Implicit in this categorisation is a deep appreciation of individual roles in partnership and the personal relationships that underpin collaboration. Attention is therefore given to relationships and how partners work together which, in turn, contributes to learning and exchange that provide insights into where improvements may be made.

The elements outlined in Table 3.5 are not exhaustive. The intention is simply to provide an indication of some of the different motivations that might be considered in each grouping. Although a mix of pragmatic and reflective motivations for working in collaborative arrangements is likely, the predominant reasons for partnering are generally found in the pragmatic categorisation and a focus on *organisational* connections that deliver outputs in the short term. In order to enhance the transformational potential of partnership, the argument here is that efforts need to be made to move away from purely pragmatic reasons for partnering towards more reflective motivations that recognise the integrative and intrinsic value of partnering that is derived from a deeper appreciation of *inter-personal* relationships.[117]

Against this background, it is crucial to acknowledge that partnership and other collaborative relationships are dynamic, both relative to their specific and changing operational contexts and to the continual negotiation that takes place between partners at both individual and organisational levels

116. Stott and Murphy (2020) Op. cit.
117. Ibid.

regarding the terms and conditions of their evolving relationship.[118] Appreciation of underlying emergent processes is thus central to an understanding of how relational values in partnership may be deepened. To explore this further, the next chapter will look at partnership in the context of transformation with further consideration of how attention to reflective motivations for partnering may enhance its potential for promoting systemic change.

118. Battisti (2009) Op. cit. and Caplan, K. and Stott, L. (2008) Defining our terms and clarifying our language. In: Svensson, L. and Nilsson, B., eds. *Partnership: As a Strategy for Social Innovation and Sustainable Change*, Stockholm, Sweden: Santérus Academic Press (pp. 23–35).

4 Assessing the transformational potential of partnership

George Orwell, in his celebrated essay *Politics and the English Language*, uses "radical transformation" as an example of the kind of phrase that numbs the brain.[1] His implication is that the expression is a tautology and that transformation is, and should be, radical. Viewed in this light, the growing number of calls for radical transformation to address complex global challenges raises questions about how transformation is understood and why its standalone status may be deemed insufficient.[2] Because transformation is increasingly positioned as the end goal of partnership, clarity around what it means, how it takes place and where multi-stakeholder collaboration can contribute to it are important matters to address.

In recent years, the term transformation has become inextricably linked with notions of partnership and collaboration. This is due, in large part, to disquiet about the state of the planet and the need for collective efforts to address environmental challenges,[3] growing inequalities, social exclusion and the denial of basic human rights.[4] These concerns are reflected in the UN 2030 Agenda for Sustainable Development *Transforming our World* which proposes a set of "bold and transformative steps" for a global shift towards inclusive and sustainable development.[5] The mobilisation of a revitalised Global Partnership for Sustainable Development involving "all countries, all stakeholders and all people" is situated as a key element for achieving this transformation.[6] In view of this positioning, an examination of how transformation is understood in

1. Orwell, G. (2013) *Politics and the English Language*, London, UK: Penguin Books (p. 16).
2. Temper, L., Walter, M., Rodriguez, I., Kothari, A. and Turhan, E. (2018) A perspective on radical transformations to sustainability: Resistances, movements and alternatives. *Sustainability Science*, 13: 747–764. https://doi.org/10.1007/s11625-018-0543-8 (p. 748).
3. Feola, G. (2015) Societal transformation in response to global environmental change: A review of emerging concepts. *Ambio* 44, 376–390. https://doi.org/10.1007/s13280-014-0582-z (p. 376).
4. See https://en.unesco.org/themes/social-transformations (accessed February 21, 2022).
5. United Nations (2015) *Transforming Our World: The 2030 Agenda for Sustainable Development*, Resolution 70/1 Adopted by the United Nations General Assembly on 25 September, New York, NY, USA: United Nations.
6. Ibid., p. 2.

DOI: 10.4324/9781003199434-5

different contexts and the extent to which partnership may contribute to the achievement of more inclusive and sustainable development seems necessary.

What is transformation?

Dictionary definitions of transformation link the term to a *major* change in form, nature or function.[7] This implies that rather than minor, incremental or partial changes, transformation is about fundamental shifts in socio-ecological systems that address "human–environment" relations in an integrated manner.[8] There is, however, disagreement among those who believe that reform of the status quo may be classified as transformational and those who argue that a radical overhaul of the prevailing socio-economic system is at the heart of transformation,[9] a difference that has been presented as "changing the rules of the game" versus "changing the game."[10] Here, the interchangeable use of transformation and adaptation is regarded as particularly problematic with concerns that a focus on the latter directs efforts towards building the resilience of the existing system rather than changing it, hence justifying "business as usual" approaches.[11]

A 2015 report by the LankellyChase Foundation describes systems change as a journey that involves connections across multiple areas and levels, including policies, routines, relationships, resources, power structures and values.[12] The suggestion here is that interactions at different levels within a system will contribute to transformation.[13] Ju Young Lee and Sandra Waddock further note that small shifts can "nudge key leverage points within a complex system" and produce large-scale change.[14] As well as macro-level transformation then, meso- and micro-level transformations, and the connections

7. See, for example, https://dictionary.cambridge.org/dictionary/english/transformation (accessed February 21, 2022).
8. See Feola (2015) Op. cit. p. 377; Geels, F., Golland, A., Lung, T., Sygna, L., Kemp, R. and Steward, F. (2018) *Perspectives on Transitions to Sustainability*, Brussels, Belgium: European Environment Agency. https://data.europa.eu/doi/10.2800/332443 (accessed January 17, 2022) and Reyers, B., Folke, C., Moore, M.L., Biggs, R. and Galaz, V. (2018) Social-ecological systems insights for navigating the dynamics of the anthropocene. *Annual Review of Environment and Resources*, 43: 267–289. http://dx.doi.org/10.1146/annurev-environ-110615-085349
9. Feola (2015) Op. cit. p 377 and Temper et al. (2018) Op. cit.
10. Wigboldus, S., Brouwers, J. and Snel, H. (2020) How a strategic scoping canvas can facilitate collaboration between partners in sustainability transitions. *Sustainability*, 12: 168. https://doi.org/10.3390/su12010168 (p. 4).
11. Blythe et al. (2018) Op. cit. p. 7.
12. Abercrombie, R., Harries, E. and Wharton, R. (2015) *Systems Change: A Guide to What It Is and How to Do It*, London, UK: LankellyChase Foundation (p. 9).
13. Pelling, M., O'Brien, K. and Matyas, D. (2015) Adaptation and transformation. *Climatic Change*, 133: 113–127. https://doi.org/10.1007/s10584-014-1303-0 and see also Stirling, A. (2014) Emancipating transformations: From controlling "the transition" to culturing plural radical progress. *STEPS Working Paper 64*, Brighton, UK: STEPS Centre, p. X.
14. Lee, J.Y. and Waddock, S. (2021) How transformation catalysts take catalytic action. *Sustainability*, 13: 9813. https://doi.org/10.3390/su13179813

between these three levels also need to be considered. These interactions mirror the contextual levels outlined in Chapter 3 and correspond to the possibility that transformation can take place at individual and organisational levels as well as globally. At the individual level, for example, shifts in personal beliefs, values and world views may be "the building blocks for group and societal transformation."[15]

While there is general agreement that transformation is unlikely to occur smoothly and is subject to "discontinuities and ruptures,"[16] its conceptualisation as a journey implies a process that embraces different phases of growth. These phases have been described variously as "sustainability transitions" and "co-evolutionary processes that include changes in modes of production, work relations and culture that take place over time."[17] Although some scholars distinguish transformation from transition, suggesting, for example, that transitions are essentially about top-down technocratic changes as opposed to the more extensive, radical and long-term changes encompassed by transformation, others indicate that the terms are not mutually exclusive and that both involve the engagement of social actors in political processes that are likely to include power struggles and conflicts relating to values.[18] In this sense, as noted by Ian Scoones, "transformation cannot be managed or controlled, but must draw on an unruly politics, involving diverse knowledges and multiple actors."[19]

Like partnership, the catch-all nature of the term transformation risks diluting its usefulness, a risk that is reinforced by suggestions that transformation may have a "dark side."[20] A generalised view that transformation is always positive and constructive is questioned by those who call for clarity around its end goals by asking who transformation is for and for what, "who gains and who loses, who has agency and who decides about the trajectory, rate and scale of changes?"[21] In addition, and in a similar manner

15. Temper et al. (2018) Op. cit. p. 760. It is worth noting here that shifts in individual thinking and behaviour may emerge as the result of "transformational moments" that precipitate new insights in response to the acquisition of new knowledge or connections with others.
16. Feola (2015) Op. cit. p. 381.
17. See Geels et al. (2017) p. 12 and see Kemp, R., Loorbach, D. and Rotmans, J. (2007) Transition management as a model for managing processes of co-evolution towards sustainable development. *The International Journal of Sustainable Development and World Ecology* 14 (1): 78–91. https://doi.org/10.1080/13504500709469709
18. Hölscher, K., Wittmayer, J.M. and Loorbach, D. (2018) Transition versus transformation: What's the difference? *Environmental Innovation and Societal Transitions*, 27: 1–3. https://doi.org/10.1016/j.eist.2017.10.007
19. Scoones, I. (2016) The politics of sustainability and development. *Annual Review of Environment and Resources* 41: 293–319. https://doi.org/10.1146/annurev-environ-110615-090039 (p. 293).
20. Blythe et al. (2018) Op. cit. p. 11.
21. Tisdall E.K.M. (2013) The transformation of participation? Exploring the potential of 'transformative participation' for theory and practice around children and young people's participation. *Global Studies of Childhood*, 3 (2): 183–193. doi: 10.2304/gsch.2013.3.2.183 (p. 190).

to arguments posed by Eric C. Poncelet[22] with regard to partnership, the transformational discourse can also be seen as undermining the role that conflict and resistance may play in transforming.[23] The fact that transformation may be awkward and create tensions further underscores the need for attention to power dynamics and the processes that underpin them.[24] This brings us back to the notion of "radical transformation" and the possibility that this term is being espoused precisely because "transformation" has been absorbed into a narrative that as well as seeking to minimise discomfort and awkwardness also limits its ambition by keeping the focus on adjusting rather than challenging existing systems and structures. Ironically, this distinction could also be construed as reinforcing Orwell's argument that language should be an instrument for expressing rather than concealing or preventing thought.[25]

Taking the debates outlined earlier into consideration, this chapter seeks to explore the ways in which partnership might promote and support transformation. It centres on the premise that transformation involves different actors working together to challenge the drivers of social and economic inequality or environmental deterioration in particular contexts, and that this necessarily involves shifts in power that will entail tension, disagreement and even conflict. Drawing on the analysis of context outlined in Chapter 3, it is further argued that transformation may be achieved through partnership when there is evidence of its added value at individual, organisational and societal levels. To further explore the transformational potential of partnership, incorporation of some of the reflective drivers outlined in Chapter 3 is proposed. The assumption here is that deeper, radical and more "comprehensive transformations"[26] may be promoted by balancing pragmatic and impact-oriented motivations for partnership with more reflective and relational elements that nurture individual and organisational learning and growth. Ultimately, by promoting ongoing stakeholder participation in decision-making and political life, the transformation that partnership might work towards could be described as a form of "social progress" that combines human development, well-being, and environmental sustainability with notions of social justice and the promotion of equal rights and opportunities for all.[27]

Consideration of the transformational possibilities of partnership and evidence to support the added value hypothesis mentioned earlier clearly demand a closer look at how partnership initiatives are monitored and

22. Poncelet, E.C. (2001) A kiss here and a kiss there: Conflict and collaboration in environmental partnerships. *Environmental Management*, 27 (1): 13–25.
23. Blythe et al. (2018) Op. cit. p. 10.
24. Tisdall (2013) Op. cit. p. 190.
25. Orwell (2013) Op. cit. p. 19.
26. Temper et al. (2018) Op. cit. p. 761.
27. See www.socialprogress.org/index/global (accessed August 9, 2021).

evaluated. This requires attention to what is captured in terms of results and impact, as well as how the process of working in this way influences outcomes at different levels in different contexts.

The partnership evaluation challenge

The issue of how partnership arrangements may best be monitored and evaluated is one that has been debated extensively by both academics and practitioners alike. Academics, for example, have routinely called for a more solid evidence base for the effectiveness of collaboration and partnership,[28] while practitioners place emphasis on the need for "fit for purpose" ways of checking on progress and assessing whether their work is achieving intended goals.[29] As a result, a number of different options have been put forward for tracking and measuring partnership. These models propose assessment from a variety of different angles, including exploration of the added value of partnership over time; partner relationships and outcomes; partnership transaction costs; accountability measures; and changes in behaviour, relationships and activities.[30]

In many ways, the confusing array of partnership assessment models on offer reflects the challenges inherent in assessing connections that are not hierarchical and composed of diverse actors. The different relationship levels in partnership arrangements make identification of exactly what to measure, and with what indicators, complex, particularly as partners are likely to have individual preferences regarding appropriate monitoring

28. El Ansari, W. and Phillips, C. J. (2001) Empowering healthcare workers in Africa: Partnerships in health-beyond the rhetoric towards a model. *Critical Public Health*, 11 (3): 231–252. http://dx.doi.org/10.1080/09581590110066676
29. The demand for simple monitoring and evaluation systems and indicators was highlighted at the virtual event: *Impact of Multi-stakeholder Partnerships: Lessons learned, indicators and tools for monitoring the added value of partnering*, jointly organised by the Platform for Multi-Stakeholder Partnerships for Implementing the 2030 Agenda (Partnerships2030) and the Partnerships Resource Centre (PrC), February 15, 2022.
30. Caplan, K., Gomme, J., Mugabi, J. and Stott, L. (2007) *Assessing Partnership Performance: Understanding the Drivers for Success*, London, UK: Building Partnerships for Development (p. 4) and see: Mitchell, J., Shakleman, J. and Warner, M. (2001) Measuring the "added value" of tri-sector partnerships. *Working Paper No. 14*, London, UK: Business Partners for Development Natural Resources Cluster; Brinkerhoff, J. (2002) Assessing and improving partnership relationships and outcomes: A proposed framework. *Evaluation and Program Planning*, 25: 215–231. http://dx.doi.org/10.1016/S0149-7189(02)00017-4; Artz, K.W. and Brush, T.H. (2000) Asset specificity, uncertainty and relational norms: An examination of coordination costs in collaborative strategic alliances. *Journal of Economic Behavior and Organization*, 42: 337–362. https://doi.org/10.1016/S0167-2681(99)00080-3; Caplan, K. (2005) Partnership accountability: Unpacking the concept. *Practitioner Note Series*, London, UK: Building Partnerships for Development, and Earl, S., Carden, F. and Smutylo, T. (2001) *Outcome Mapping: Building Learning and Reflection into Development Programs*, Ottawa, Canada: International Development Research Council.

and evaluation systems.[31] Attempting to appraise partnership is further complicated by the fact that partnership goals are frequently unclear. In this regard, Derick W. Brinkerhoff observes that while the drawing up of "compatible and convergent objectives" by partners is a logical starting point for any partnership, this is complicated by three key challenges: the incompatibility of multiple interests and existence of hidden agendas; power differentials among actors due to differences in resource levels, capacity or political leverage and the fact that partner objectives may change over time.[32]

This issue of hidden agendas is of particular importance because, as noted in Chapter 3, when partners are not upfront about their reasons for partnering, partnership goals may be unrealistic and over ambitious or, conversely, diluted to the "lowest common denominator," thus limiting opportunities for achieving transformation. Difficulties in deciding exactly what needs to be assessed and why may also be combined with standard concerns about attribution and the fact that changes often occur well after interventions such as partnership have completed their work.[33] Assessing partnership and its impact is thus aptly likened to measuring "a moving target" (see Figure 4.1).[34]

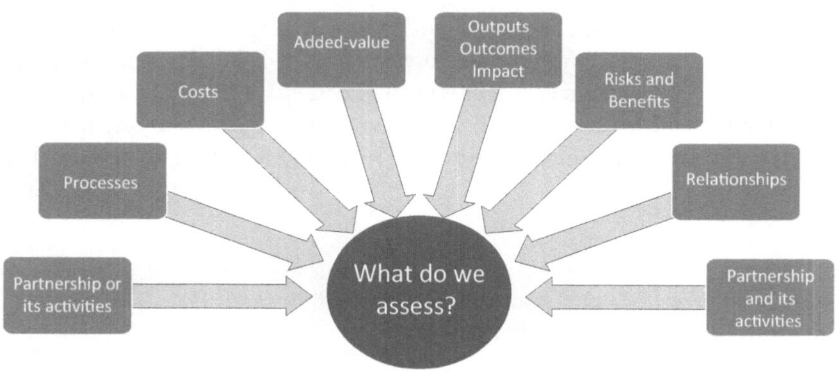

Figure 4.1 The challenge of assessing partnership

Source: Adapted from Caplan et al. (2007)[35]

Credit: Building Partnerships for Development in Water and Sanitation (BPD)

31. Caplan et al. (2007) Op. cit. and Rein, M. and Stott, L. (2009) Working together: Critical perspectives on six cross-sector partnerships in Southern Africa. *Journal of Business Ethics*, 90 (1): 79–89. https://doi.org/10.1007/s10551-008-9915-9 (pp. 85–86).
32. Brinkerhoff, D.W. (1999) Exploring state-civil society collaboration: Policy partnerships in developing countries. *Nonprofit and Voluntary Sector Quarterly*, 28: 59–86. https://doi.org/10.1177%2F089976409902801S01 (p. 61).
33. Caplan et al. (2007) Op. cit. pp. 16–17.
34. El Ansari, Phillips and Hammick (2001) Op. cit. p. 220; Kolk, A., Van Dolen, W. and Vock, M. (2010) Trickle effects of cross-sector social partnerships. *Journal of Business Ethics*, 94 (Supplement 1): 123–137. https://doi.org/10.1007/s10551-011-0783-3 (p. 123).
35. Adapted from Caplan et al. (2007) Op. cit. p. 3.

The patchy nature of partnership results, which is compounded by the paucity of partnership monitoring and evaluation systems, has led a number of writers to conclude that "partnerships" have failed to live up to their expectations.[36] A sense that "the development field is littered with aspirational partnerships that fall short of executing their ambitious goals"[37] is reiterated by Philipp Pattberg and Oscar Widerberg who found that many of the Type II partnerships developed after the 2002 WSSD in Johannesburg showed limited overall effectiveness in relation to their stated goals and ambitions.[38] More than five years after they began, 211 partnerships from a sample of 340 in total were found to be inactive, lack outputs or unable to match their stated aspirations with their declared activities.[39] This "failure" is not limited to WSSD partnerships. Among large global partnerships, although some show success in problem-solving,[40] partly because of poor tracking systems, there appears to be little evidence of their "net added value" compared to existing institutional arrangements for addressing development concerns.[41] More generally, as well as an inability to deliver on governance objectives, the continued marginalisation of key and relevant stakeholders, including private sector actors, has also been documented.[42] This has been compounded by a sense that most partnership arrangements are donor or "Northern driven" and lack local-level participation from "the South."[43]

36. Tomlinson, F. (2005) Idealistic and pragmatic versions of the discourse of partnership. *Organization Studies*, 26 (8): 1169–1171. https://doi.org/10.1177%2F0170840605055338 (p. 1169); Beisheim, M. (2012) Partnerships for sustainable development: Why and how Rio + 20 must improve the framework for multi-stakeholder partnerships. *SWP Research Paper*, Berlin: Stiftung Wissenschaft und Politik, German Institute for International and Security Affairs (p. 6); and Patscheke, S., Barmettler, A., Herman, L., Overdyke, S. and Pfitzer, M. (2014) Shaping global partnerships for a post-2015 world. *Stanford Social Innovation Review*, Spring: 2–9 (p. 2).
37. Patscheke et al. (2014) Op. cit. p. 2.
38. In order to distinguish them from Type 1 arrangements promoted by governments, these arrangements were known as Type II partnerships or "voluntary" coalitions among different actors to implement WSSD goals Ivanova, M. H. (2003) Partnerships, international organizations, and global environmental governance. In: Witte, J. M., Streck, C. and Benner, T. eds. (2003) *Progress or Peril? Partnerships in Global Environmental Governance: The Post-Johannesburg Agenda*, Washington, DC, USA: Global Public Policy Institute, pp. 9–36 (pp. 14–15).
39. Pattberg, P. and Widerberg, O. (2016) Transnational multistakeholder partnerships for sustainable development: Conditions for success. *Ambio* 45: 42–51. https://doi.org/10.1007/s13280-015-0684-2 (p. 44).
40. For example, the Global Alliance for Vaccines and Immunization (GAVI), which offers funding for vaccines and health system strengthening support and the Forest Stewardship Council (FSC) which certifies timber.
41. Bezanson and Isenman (2012) Op. cit. p. 24.
42. Pattberg and Widerberg (2016) Op. cit. p. 44.
43. Bäckstrand, K. (2006) Multi-stakeholder partnerships for sustainable development: Rethinking legitimacy, accountability and effectiveness. *European Environment*, 16: 290–306. https://doi.org/10.1002/eet.425 (p. 299).

Notwithstanding the importance of these critiques, the criteria used to assess partnership generally give little or no attention to the "hidden" or unexpected benefits of partnering. Such benefits may accrue even when partnership has been judged as ineffective or too costly. In this regard, rather than a focus on outputs and outcomes, it is important to acknowledge that "collaborative advantage" may be derived from the process of partnering and the development of relationships.[44] Most partnership evaluations focus on measuring effectiveness in an instrumental manner through quantitative assessments of short-term tangible outputs derived from joint activities. In addition to weak analysis of medium-term outcomes and long-term impact, such appraisals do little to assist in understanding how partner relationships influence results and why partnering may be preferable to working in projects managed by single organisations or through traditional contract-based relationships. In view of evidence linking partnership effectiveness to good process management, greater consideration of how partners work together in order to meet their goals is important.[45] As Joanne Burke notes, "the way that partners manage their interaction and invest in their relationship – *how they collaborate* – is inextricably linked to the overall effectiveness of the partnership and *what* it achieves."[46]

Emphasis on the process of partnering and the benefits that may ensue from this is endorsed by findings from the six Southern African partnership initiatives where, in spite of limited outcomes, the value of partnering appeared to lie in its potential for promoting wider connections and long-term change[47] (see Table 4.1). Although review procedures in these partnership initiatives

Table 4.1 Partnership results in the Southern African case studies

Partnership		***Results***	
	Aim	***Outcomes***	***Processes***
Chamba Valley Partnership	To increase small-scale farming income by supplying a supermarket chain with local produce	10/98 farmers selling to Shoprite	Individual farmers had more capacity and confidence
Small-scale Sugarcane Farming Communities Partnership	To improve livelihoods of small-scale sugarcane growers	No data available	Integration of affected communities in political processes of post-apartheid South Africa

44. Huxham, C. and Vangen, S. (2004) Doing things collaboratively: Realizing the advantage or succumbing to inertia? *Organizational Dynamics*, 33 (2): 190–201. http://dx.doi.org/10.1109/EMR.2004.25132 (p. 200).
45. Pattberg and Widerberg (2016) Op. cit. p. 47.
46. Burke, J. (2018) Improving partnerships: Reflecting, reviewing and revising. In: Stott, L. ed. *Shaping Sustainable Change: The Role of Partnership Brokering in Optimising Collaborative Action*, London, UK: Greenleaf Publishing, Routledge, Taylor and Francis Group.
47. Rein and Stott (2009) Op. cit. p. 86.

Partnership		*Results*	
	Aim	*Outcomes*	*Processes*
Zambia Business Coalition on HIV/AIDS	To link businesses with NGOs and government to tackle HIV/AIDS pandemic	- Increase in membership - No figures for numbers of people being treated and supported	Wider awareness about HIV/AIDS and links with business coalitions in other African countries
Amangwe Village	To promote a holistic healthcare centre with and for people living with HIV/AIDS	Limited statistical data available	No data available
Mthashana FET College Partnership Programme	To support learning and skills development	No data available	Slow embedding in government policy
Sharing Responsibility for Higher Education Partnership	To engage businesses in improving educational infrastructure and teaching conditions	- Slight increase in award of scholarships - Some environmental improvements	Awareness of the role the private sector might play in supporting higher education and ensuring the development of a qualified workforce

Source: Adapted from Stott (2017)[48]

were largely absent or ad hoc, and data on the tangible impact of their activities were hard to identify, a key conclusion from the research was that the process of working in partnership provided openings for different stakeholders to express and draw attention to their needs and concerns.[49]

In the long term, it appears that sustainability of the more intangible benefits of working in partnership will depend on the identification of real-life changes that would not have happened, or would have happened only at greater cost or more slowly, without partnership.[50] While it is difficult to review the counterfactual, according to a number of representatives from ESF Managing Authorities, after several decades of promoting the "partnership principle" in Europe, disadvantaged and marginalised groups have

48. Stott, L. (2017) *Partnership and Social Progress: Multi-Stakeholder Collaboration in Context.* Ph.D. Thesis, University of Edinburgh, UK (p. 57) and see also Rein, M., Stott, L., Yambayamba, K., Hardman, S. and Reid, S. (2005) *Working Together: A Critical Analysis of Cross-Sector Partnerships in Southern Africa*, Cambridge, UK: University of Cambridge Programme for Industry.
49. Ibid.
50. As this kind of evidence often emerges after a partnership arrangement has ended, this raises questions about how stakeholders track and record results when their work together is over.

gained a stronger voice in the political arena.[51] Partnership arrangements in Austria, Germany, Ireland and Sweden, for example, appear to have assisted the integration of grassroots concerns in development programmes.[52] Here, "multi-objective, multi-layered and multi-stakeholder" connections are seen as having contributed to "innovative local development strategies and the breaking down of institutional and organisational barriers that impede improved approaches for dealing with complex problems on the ground."[53] Partnership relationships within, between and across different countries, regions, sectors and organisations in Europe are further viewed as reinforcing "social capital" and supporting positive change within organisations. One of the interviewees in the 2008 ESF study described this process as one that included: "dialogue, experience exchange and improvement of routines and processes in the organisations involved."[54] Ten years later, a participant in the ESF Transnational Platform's Thematic Network on Partnership noted that "more than just a concept, true partnerships are the most difficult, rewarding, and effective form of decision-making available to us in Europe."[55]

In the Latin American cases, addressing and giving voice to community concerns and ensuring active roles for community members in co-creating service models were welcomed. A member of the *Ciudad Saludable* initiative described this as a model in which "the aim is to support processes that change the vision. I do it, we do it together and then you do it." (see Box 4.4). As well as tangible improvements in service provision, evidence also suggests that the partnership approaches adopted have contributed to changes in government policies and norms that embrace collaborative approaches and give greater space for their work. In Peru, for example, the positive relationship between *Acciona Microenergía Perú* (AMP) and national public bodies ensured clarity around regulations and new energy technologies in country-wide service expansion plans (see Box 4.1).[56] Meanwhile,

51. Stott, L. (2008) *How European Social Fund Managing Authorities and Intermediate Bodies Support Partnership*, Brussels: European Commission (p. 22) and Stott, L. (2019) *How European Social Fund Managing Authorities and Intermediate Bodies Support Partnership*, Revised edition, Brussels, Belgium: European Commission (p. 18).
52. Stott, L. and Scoppetta, A. (2013) Promoting local economic development through partnerships in Europe. *Skills@Work: Theory and Practice Journal*, 6: 2–12 (pp. 6–8).
53. Ibid., p. 11.
54. Stott (2008) Op. cit. p. 20.
55. Cited in Stott, L. (2018) Review of the European Code of Conduct on Partnership (ECCP), *Technical Dossier No. 7*, Brussels, Belgium: DG Employment, Social Affairs and Inclusion, EU (p. 5).
56. Egido, M.A. (2014) Luz en casa: Access to sustainable energy in rural communities. In: Peru Martínez, A. ed. *eHealth in Rural Areas: Access to Medical Care, Training and Prevention in Guatemala, Partnerships for Innovation in Access to Basic Services Case Study*, Washington, DC, USA: Multilateral Investment Fund/Inter-American Development Bank (MIF/IDB) and Madrid, Spain: Innovation and Technology for Development Centre/*Universidad Politécnica de Madrid* (itdUPM).

Box 4.1 *Luz en Casa* access to sustainable energy in rural communities, Peru

In 2009, *Acciona Microenergía Perú* (AMP), a social enterprise founded by the *Acciona Microenergía* Foundation (FUNDAME), launched the *Luz en Casa* (Light at Home) programme to supply electricity to rural inhabitants of the Department of Cajamarca in Peru using Solar Home Systems (SHS).[57] By 2013, the Partnership had installed 3,000 SHS which supplied residential homes with low consumption lighting and energy outlets. The *Luz en Casa* programme was well accepted by the community and the default rate was extremely low. As well as the social benefits of improved access to electricity and mobile communication, household costs were reduced as the service was cheaper than paying for kerosene and candles. Close collaboration with community users took place through local Photovoltaic Electrification Committees (*Comités de Electrificación Fotovoltaica* or CEF) which assisted with service inspections, tariff collection and protection of the SHS. The similarity of the CEF to traditional organisational structures and the promotion of equitable gender representation meant they were well accepted. AMP worked to capacity-build members of the community to use the SHS and trained a network of local technicians to install and maintain them. Qualified technicians were also offered support to set up micro-businesses that could service SHS installations as well as sell equipment such as lamps, bulbs, mobile chargers and power adapters. AMP further responded to consumer demands for improved services by introducing higher strength LED lamps to boost lighting and the use of mobile phones to transmit repair requests and make payments, thus improving CEF fee collection systems that often involved extensive travel and exposure to the risk of theft.

The development of a positive relationship between AMP, the Ministry of Energy and Mines and the Energy and Mining Investment Supervisory Body ensured clarity around regulatory requirements. As a result of an ongoing dialogue at this level, AMP was granted Peru's first photovoltaic-based electricity concession in May 2012. The pay-for-service model adopted by AMP was also made affordable at the household level through an agreement with the government whereby a higher fee for those who consumed more energy enabled lower tariffs for off-grid users receiving services from renewable energy sources. This arrangement allowed AMP to assume the costs of service installation, operation and maintenance, and offer customers a

57. A Solar Home System (SHS) supplies residential electric power using solar panels as the main power source.

fair user fee based on their economic capacity and ability to pay. Due in large part to the positive impact of the *Luz en Casa* programme, the Peruvian government launched a scheme to install half a million SHS throughout the country.

the advocacy work of *Ciudad Saludable* contributed to the comprehensive focus of Peru's General Law for Solid Waste, one of the first national laws to integrate regulations for recyclers (see Box 4.2).

These "results" suggest that multi-stakeholder collaboration may be transformational by combining policy level changes, shifts in individual and organisational views, behaviours and ways of working, and the empowerment of vulnerable and marginalised stakeholders. Furthermore, internalisation of the learning from partnering can also enhance a deeper shared understanding of the value and importance of other sectors and their roles in society. Clearly then, improved partnership monitoring and evaluation systems are required that are able to capture the added value of partnering, both as a tool and as a process.

In order not to overburden partners with too many assessment activities, and in response to practitioner demands for simpler review methods, Ken Caplan et al. suggest that evaluation of the results of partnership activities may be conducted using standard project monitoring and evaluation frameworks.[58] The authors further propose a "health-check" approach to explore how partners are working together that examines partnership performance and effectiveness by analysing the drivers that promote or inhibit partnering at three interconnected levels: the external context in which a partnership is working; the organisational environment of each partner and among individuals representing partner organisations.[59] Other methodologies that have been put forward for these kinds of assessments include a framework developed by Jennifer M. Brinkerhoff that aims to improve partnership practice and explore a partnership's contribution to performance and outcomes by reviewing evolving partner relationships[60] and a Partnership Learning Loop (PLL) tool that seeks to strengthen collaboration between partners by looking at different partnership layers in order to provide insights into how a partnership functions, how it adds value and how it evolves over time.[61] More recently, the PrC and the Partnerships 2030 Platform facilitated by the German development agency, GIZ, have suggested a flexible multi-layered

58. See, for example, https://tools4dev.org/resources/how-to-write-a-monitoring-and-evaluation-framework/
59. Caplan et al. (2007) Op. cit.
60. Brinkerhoff (2002) Op. cit.
61. See www.learningloop.nl/ (accessed February 22, 2022).

impact measurement pathway that explores partnership outcomes at individual, organisational, partnership, sectoral and societal levels.[62]

Those involved in the development of these models indicate that an important first step in addressing the evaluation challenge is for partners to agree on exactly what they want to measure and why. They also suggest that integrating monitoring and evaluation of the partnering process into the fabric of a partnership is needed from the start, and that a nuanced appreciation of context and how it influences particular collaborative approaches are necessary. As noted in a report by the Partnership Brokers Association (PBA), partnership activities are impacted by a complex mix of external and internal contextual issues, and understanding how partners navigate these is critical to the successful achievement of their goals.[63] It should be noted once again that, while it is tempting to propose a wider range of criteria for partnership assessment, those working in partnership consistently demand straightforward measures for doing this that do not overload or complicate their work.

Added value and transformation

With the aforementioned caveats in mind, a partnership review approach is proposed here that explores the transformational potential of partnership in relation to the societal, organisational and individual added value that working in this way might offer. This approach focuses on the outcomes of collaboration and how partners work together to achieve these.[64] The idea here is that partnership arrangements are more likely to be effective and have a societal impact if clear organisational *and* individual benefits are derived from partnering.[65] Such an approach resonates with calls for consideration of how "partnerships can address the 'social good' in many more subtle ways, as well [as] via stakeholder interactions that might trickle from one level to another."[66] Some of the outcomes that might demonstrate the positive societal contribution of partnership are outlined in Table 4.2.

The notion of partnership adding value to individuals, organisations and society as a whole is centred on the idea that, rather than seeking to identify concrete results from short-term transactions, we need to explore the potential partnership offers for systems change in relation to the policies, behaviours, structures, routines and values alluded to by the LankellyChase

62. See www.partnerschaften2030.de/wp-content/uploads/2021/05/Impact-Narrative-Visual-and-Tool.pdf (accessed February 22, 2022).
63. Tennyson, R., Stott, L, Marhubi, A. and Wood, E. (2016) The necessity of transformation, emerging partnership lessons from diverse contexts. *Report for the Promoting Effective Partnering (PEP) Facility*, London, UK: Partnership Brokers Association.
64. Caplan et al. (2007) Op. cit. p. 3.
65. Ibid., p. 5.
66. Kolk, Van Dolen and Volk (2011) Op. cit. p. 123.

Table 4.2 Results that might demonstrate partnership added value

	Short-term results	***Longer-term outcomes***
Individual partner representatives	• Access to new/improved products and services • Acquisition of new knowledge/skills • Access to new opportunities	• New opportunities • Enhanced confidence • Ability to influence organisations • Improved quality of life
Partner organisations	• Improved stakeholder relationships • New markets for products and services • Transactional efficiency • Improved reputation/public recognition • Acquisition of knowledge/skills • Networking and information exchange • Access to funding/resources	• Policy influence/impact • More integrated organisational approaches • Improved working relationships • Heightened ability to fulfil the mission • Innovative ways of problem-solving • Better ability to address risks
Target groups and wider society	• Acquisition of knowledge/skills • Learning opportunities • Improved job performance • Effective use of time and resources	• Changes in practice, attitudes and behaviour • Improved quality of life • Greater confidence/stronger voice in political arena • Sustainable solutions to development challenges

Source: Stott (2017)[67]

Foundation.[68] To do this, it is helpful to distinguish transformational partnership from other types of partnership.

In an article on strategic collaboration between non-profit organisations and businesses, James E. Austin outlines a collaborative continuum consisting of three stages: philanthropic, transactional and integrative.[69] In this continuum, partners deepen their connection as they move towards integrative relationships where societal value is created by combining the distinctive competencies and resources of their members. This scale has been built upon by Austin and Maria May Seitanidi to create a "Value Creation Spectrum" which helps partners to explore their potential for generating meaningful shared value in relation to four stages of collaboration: philanthropic, a charitable relationship based on unilateral transfer of funds from

67. Stott, L. (2017) *Partnership and Social Progress: Multi-Stakeholder Collaboration in Context.* Ph.D. Thesis, University of Edinburgh, UK (p. 55).
68. Abercrombie et al. (2015) Op. cit.
69. Austin, J.E. (2000) Strategic collaboration between nonprofits and businesses. *Nonprofit and Voluntary Sector Quarterly*, 29 (1): 69–97. https://doi.org/10.1177%2F0899764000291S004 (p. 91).

one party to another; transactional, in which there is "reciprocal exchange" of resources through activities such as sponsorships and personal engagements; integrative, where value is created by combining distinctive partner competencies and resources, and transformational, whereby value is derived from innovative co-creation processes between partners which encourage lasting change within organisations and their staff, as well as in broader social, economic or political systems.[70]

Austin and Seitanidi's "Value Creation Spectrum" resonates with similar frameworks that have been developed to categorise UN-Business Partnerships[71] and Business-NGO arrangements.[72] UN-Business Partnerships, for example, are classified by the UN Global Compact LEAD Task Force as philanthropic, opportunistic, strategic and transformational, while Barbara Gray and Jenna Stites group Business-NGO partnership initiatives as reactive, transactional, integrative and transformational in relation to the scope they cover and the extent to which partners assume shared responsibility. These classifications have been combined in Figure 4.3 in a four-stage spectrum that includes philanthropic relationships and initiatives developed in response to a mandate or crisis on the one hand and transformational partnership arrangements that engage more deeply with stakeholders and leverage the core competencies of all partners in order to "restructure the rules of the game" on the other.[73]

While the continuum presented in Figure 4.2 offers useful insights into transformational collaboration, it has several drawbacks. First, it is focused primarily on relationships that involve the private sector and the added value that might accrue to business by working in partnership.[74] Second, it is centred upon an understanding of partnership as a structural form and does not engage deeply with aspects relating to the intrinsic worth of partnering. It is also worth pointing out that the term "transactional" to describe a particular partnership type could be construed as something of a misnomer as all partnership arrangements involve some form of transaction or exchange.

To address these shortcomings and explore the core elements of transformational partnership arrangements more deeply, it is helpful to return to

70. Austin, J.E. and Seitanidi, M.M. (2012) Collaborative value creation: A review of partnering between nonprofits and businesses: Part I. Value creation spectrum and collaboration stages. *Nonprofit and Voluntary Sector Quarterly*, 41 (5): 726–758. https://doi.org/10.1177%2F0899764012450777 (p. 736).
71. UN Global Compact LEAD Task Force (2011) *Catalyzing Transformational Partnerships between the United Nations and Business*, New York, NY, USA: UN Global Compact Task Force (p. 9).
72. Gray, B. and Stites, J.P. (2013) *Sustainability Through Partnerships: Capitalizing on Collaboration* Canada: Network for Business Sustainability, pp. 24–25. nbs.net/knowledge (accessed February 22, 2022).
73. The Global Compact LEAD Task Force (2011) Op. cit. pp. 9–11; Gray and Stites (2013) Op. cit. p. 14.
74. Porter, M.E. and Kramer, M.R. (2011) The big idea: Creating shared value. *Harvard Business Review*, 89: 2–17.

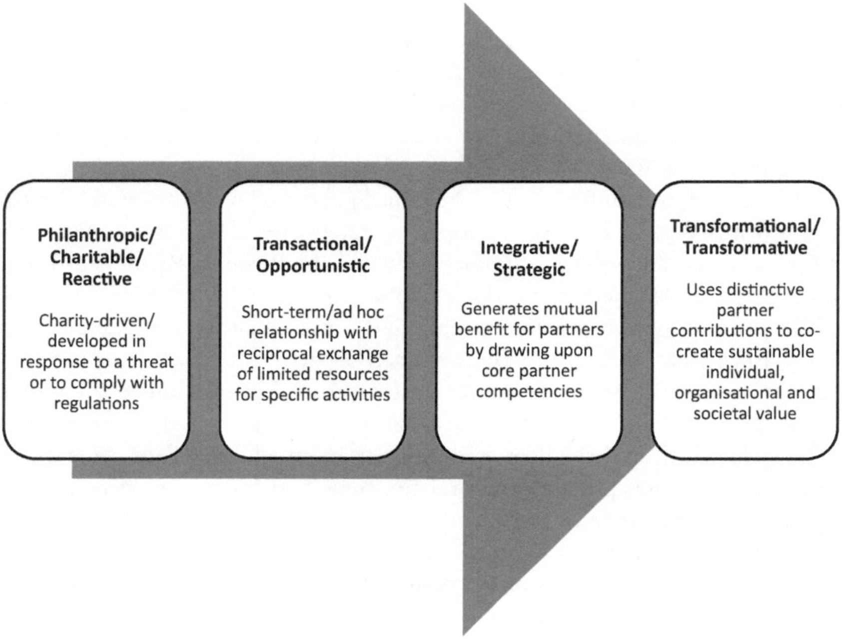

Figure 4.2 Spectrum of partnership types

the distinction made between pragmatic (partnership as a means to an end) and reflective (partnership as an end in itself) incentives for partnering. The hypothesis here is that both these elements need to be fully integrated within transformational partnership arrangements so that, as well as a focus on results and compliance in order to get the work done, ample attention is given to the quality of partnering processes and relationships. A focus on relationship-building rests fundamentally on deeper recognition of the interpersonal connections that inform partnership, how these link to organisational interactions and how the values, motivations and dynamics they encompass influence both the development and outcomes of diverse collaborative arrangements. As Riane Eisler reminds us, it is the combination of individual and collective actions that are the "sparks for systems transformation."[75] An appreciation of the intrinsic qualities of collaboration is central to this.[76]

75. Eisler, R. (2002) *The Power of Partnership: Seven Relationships That Will Change Your Life*, California, USA: New World Library (p. xxi).
76. See Eisler, R. (1987) *The Chalice and the Blade, Our History, Our Future*, San Francisco, CA, USA: Harper and Row; Esiler, R. (2008) Our great creative challenge: Rethinking human nature: And recreating society. In: Richards, R. ed. *Everyday Creativity and New Views of Human Nature: Psychological, Social, and Spiritual Perspectives*, Washington, DC, USA: American Psychological

Richard Sennett's "spectrum of exchange" offers a useful way of exploring these connections further. In the book *Together, The Rituals, Pleasures and Politics of Cooperation*, Sennett sets out five forms of exchange: altruistic exchange which focuses on gift-giving; win–win exchange which involves overt reciprocity; differentiating exchange in which there is an appreciation of distinctiveness; zero-sum exchange in which one party dominates at the expense of another, and winner-takes-all exchange in which one party wipes out another.[77] By combining some of the elements of these forms of exchange with the typologies presented in Figure 4.2, an updated schema for exploring partnership arrangements in relation to their potential for transformation is offered in the following discussion framework.

Exploring the potential for transformation

The aim of the framework shared here is to reinforce the need for a balance between the pragmatic and reflective dimensions of partnership presented in Chapter 3 and, using a transformational lens, explore the depth of change that we might expect from initiatives that sit within different partnership categories.[78] To do this, Table 4.3 delineates four possible partnership "types":[79]

- **Tactical partnership** in which partners aim to achieve a specific task with a limited or immediate end in view
- **Targeted partnership** which is based on working with a specific partner or partners in order to ensure that the right resources are pooled to meet a particular need or task
- **Transversal partnership** in which partners seek to maximise outcomes by ensuring different partner hierarchies and functions intersect in a horizontal manner and cut across silos
- **Transformational partnership** in which partners work to achieve long-lasting structural or systemic change

Association, pp. xiii: 261–285. http://rianeeisler.com/wp-content/uploads/2014/06/riane-eisler.pdf (accessed January 6, 2017); Eisler, R. (2015) Human possibilities: The interaction of biology and culture. *Interdisciplinary Journal of Partnership Studies*, 1 (1): 1–39 https://doi.org/10.24926/ijps.v1i1.88; Leadbeater, C. (2012) *It's Co-Operation, Stupid, Why Richard Dawkins, Thomas Hobbes and Milton Friedman Got It Wrong*, London, UK: Institute for Public Policy Research; Sennett, R. (2013) *Together: The Rituals, Pleasures and Politics of Cooperation*, London, UK: Penguin Books; and Bregman, R. (2020) *Humankind: A Hopeful History*, London, UK: Bloomsbury Publishing.

77. Sennett, R. (2013) *Together: The Rituals, Pleasures and Politics of Cooperation*, London, UK: Penguin Books (pp. 72–86).
78. Wigboldus et al. (2020) Op. cit. p. 3.
79. I am grateful to Ken Caplan for assisting me in the development of these categories.

Table 4.3 Assessing the transformational potential of partnership

	Tactical	*Targeted*	*Transversal*	*Transformational*
Focus and drivers	- Concrete project type focus - Multiplicity of contextual factors not fully considered	- Developed in response to specific issue/need - Strong task response focus - Short-term/ad hoc relationship - Works within status quo – "business as usual" models	- Focus on institutional strengthening in order to address gaps - Embedded within particular contexts - Interest in reform and improvement - Attention to different partners drivers	- Focus on systems change - Addresses connections between external, organisational and individual drivers
Resource exchange	- Donor–recipient type relationship based on unilateral transfer of resources (usually financial)	- Reciprocal exchange of limited resources for specific activities	- Use of core partner competencies to develop partner and societal value	- Use of distinctive partner contributions to ensure individual, organisational and societal value
Representation and participation	- Partner selection restricted to known actors - Limited consultation with stakeholders	- Partner selection based on known quantities - Opportunistic cooperation with wider stakeholders at specific intervals	- Efforts made to ensure partner diversity and seek continuous engagement of partners and wider stakeholders	- Seeks engagement with "non-traditional" partners - Stakeholder engagement tailored to needs of particular groups and changing circumstances
Governance and accountability	- Top-down system of governance - Limited space for experimentation and innovation	- Initiating partner assumes a strong lead role - Difficult to balance accountability with innovation – tends towards one or other	- Distributed governance - Attempts to secure adequate space for innovation while also promoting accountability	- Strong horizontal ownership - Attention to power dynamics that limit space for innovation
Relationship building	- Partnership brokers play a minimal role - Tension and conflict ignored or suppressed	- Partnership brokers place emphasis on getting job done - Little room for disagreements to surface	- Partnership brokers provide space for tensions and disagreement to surface but the emphasis is on limiting/managing differences	- Partnership brokers allow space for "difficult" conversations - "Productive conflict" accepted/no attempt to shy away from tension
Learning and embedding	- Little change within partner organisations - Weak systems connections	- Engages with wider systems but no long-term impact within partner organisations	- Emphasis on shared learning with efforts to mainstream results	- Learning internalised and results mainstreamed at partner and societal levels

Each of these categories is examined in relation to a set of core interrelated elements that are central to how they operate. Following a description of these features, attention is given to assessing where some of the case studies used in this book might sit within the groupings suggested. The intention is to provide a flexible review framework to assist discussion among partners about interest in, and advances towards, the pursuit of a transformational trajectory.

It is important to emphasise that this representation is *not* arranged as an evolutionary continuum. Although partnership arrangements may evolve across these classifications, the interconnected internal and external contextual variables that drive them suggest that they are unlikely to do so in a linear manner. As well as embracing elements across the different types, partnership initiatives may also move back and forth between them as they develop.

Focus and drivers

Although there is some discrepancy about whether transformational partnership arrangements are likely to start with a transformational intention or whether this focus may be more evolutive,[80] a holistic approach and systems perspective is central to them. This is likely to be reflected in goals that focus on reshaping rules, norms and behaviours that challenge the status quo and traditional ways of doing things. Austin and Seitanidi's assertion that "the collaboration's transformative effects would not only be in social, economic or political systems but also change each organization and its people in profound, structural, and irreversible ways"[81] further suggests that attention will be paid to individual, organisational and external drivers and the added value that collaboration may offer at each of these levels. Because they seek to promote lasting systemic change, transformational relationships will also need to be stronger than those that focus on short-term goals.[82]

A focus on systems clearly distinguishes transformational partnership arrangements from those that are tactical or targeted. In line with the "reactive" partnership category proposed by Gray and Stites, tactical partnership arrangements are understood here as those that "embrace threat-induced, compliance or charity-driven responses."[83] Their intention

80. Austin and Seitanidi (2012) Op. cit. p. 737.
81. Ibid., p. 722.
82. Nowell, B. (2009) Profiling capacity for coordination and systems change: The relative contribution of stakeholder relationships in interorganizational collaboratives. *American Journal of Community Psychology*, 44:196–212. https://doi.org/10.1007/s10464-009-9276-2 (p. 209).
83. Gray and Stites (2013) Op. cit. p. 25.

is to address a particular issue or undertake a task through collaborative arrangements that are pragmatic, short term and often ad hoc. In charitable or philanthropic arrangements, for example, organisational priorities are primarily about gift-giving and "discrete efforts" that focus on "public relations and financial contributions."[84] Rather than being "totally selfless", such "altruism" may be viewed as one in which the giver expects to get something back.[85] In targeted arrangements, meanwhile, the emphasis is usually on short-term gain with organisational incentives for participation often based on improving reputation or image.[86] Such initiatives work primarily within the status quo and generally reinforce standard ways of doing things. Pragmatic in nature and focused on a concrete need, partners are unlikely to possess "a collaborative vision . . . reflective of multiple values and worldviews."[87]

Transversal partnership arrangements are likely to have a strong focus on strengthening institutions, and the links between them, in order to better deliver existing policies and comply with rules and regulations.[88] As such, they will pay attention to organisational incentives and the added value that the relationship between different partners can bring to wider society in the longer term. In these arrangements, consideration will also be given to individual motivations for partnering and to the incorporation of more reflective elements, including relationship-building processes. Here, Sennett draws an analogy with nest-building in which, as well as sharing in its construction, members of a nest also benefit from the result.[89] A transversal partnership, however, also tends to be strongly nested within the status quo and largely focused on reforming and improving what exists as opposed to replacing it with something new. This contrasts with transformational arrangements that focus on changing systems, making cross-cutting societal linkages and working with short-, mid- and long-term outcomes in mind. Drawing extensively upon previous learning and experience,[90] these initiatives explore and seek to align the incentives of both internal and external stakeholders to ensure responsiveness to particular needs.[91] The links between individual, organisational and societal motivations for partnering will also be reinforced, alongside clear acknowledgement that *how* partners work together will be reflected in their results and impact.

84. Global Compact LEAD Task Force (2011) Op. cit. p. 9.
85. Sennett (2013) Op. cit. pp. 74.
86. Gray and Stites (2013) Op. cit. p. 24.
87. Ibid., p. 42.
88. Thanks again to Ken Caplan for this insight.
89. Sennett (2013) Op. cit. p. 75.
90. Gray and Stites (2013) Op. cit. p. 26.
91. Austin and Seitanidi (2012) Op. cit. p. 744.

Box 4.2 Ciudad Saludable, Peru

The NGO *Ciudad Saludable* established an integrated model for waste management in Lima that expanded to 20 cities across Peru. Financed from donor and government grants, public funds and waste management consultancy activities, the model addressed the entire solid waste value chain by linking together three key elements: advocacy at the municipal level to reinforce a comprehensive solid waste management system; social and economic inclusion of recyclers and environmental awareness-raising. A diverse set of partnership arrangements between stakeholders such as private companies, central, regional and local government, educational institutions, recyclers and communities was channelled into three cross-cutting programmes:

The **Zero Rubbish Programme** to change policies and practices through an integrated system of solid waste management by working with local and regional governments, businesses and the general public to ensure that all reusable materials were recycled and that unusable waste was disposed of in controlled landfills.

The Recycler Programme to assist recycler collectives to create formal associations and to develop inclusive businesses to collect, process, manage and recycle solid waste. Recyclers were provided with equipment such as *motofurgones* (small vehicles able to negotiate narrow transport routes) and access to finance through microcredit and training programmes.

The Environmental Citizens Programme to engage in activities with the wider public in order to promote awareness about waste management. Local Environmental Management Committees were formed to manage solid waste collection, separate and market recyclable materials, participate in the monitoring of microenterprises established by recyclers, and ensure that non-recyclable solid waste was disposed of in controlled landfills. Partnership connections were also created with local and national businesses to assist them to design and implement waste separation systems, with educational institutions to teach school children about recycling and with universities to promote research and training activities related to waste management.

Resource exchange

One of the main reasons that partnership initiatives are established is to bring together actors with diverse resources, strengths, experiences and approaches.[92] However, priority is often given to financial contributions

92. Mundy, J. (2018) Embedding ethical and principled partnering approaches. In: Stott, L. ed. *Shaping Sustainable Change: The Role of Partnership Brokering in Optimising Collaborative Action*, London, UK: Greenleaf Publishing, Routledge, Taylor and Francis Group.

which, in consequence, privileges partners that provide monetary resources. In tactical partnership arrangements dependent upon donor funding, for example, resource flows are generally unidirectional from one partner to another.[93] Rather than a relationship between equals, such an arrangement is thus likely to reinforce traditional donor–recipient or project-style relationships. In a targeted partnership arrangement, there will be "more reciprocal"[94] exchange between the different partners and "higher resource complementarity"[95] as efforts are made to draw upon the core competencies of the parties involved in order to meet a common goal.

In both transversal and transformational partnership initiatives, as well as clear recognition that financial resources are just one of a range of possible inputs that partnership arrangements may draw upon, including knowledge, skills, experience, products, venues, networks and political leverage, there is also acknowledgement that contributions need to be linked to the core competencies of the partners involved in order to enhance the value of working together.[96] The difference between these two forms of relationship is that in transformational arrangements, there will be a stronger appreciation of the *distinctive* contribution of each partner to the partnership arrangement and how this can support the common good.[97]

Representation and participation

Although partner diversity is hailed as one of the key reasons for collaboration, a majority of partnership arrangements tend to work with organisations,

Box 4.3 Territorial Employment Pacts in Austria[98]

Territorial Employment Pacts (TEPs) are cooperation structures that operate in the field of labour market policy in Europe. These contracted regional partnerships aim to better link employment policy with other policies in order to improve the employment situation at regional and local levels. In 1997, following positive results from pilot pacts, TEPs were established in all nine Austrian provinces under the auspices of the Federal Government. The TEPs brought together the

93. Austin and Seitnaidi (2012) Op. cit. p. 738.
94. Sennett (2013) Op. cit. p. 75.
95. Austin and Seitanidi (2012) Op. cit. p. 739.
96. Caplan and Stott (2008) Op. cit. p. 30.
97. Sennett (2013) Op. cit. p. 82.
98. Federal Ministry of Labour, Social Affairs and Consumer Protection and Centre for Social Innovation (2009) *Brochure on Territorial Employment Pacts in Austria*, Vienna, Austria: BMASK and ZSI; and Scoppetta, A. (2013) The Austrian TEP model. *Presentation at ESADE VI Annual Conference: Promoting Social Innovation through Collaboration*, Barcelona, Spain, 20 February.

Public Employment Service, Provincial Governments, Federal Social Welfare Offices, social partners and other stakeholders in joint programmes for employment that were implemented with a coordinated Pact budget. Characterised by autonomy in decision-making and flexible organisation, the structure and tasks of each TEP were tailored to specific regional needs. In the 2007–13 ESIF programming period, TEPs were able to experiment with different measures for the integration of those furthest away from the labour market. In Tyrol, for example, initiatives involved training young, disadvantaged women; in Lower Austria, efforts were directed towards labour market access via training programmes and assistance to start-ups, while in Vienna, the TEP offered innovative counselling and integration projects using a model of flexible cross-partner cooperation.

The TEPs generated a series of methodological innovations such as integration chains that combined actions and target groups; process innovations enabling more transparent, efficient and effective project and programme management; systemic innovations such as the restructuring of data and interface management for social welfare beneficiaries, and structural innovations such as pilots for one-stop-shops and pioneering demand-oriented minimum wages. An Austria-wide coordination unit, Kooo, subsidised by the Federal Government provided support to the TEPs and promoted a strong learning culture at regional, national and international levels.

groups and individuals that they know and are familiar with.[99] Those exploring partnership arrangements developed to meet the targets of the SDGs have noted that the transformations necessary for achieving targets require much greater diversity and inclusiveness.[100] Among the arguments for engaging with different actors in partnership initiatives are access to new and more innovative ideas and ways of working that can assist in the development of solutions to "wicked" problems, greater societal involvement in "collective problem-solving"[101] and the possibility of addressing entrenched power relations.[102]

99. Stott (2018) Op. cit. p. 11.
100. Stott and Scoppetta (2020) Partnerships for the Goals: Beyond SDG 17. *Revista Diecisiete: Investigación interdisciplinar para los Objetivos de Desarrollo*, 2: 29–38. doi: 10.36852/2695-4427_2020_02.02 (p. 33).
101. GCPSE and UNDP (2016) *Citizen Engagement in Public Service Delivery: The Critical Role of Public Officials,* Singapore: UNDP Global Centre for Public Service Excellence (p. 2)
102. Gupta, J. and Vegelin, C. (2016) Sustainable development goals and inclusive development. *International Environmental Agreements* 16: 433–448. https://doi.org/10.1007/s10784-016-9323-z (pp. 444–445).

Tactical and targeted partnership arrangements tend to involve partners who know one another and have worked together on previous occasions. In this sense, they are more risk averse than transversal and transformational partnership arrangements that actively seek to engage with non-traditional stakeholders in sustained interactions that work towards societal objectives while responding to the needs of all partners.[103] In addition, in tactical and targeted initiatives, stakeholders tend to be engaged in an ad hoc manner or at specific points such as design or evaluation phases. This contrasts with transversal and transformational arrangements where the involvement of partners and stakeholders is continuous throughout partnership life cycles.[104]

Transformational partnership initiatives may be distinguished from transversal partnership arrangements in that, as well as recognising that actor distinctiveness has practical value,[105] *appropriate* stakeholder participation is sought. This suggests a more refined understanding of partner contributions that is linked to the relevance, timing and "fit" of diverse inputs in different contexts. In this way, the right set of partners and stakeholders will be engaged to address specific issues and challenges.[106] Transformational partnership arrangements ultimately rest upon contextually relevant approaches that take cognisance of diverse voices to inform particular initiatives. According to the UN Global Compact LEAD Task Force, by drawing upon the "network effect" of different actors, collaboration in this type of partnership initiative can "reach a tipping point of social change."[107] Gray and Stites further observe that managing and integrating different stakeholder expectations, and their partnership efforts, can empower by giving an equal voice to the stakeholders with whom they partner.[108]

Governance and accountability

Simon Zadek has argued that the transformational potential of partnership is directly linked to the extent to which accountable decision-making processes are in place that respond legitimately to stakeholder concerns.[109] This legitimacy is based upon the existence of clear governance structures, operational guidelines and procedures for working together, as well as clarity about the roles and responsibilities of those involved.[110] Ken Caplan further advises that as well as being accountable to one another, and to

103. Gray and Stites (2013) Op. cit. p. 25.
104. Stott (2018) Op. cit. pp. 20–21.
105. Sennett (2013) Op. cit. p. 82.
106. Pattberg and Widerberg (2015) Op. cit. p. 46; Stott (2018) Op. cit. p. 17.
107. Global Compact LEAD Task Force (2011) Op. cit. p. 13.
108. Gray and Stites (2013) Op. cit. p. 26.
109. Zadek, S. (2007) Collaborative governance: The new multilateralism for the 21st century. *Global Development* 2.0, Washington, DC, USA: Brookings Institute (p. 11).
110. Global Compact LEAD Task Force (2011) Op. cit. p. 9.

external stakeholders, partners will also operate within relevant regulatory frameworks.[111] Because a strong criticism of partnership is that, under the guise of collaborative governance, the role of state actors is undermined or distorted,[112] close links to policy environments are particularly important, especially when partnership goals relate to public service provision or the achievement of national development targets.[113]

Caplan helpfully defines accountability as incorporating three key elements: compliance, where partners know what is required of them to achieve objectives with clear standards and commitments in place to which they must adhere; transparency, where accessible information exists on decisions and related actions, performance and expected outcomes for partners, and responsiveness, where stakeholder feedback is carefully considered and responded to so that the reasons why a particular decision or action has been taken can be publicly demonstrated. These elements of accountability may be validated in some form of partnership agreement signed by the parties involved.[114]

In tactical partnership arrangements, governance functions are likely to be minimal with an initiating partner or donor exercising decision-making powers and stipulating accountability requirements.[115] Partner agreements are often bilateral in nature, involving a funder and one of the partner organisations assuming an administration role on behalf of the partnership. Compliance will generally be one-sided with little information shared and minimal consideration of wider stakeholder feedback. Targeted arrangements will generally have some form of governance structure in place, with particular attention paid to the roles and responsibilities of partners so that compliance is ensured. Less attention, however, will be paid to transparency and responsiveness.

Because transversal partnership arrangements generally require the deployment of more valuable core partner resources and have greater societal ambitions, they will demand stronger management and leadership.[116] As well as an emphasis on partner compliance, they will also share information related to partner decisions and standards transparently and be responsive to wider

111. Caplan, K. (2005) Op. cit. p. 2.

112 Schäferhoff, M., Campe, S. and Kaan, C. (2007) Transnational public-private partnerships in international relations: Making sense of concepts, research frameworks, and results. *SFB-Governance Working Paper Series*, No. 6, Berlin, Germany: DFG Research Center. ISSN 1079–1760 (p. 13) and Beisheim (2012) Op. cit. p. 6.

113. Stott, L. (2010) *The Partnering with Governments Navigator, Building Effective Collaboration With the Public Sector in Africa*, London, UK: International Business Leaders Forum and Eschborn, Germany: GTZ (p. 10).

114. For more on partnership agreements see: Evans, B., McMahon, J. and Caplan, K. (2004) *The Partnership Paperchase: Structuring Partnership Agreements in Water and Sanitation in Low-Income Countries*, London, UK: Building Partnerships for Development.

115. Austin and Seitanidi (2012) Op. cit. p. 738.

116. Ibid., p. 743.

stakeholder demands. Communication between partners is likely to be fluid with regular interaction and meetings. The importance of linking collaborative activities to public policy frameworks and the establishment of good connections with government agencies will also be evident. Transformational partnership initiatives will build upon these elements, often through the signing of a jointly developed partnership agreement. The idea of inclusive governance that gives attention to how decisions are made and who is included in decision-making processes will also be apparent. Finally, emphasis will be placed on ensuring that accessible and transparent channels exist for different groups of external stakeholders to connect with their work.

Although accountability is important, Eisler contends that partnership systems require flexible hierarchies that provide space to inspire rather than control.[117] The argument here is that accountability measures should not stifle collaborative arrangements by reducing room for testing and meaningful learning. The need for a balance between accountability and space for innovation is echoed by Caplan who contends that clarity around partnership systems, structures, roles and responsibilities must accommodate change and allow for experimentation with new ways of doing things. "The ideal partnership," he suggests, "would be framed as . . . maximising innovation and creativity whilst ensuring accountability, focusing on delivery whilst capturing lessons to influence the rules."[118]

Rather than seeking a balance between accountability and flexibility, tactical and targeted partnership arrangements will tend towards the former, particularly with regard to ensuring compliance. Transversal arrangements are likely to seek equilibrium between the two albeit in an unsystematic manner. Transformational initiatives, however, will strive to provide frameworks for collaborative activities in which "people are able to rely on norms of reciprocity and peer-to-peer learning to enforce sanctions, rather than material incentives and abstract rules, both of which tend to undermine cooperation."[119]

Relationship-building

One of the main arguments in this book is that investment in the partnering process is central to collaborative effectiveness and, in consequence, that the transformational potential of partnership rests upon transformative participation. To move beyond what Gray and Stites describe as "mere

117. Eisler (2015) Op. cit. p. 6.
118. Caplan, K. (2003) *Plotting Partnerships: Ensuring Accountability and Fostering Innovation, Practitioner Note Series*, London, UK: Building Partnerships for Development (p. 4).
119. Leadbeater (2012) Op. cit. p. 44.

transactional exchanges," partners need to be willing to "open themselves, recognize their blind spots and rigid preconceptions, and enter into a process of genuine mutual influence."[120] Here, careful attention to process factors and the nature of interactions among partners is necessary.[121] Such relationship-building will involve exploring and managing differences so that cultures can be bridged and trust built among partners.[122] A vital role can be played here by a partnership broker, convener or facilitator to cement relationships through the fostering of collaborative spaces in which issues and challenges are shared, including those that may be problematic or cause tension.[123]

In a tactical collaboration, there is likely to be little interaction of this nature between partners as their connection is generally hands-off and top-down. In targeted arrangements, some attention will be given to process and relationship-building, but the priority will be on working towards tangible impact. Indeed, the partnership broker role in this type of initiative is often limited to ensuring that partners meet planned goals in a timely manner. In transversal initiatives, on the other hand, the link between good process and results will be clear and partners will be able to negotiate with one another in an open-ended manner while dealing with ambiguity.[124] The value of informal exchange between partners can also be mutually affirming as relationships are forged through spontaneous interaction outside of formal cooperation processes.[125]

In transformational partnership initiatives, appreciation of the intrinsic qualities of collaboration can enhance deeper levels of engagement and learning. This type of partnership arrangement may be understood as working across shifting interfaces or boundaries where differences may be revealed and self-understanding stimulated.[126] Such interactions can add value through "dialogic" or "differentiating" exchange based upon recognition of the distinctive contribution of the actors involved. Through this connection, even though agreement may not always be reached, "people may become more aware of their own views and expand their understanding of the other."[127] In such arrangements, the facilitation of collaborative spaces can provide opportunities for "asking provocative questions, offering sensitive disclosures, opening the agenda to pursue spontaneous ideas, and

120. Gray and Stites (2013) Op. cit. p. 44.
121. Ibid., p. 41.
122. Global Compact LEAD Task Force (2011) Op. cit. p. 9.
123. Baksi, B. (2018) Building on diversity. In: Stott, L. ed. *Shaping Sustainable Change: The Role of Partnership Brokering in Optimising Collaborative Action*. London, UK: Greenleaf Publishing, Routledge: Taylor and Francis Group (pp. 64–65).
124. Sennett (2013) Op. cit. p. 76.
125. Ibid., p. 78.
126. Ibid., p. 79.
127. Ibid., p. 19.

valuing the other in attitudes and acts."[128] These opportunities can, in turn, assist in building trust among those involved.[129]

Learning and embedding

As well as ensuring added value for society, organisations and individuals, Austin and Seitanidi suggest that transformational partnership is based upon "shared learning about social needs and partners' roles in meeting those needs."[130] This focus on learning is explored by Susan Buck Sutton and Daniel Obst who note that institutional partners in transactional partnership initiatives in the field of education remain largely "separate and unaffected" by the relationship.[131] Transformational collaborations, meanwhile, permeate organisations so that different units and teams, and the individuals within them, are altered by working in partnership. This institutional change may encompass improvements in human resource development, engagement in more dynamic networks, better communication and opportunities for "getting out of the box."[132] Such opportunities may be derived from processes of experimentation in which partners jointly "test" out new ideas and approaches. As well as combining resources, transformational partnerships will, then, view partner connections as "sources of institutional growth and collaborative learning."[133]

In tactical initiatives, the institutionalisation of learning and experimentation will be minimal with little internal change among partners as a result of collaboration. An exception to this may be a situation in which individual "gift-givers" in charitable partnership arrangements are motivated more deeply by a desire to act well than an interest in praise or reward.[134] Those involved in tactical and targeted partnership arrangements are likely to view testing processes as risky, often due to concerns about time and the need to focus on delivery within prescribed deadlines. In targeted relationships, although there may be changes in the way individuals and organisations work as a result of partnering, learning will not be acted upon proactively or viewed as essential to informing further change.

128. Sloan, P. and Oliver, D. (2013) Building trust in multi-stakeholder partnerships: Critical emotional incidents and practices of engagement. *Organization Studies*, 34 (12): 1835–1868. https://doi.org/10.1177%2F0170840613495018 (p. 1862).
129. Ibid.
130. Austin and Seitanidi (2012) Op. cit. p. 744.
131. Buck Sutton, S. and Obst, D. (2011) The changing landscape of international partnerships. In: Buck Sutton, S. and Obst, D. eds. *Developing Strategic International Partnerships, Models for Initiating and Sustaining Innovative Institutional Linkages*, New York, NY, USA: Institute of International Education. ISBN-10: 0872063445 (p. xvii).
132. Tennyson, R. (2011) *The Partnering Toolbook*, London, UK: The Partnering Initiative (IBLF) (p. 31).
133. Buck Sutton and Obst (2011) Op. cit. p. xvii.
134. Sennett (2013) Op. cit. p. 74.

Box 4.4 eHealth in rural areas, Guatemala

In 2008, the Guatemalan NGO TulaSalud established a partnership initiative to address high maternal and infant mortality rates among Indigenous communities in remote rural areas of the Department of Alta Verapaz using information and communications technology (ICT). With financial support from the Canadian-based Tula Foundation, TulaSalud's health service model included the Ministry of Public Health and Social Assistance, the Health Department of Alta Verapaz, Cobán National School of Nursing and Cobán Hospital. The three core components of the partnership included:

Tele-education – training local nursing assistants and technicians using videoconference systems. As well as assisting TulaSalud with the selection of applicants, the Cobán National School of Nursing provided premises for training in remote locations. The Ministry of Public Health and Social Assistance established the training requirements for the distance learning courses and covered most of the teaching costs.

Tele-medicine – supporting local community facilitators to provide healthcare in remote areas. The Health Department of Alta Verapaz selected the areas in which the work would take place and health service providers then chose basic healthcare teams and community facilitators. Endorsed by their communities and paid a small stipend for their work by the Ministry of Public Health and Social Assistance, community facilitators were equipped with a mobile phone to make diagnostic inquiries and supply patient information to doctors and nursing staff based in health centres and hospitals, as well as receive ongoing training.

Teenage health protection and prevention – to ensure long-term change through health education and awareness-raising, TulaSalud and the Health Department of Alta Verapaz jointly developed the *X'beil li Kawilal* (Path to Health) initiative. The programme supported young Indigenous female leaders to work with adolescent girls on issues such as prevention of teenage pregnancies, improvement of self-esteem, life-planning and decision-making.

Considerable efforts were made by TulaSalud and the Tula Foundation to ensure financial support as the public health system assumed control of the programme. An Advisory Board with representatives from all partners was established to manage the initiative and promote the active involvement of public health authorities. The Cobán National School of Nursing eventually took over full responsibility for the training of nursing technicians, community facilitators were incorporated into the local rural health system and the salaries of staff involved in the telemedicine service were paid by Cobán Hospital.

Both transversal and transformational initiatives will encourage and make space for experimentation and see this as an opportunity to learn from what works and what does not. Review and feedback processes will also help to systematise lessons about apparent "successes" and "failures" which may be shared with other practitioners as well as planners and policy makers. Meanwhile, an environment that is conducive to individual trust-building will enable the development of a unique partnership identity that consolidates relationships and binds partners together more firmly.[135] Here, as noted by Maria May Seitanidi and Andrew Crane, trust-based connections can demonstrate "partnership embeddedness."[136] A "we" rather than "us" and "them" mentality can also strengthen the ability of partners to better address challenges.[137] In transformational arrangements, such embeddedness further implies a progression away from purely instrumental and pragmatic notions of partnership towards the institutionalisation of more joined-up, reflective and co-created approaches. Ros Tennyson further notes that this involves individual engagement and growth, "true collaboration transforms the individuals that engage in it consciously: partners help each other grow personally and professionally while accomplishing the objectives of the partnership."[138]

A link can be made here to the notion of reflective practice which has been defined as the capacity to reflect on action and engage in a process of continuous learning in which attitudes, processes, values and assumptions are questioned.[139] By encouraging a focus "outside oneself," Sennett believes that this kind of dialogic exchange can promote empathy.[140] This is endorsed by Charles Leadbeater and Riane Eisler who both regard empathy as central to genuine cooperation.[141] Given the emphasis placed on the full acknowledgement of the value of distinct competencies and resources in transformational partnership arrangements, and the need to understand different partner incentives for engaging in collaboration, insistence on a connection that is "real and personal" so that "the people taking part are more able to put themselves in the other person's shoes" is apposite here.[142] This implies a focus on individuals, as well as organisations, and the possibility

135. Ibid.
136. Seitanidi, M.M. and Crane, A. (2009) Implementing CSR through partnerships: Understanding the selection, design and institutionalization of nonprofit-business partnerships. *Journal of Business Ethics*, 85: 413–429. https://doi.org/10.1007/s10551-008-9743-y (p. 422).
137. Ibid., p. 421.
138. Tennyson (2011) Op. cit. p. 25.
139. Hundal, S. (2016) The value of reflective practice for partnership brokers. *Betwixt and Between The Journal of Partnership Brokering*, (6). http://partnershipbrokers.org/w/journal/the-value-of-reflective-practice-for-partnership-brokers/ (accessed February 19, 2022) and see also https://learningforsustainability.net/reflective-practice/ (accessed February 19, 2022).
140. Sennett (2013) Op. cit. p. 22.
141. Leadbeater (2012) Op. cit. p. 44 and Eisler (2015) p. 19.
142. Leadbeater (2012) Op. cit. p. 40.

that by improving quality of life, a "healthy" collaborative connection may be intrinsically good.

Application to practice: a new way of assessing partnership?

Exploration of where different partnership arrangements sit in Table 4.3 may assist assessments of how far they are adding value for society, partners and individuals, and if (or where) further action is needed to promote this. Due to the time and resource implications of working in partnership, if a move towards transformation is not taking place, questions may be asked about whether a collaborative relationship is in fact worth pursuing.[143] Those involved in tactical and targeted collaborations might therefore investigate whether there is appetite among partners for engaging in efforts to become more transformational and, if not, whether they may want to continue to work in partnership. Such thinking is in line with work on partnership evaluation which suggests that the validity of a partnership approach may be tested by asking whether the results sought could be achieved more easily through alternatives such as contractual arrangements, traditional project formats or single-sector programmes.[144]

For transversal arrangements, discussion among partners may centre on how far partners are content to engage in reform-type efforts or whether they wish to deepen possibilities for change. In a transformational initiative, meanwhile, questions about the extent to which the results of partnership arrangements, and the processes they have facilitated, are sustained through socially embedding and integration within policies and institutions are pertinent.[145] This deliberation will involve exploring whether the collaborative work has been completed and may thus be disbanded or whether partners wish to build upon the connection and engage in further work together. Here, we return to the idea that partnership arrangements of a structural nature may best serve as non-permanent or transitional mechanisms until the results or practices they advance become institutionalised and part of everyday practice.[146] In this regard, the idea that the pressures of being temporary and transitional may actually increase the potential for transformation is worthy of reflection.[147]

In order to further explore the usefulness of the discussion framework offered here, it is helpful to use some of the examples from the Case Study

143. Stott, L. (2019) Partnerships for sustainable development: The monitoring and evaluation challenge. *Great Insights, European Centre for Development Policy Management (ECDPM)*, 8 (1): 28–30.
144. Caplan et al. (2007) Op. cit. p. 7.
145. Tennyson (2011) Op. cit. pp. 29–31.
146. Caplan and Stott, 2008:26.
147. Halper, E. (2009) *Moving On: Effective Management for Partnership Transitions, Transformations and Exits*, London, UK: International Business Leaders Forum (p. 14).

Map (Table 1.1). While a number of the cases combine elements from different categories, others can be clearly positioned within a single classification. The Amangwe Village and Sharing Responsibility for Higher Education Partnership initiatives, for example, could be described as tactical arrangements that operated in a similar manner to a project with vertical rather than horizontal governance arrangements, a focus on the granting of funds as opposed to interest in combining core partner competencies, and limited efforts to engage deeply with different groups of stakeholders.

The Chamba Valley Partnership, meanwhile, may be viewed as a targeted partnership arrangement. Here the basis of reciprocity and exchange of resources in relation to core competencies was clear, but the lack of adequate governance arrangements and limited attention to nurturing stakeholder engagement processes were also notable. This contrasts with the more transversal stance of the Zambia Business Council on HIV/AIDS (ZBCA) partnership and several of the European Social Fund (ESF) initiatives in which the participation of different actors was actively encouraged because of the varied nature of their resource contributions and competencies. Close attention to governance arrangements and the regularisation of meetings and activities was also observed in these initiatives, alongside the use of review mechanisms that assessed the achievement of milestones.

The collaborative initiatives to improve access to basic services in Latin America and South Africa could be categorised as transformational.[148] These models worked in the short term to provide an early demonstration of tangible change such as the provision of photovoltaic electricity in the *Luz en Casa* study in Peru (see Box 4.1) or maternal health services in the e-Health partnership in Guatemala (Box 4.3).[149] As well as encouraging experimentation in order to assess what kind of approaches and activities would best suit the particular contexts in which they were working, efforts were made to ensure that new ways of doing things become part of the organisational cultures of the partners. In the Guatemala case, for example, government agencies began to take over the health education activities and costs initially assumed by other partners.[150] In the longer term, as shown in the cases of *Luz en Casa* and *Ciudad Saludable* in Peru, the partnership models led to positive changes in regulatory frameworks for energy and waste management, respectively.[151] The learning gained through continuous exchanges of knowledge and experience also promoted a sense that the intrinsic value of partnership contributed to sustainable change.[152]

148. Stott, L. (2014) *Partnerships for Innovation in Access to Basic Services*, Washington, DC, USA: Multilateral Investment Fund/Inter-American Development Bank (MIF/IDB) and Madrid, Spain: Innovation and Technology for Development Centre/*Universidad Politécnica de Madrid* (itdUPM).
149. Ibid., pp. 9–11.
150. Ibid., p. 14.
151. Ibid., pp. 10 and 22.
152. Ibid., p. 39.

Among the examples situated between the different classifications in Table 4.3 are the partnership principle promoted by the European Commission and the Austrian TEPs. The partnership principle is clearly transformational in intent, promoting as it does the involvement of different societal actors in EU projects and programmes as a routine way of operating. However, the assimilation of the principle in different Member States has varied with regard to the depth of its implementation both within the ESF and across other funds. Current endeavours to enhance and endorse the partnership principle in the 2021–27 ESIF programming period indicate that, while there is clearly work to be done to engage more diverse partners and deepen the connections that have been established, efforts are needed to reinforce connections across different EU funds and programmes.[153] Ongoing work to consolidate the partnership principle across EU Member States also highlights the importance of acknowledging the time and dedication needed to position, develop and embed processes that enhance multi-level governance and stakeholder engagement in disparate contexts.

The Austrian TEPs (see Box 4.2) were disbanded in 2014 due to a national policy level shift away from proactive involvement in promoting these arrangements to the assumption of a more hands-off administrative role. In spite of this, the transversal processes developed by the nine TEPs appear to have become rooted in institutional practice with evidence to suggest they have had lasting effects on the way different actors work together, and acceptance of the need for robust connections to address access to employment and social exclusion at the regional level.[154] The TEPs also became a model for addressing access to employment across Europe and motivated an enabling environment for working in this way at the levels of both policy and practice.[155] This example is of further interest because, in common with some of the other partnership arrangements developed under the umbrella of the ESF, it suggests that partnership can become more dynamic and innovative over time, even when established in a top-down manner.[156]

The examples of the EU's partnership principle and the Austrian TEPs indicate that a check on the current status of the partnership arrangements used in this book may help to confirm whether or not they have promoted added value and lasting change, both for the individuals and organisations involved, as well as more widely. As most of the examples mentioned here offer a snapshot of partnership arrangements at a particular time in the past, such information is, unfortunately, not easy to find. This difficulty, which is notable in both academic and practitioner materials, is indicative of a

153. The recent launch of the European Community of Practice on Partnership (ECoPP), which has been established to develop learning exchange between countries, actors and funds, provides an example of this.
154. Scoppetta, A. Personal communication. February 8, 2022.
155. Stott and Scoppetta (2013) Op. cit. p. 7.
156. Stott (2008) Op. cit. pp. 40–41.

partnership knowledge gap and suggests that more work needs to be done to better capture partnership stories and trajectories.

Although further research is required to confirm its status and activities, Amangwe Village is registered as a community-based non-profit organisation that offers a holistic healthcare approach to adults and children infected and affected by HIV/AIDS.[157] This implies that, while it may still be engaged in partnership connections, it has elected to operate in a more traditional manner. The Sharing Responsibility for Higher Education Partnership no longer exists, but testimonies indicate that it created a strong connection between the private sector and the two universities involved with business leaders continuing to make financial and in-kind contributions, particularly to the University of Zambia (UNZA).[158]

The Chamba Valley Partnership ended a few years after the EC-Prep study. However, due to the links made through the initiative, some of the farmers continued to supply produce to local stores. More recently, farmers in the area appear to have been able to take advantage of a revived collaborative arrangement with the Zambia Inclusive Business Faculty to sell produce to Shoprite through a partnership that began through another connection with Freshmark.[159]

The Zambia Business Council on HIV/AIDS (ZBCA) seems to have been absorbed in a wider national health coalition. This movement corresponds to changes among other business groupings working on HIV/AIDS in Africa which, while accepting that HIV/AIDS remains a high priority, have elected to focus on wider wellness approaches supported by the business sector that include other communicable and non-communicable diseases.[160] In line with similar coalitions in the region, the integration of ZBCA's work within a wider national health strategy thus confirms the transversal nature of this partnership and indications of its absorption into existing institutions and policies.

As well as permeating institutions, the basic service provision partnership models in Latin America and South Africa have become consolidated within wider programmes and organisational initiatives. This institutionalisation can be linked both to the achievement of positive results and to the effectiveness of ongoing collaborative processes. In 2015, a study found that as a result of the telemedicine initiative in Guatemala, maternal and child mortality rates were lower than the provincial average (which included

157. See www.facebook.com/Amangwe-Village-409545382454791/ (accessed March 1, 2022).
158. Yambayamba, K. Personal communication. February 24, 2022.
159. Zambia Business in Development Facility (ZBiDF) Case Study the Consortium of Fresh Fruit and Vegetable Producers' Partnership (FPP). www.inclusivebusiness.net/sites/default/files/wp/FPPCaseStudy_Web.pdf (accessed March 1, 2022).
160. The South African Business Coalition on Health and Aids (2012) Healthy workplaces shaping healthy communities. *Strategy Document*. www.sabcoha.org/wp-content/uploads/bsk-pdf-manager/10_Strategy-Document_source-doc.pdf (p. 6) (accessed March 21, 2022).

urban areas).[161] The tele-capacity building and education programmes have also expanded to an additional five provinces.[162] Meanwhile, the sanitation partnership initiated by Water for People has been consolidated within the organisation's wider activities in Bolivia which revolve around a programme that focuses on water and sanitation services for all,[163] and the AMP Solar Home Systems model developed in Peru has been successfully adapted in Mexico and Panama.[164] In South Africa, as a result of partnership arrangements with institutions such as the University of KwaZulu-Natal (UKZN), eThekwini Water and Sanitation (EWS) has received global recognition for its progressive policies and innovative WASH service delivery.[165] *Ciudad Saludable* has also continued to extend its collaborative activities in the field of waste management in Peru[166] where its founder, Albina Ruiz, has noted that, in addition to legal advances, systemic change rests upon continued efforts to ensure that these are implemented in practice. Transformational approaches, she believes, should address the interests and concerns of all relevant actors through change processes that are conducted with humility, sincerity and respect.[167]

Against a global context in which partnership is positioned as central to the achievement of the SDGs and promoted as offering solutions to "wicked" problems, the pressure for partnership arrangements to demonstrate results is high. To ensure the development of more ambitious forms of collaboration, a stronger evidence base for partnership effectiveness that assesses both process *and* results is clearly necessary. However, attempting to gather evidence for partnership effectiveness is an enormous challenge. As well as the complex nature of the relationships involved and lack of clarity around their goals, achieving change in attitudes and practice through partnership processes takes considerable time.[168] In addition, because partnership arrangements are challenging to build and maintain, and often place enormous demands on partners, adding too many complex layers to review procedures, or insisting upon prescriptive and "one size fits all" approaches, may not be helpful. Instead, the best way forward may be to concentrate on

161. Martínez-Fernández, A., Lobos-Medina, I., Díaz-Molina, C.A., Chen-Cruz, M.F., Prieto-Egido, I. (2015) TulaSalud: An m-health system for maternal and infant mortality reduction in Guatemala. *Journal of Telemedicine and Telecare*, 21 (5): 283–291.
162. See www.tulasalud.org/telecapacitacion (accessed March 25, 2022).
163. See www.waterforpeople.org/everyone-forever/ (accessed March 25, 2022).
164. See www.acciona.org/es/peru/luz-en-casa/?_adin=11651403501 (accessed March 1, 2022).
165. Sindall, R., Mercer, S.J., Sutherland, C., Buckley, C.A., Gounden, G., Pillay, C. and MacLeod, N. (2018) Municipal-academic partnerships for innovation in sanitation delivery: A case study in Durban, South Africa. *Loughborough University: Conference Contribution*. https://hdl.handle.net/2134/35948
166. See www.ciudadsaludable.org/ (accessed March 1, 2022).
167. See https://es2latam.vc4a.com/blog/2021/07/23/como-generar-cambios-sistemicos-albina-ruiz-ciudad-saludable-peru/ (accessed March 25, 2020).
168. Stott (2019) Op. cit.

partnership review processes that support partners to explore the transformational potential of their collaboration with frank examinations of their incentives for working together, and reflection on their plans, strategies and relationships. This will necessarily require attention to issues of participation and power.

5 Transformative participation

A review of the corporate-community partnerships initiated by the Shell Petroleum Development Company (SPDC) in the Niger Delta in the early 2000s describes some of the challenges encountered as a generalised view among communities that the company was a resource provider rather than a partner; difficulties in forming stable relationships due to high community mobility rates; the absence of partners with adequate capacity and local-level acceptance.[1] The author, Olagoke Macaulay, also notes:

> The complexity and sensitivity of mainstreaming youth and gender issues in partnership negotiations (in a society which traditionally gives only *little* voice to children and women) without precipitating *unhelpful* socio-cultural disequilibrium.[2]

This anecdote is a reminder that the partnership playing field is not a level one and that the notions of horizontal decision-making and power-sharing espoused by partnership are difficult to carry out in practice. As well as limited avenues for expressing their views, recognition of distinctive stakeholder contributions and concerns may be impeded by "powerful" players "leading" and speaking on behalf of others. Furthermore, attempts to change levels of participation can, as Sarah C. White notes, become a focus for

1. Macaulay, O. (2005) The challenge of corporate-community engagement: A case study. *Partnership Matters, Current Issues in Cross-Sector Collaboration*, 3: 27–28, London, UK: The Partnering Initiative (pp. 27–28). It is worth noting here that, while the given rationale for these relationships was the company's desire to address "socio-economic, political and environmental hazards" (Macaulay, 2005:27) associated with oil and gas production, these relationships must be seen as part of SPDC's efforts to repair the damage caused by the Shell–Ogoni conflict and the highly publicised deaths of Ken Saro Wiwa and Ogoni leaders in 1995 by Nigeria's military government, see Boele, R., Fabig, H. and Wheeler, D. (2001) Shell, Nigeria and the Ogoni: A study in unsustainable development: The story of Shell, Nigeria and the Ogoni People: Environment, economy, relationships: Conflict and prospects for resolution. *Sustainable Development*, 9: 74–86. https://doi.org/10.1002/sd.161
2. Macaulay (2005) Op. cit. p. 28.

DOI: 10.4324/9781003199434-6

struggle.[3] To analyse the extent to which partnership might "transform," it is therefore fundamental to look more deeply at how (and to what extent) *different* stakeholders participate in partnership arrangements in practice. Such an inquiry inevitably involves exploring power dynamics.

Stakeholder participation and transformation

If, as we have suggested in Chapter 4, the involvement of stakeholders in transformational partnership arrangements is likely to be deeper and more extensive than in more tactical and targeted forms of collaboration, the nature of stakeholder participation and the different forms that it may assume, as well as the issues and challenges it entails, need to be studied. This involves questioning the widespread notion that transformation is "apolitical, inevitable, or universally beneficial"[4] and acceptance that it can also "create tensions or be uncomfortable."[5] Significant change, as we have noted, may mean shifts in power that are problematic in relation to "who gains and who loses."[6] This indicates the need for a clear understanding of power relations and how they might "direct, block or distort" transformational outcomes in particular contexts.[7]

A semantic clarification relating to the usage of the terms "transformational" and "transformative" is necessary at this point. While the expressions are often used interchangeably, in some fields, particularly those related to leadership, the adjective "transformative" has been positioned as more radical than "transformational."[8] In this book, however, the term "transformational" is used as an umbrella term for significant change produced by partnership arrangements and "transformative" for the actions that might lead to or cause transformation.[9] The focus of this chapter is thus on the role

3. White, S.C. (1996) Depoliticising development: The uses and abuses of participation. *Development in Practice* 6 (1): 6–15. https://doi.org/10.1080/0961452961000157564 (p. 6).
4. Blythe, J., Silver, J., Evans, L., Armitage, D., Bennett, N.J., Moore, M.L., Morrison, T.H. and Brown, K. (2018) The dark side of transformation: Latent risks in contemporary sustainability discourse. *Antipode, a Radical Journal of Geography*, 50 (5): 1206–1223. doi.org/10.1111/anti.12405 (p. 13).
5. Tisdall, E.K.M. (2013) The transformation of participation? Exploring the potential of 'transformative participation' for theory and practice around children and young people's participation. *Global Studies of Childhood*, 3 (2): 183–193. doi: 10.2304/gsch.2013.3.2.183 (p. 190).
6. Blythe et al. (2018) Op. cit. p. 11.
7. Pelling, M., O'Brien, K. and Matyas, D. (2015) Adaptation and transformation. *Climatic Change*, 133: 113–127. https://doi.org/10.1007/s10584-014-1303-0
8. Hewitt, K.K., Davis, A. and Lashley, C. (2014) Transformational and transformative leadership in an innovative partnership-based leadership preparation program. *Journal of Research on Leadership Education*, 9 (3): 225–253. doi: 10.1177/1942775114552329
9. Lonsdale, K., Pringle, P. and Turner, B. (2015) *Transformative adaptation: what it is, why it matters and what is needed*, Oxford, UK: University of Oxford, UK Climate Impacts Programme (UKCIP). (p. 6).

that "transformative participation" might play in contributing to transformational partnership arrangements.

As stakeholder involvement is central to the idea of partnership, the expectation is that transformative partnership participation should possess a meaningful degree of agency. In this regard, a useful distinction may be made between "invited participation" in which "spaces are created through invitations to participate" (by an external agency) and "autonomous participation" in which people create these spaces for themselves.[10] While "invited participation" is common in traditional projects and programmes, in theory, it is ill suited to the collective decision-making processes that partnership implies. However, due to the diverse nature of different partners and their representatives, as well as interactions with wider stakeholders, developing autonomous partnership participation processes can be a challenge. It therefore seems important to examine what works best in different contexts while accepting that distinct levels of stakeholder participation may be needed both concurrently and at different times.[11] To explore partnership participation further, it is helpful to begin by looking at who partnership stakeholders are and what levels of power may exist between them.

Stakeholders and levels of power

Partnership arrangements are composed of stakeholders that we might describe as "internal" and "external."[12] "Internal stakeholders" are partners who contribute resources to a partnership arrangement, assume risks on its behalf and stand to gain benefits from it. "External stakeholders," meanwhile, can be broadly divided into "interested observers" who exert power and influence upon a partnership arrangement (such as donors) and "risk bearers" who are influenced by a partnership arrangement (such as community members) (see Figure 5.1).

In this categorisation, emphasis is placed on understanding the nature of the risks that different partners carry on behalf of a partnership initiative in relation to the resources they commit to it, particularly as financial resources appear to give certain stakeholders greater weight in partnership decision-making processes. However, although important, resource contributions alone do not define the nature of participation in partnership. The power derived from overlapping modes of economic, political, social and cultural power may also exert influence on participation. Shifting "points of power" that are shown in behaviours such as

10. Cornwall, A. (2008) Unpacking 'participation': Models, meanings and practices. *Community Development Journal*, 43 (3): 269–283. http://dx.doi.org/10.1093/cdj/bsn010 (p. 275).
11. Tisdall (2013) Op. cit. p. 190.
12. Stott, L. (2009) Stakeholder engagement in partnerships: Who are the 'stakeholders' and how do we 'engage' with them? *BPD Research Series*, London, UK: Building Partnerships for Development (p. 2).

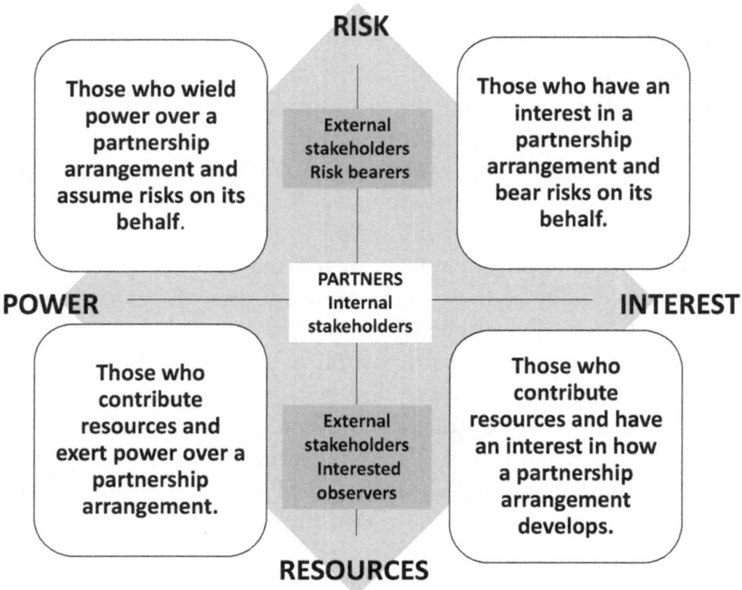

Figure 5.1 Matrix for identifying partnership stakeholders

Source: Stott (2009)[13]

Credit: Building Partnerships for Development in Water and Sanitation (BPD)

"authority, inducement, coercion, seduction, manipulation, persuasion and negotiation" at both organisational and personal levels are also likely to have an impact on partnership participation.[14] Partnership arrangements may thus be seen as "distinctive "arenas of power" where the emphasis on participation and consensus shapes power relations in particular ways.[15]

Partnership processes, as we have noted, are conditioned by context, and, as a result, stakeholder participation in them is likely to reflect wider societal power relations.[16] Furthermore, "partnerships are not static and just as power is articulated as an infinite number of iterative steps, so too is partnership."[17] Because diverse stakeholders may have different interests in partnership at different times, efforts are required to ensure their *appropriate* participation

13. Ibid., p. 6.
14. Derkzen, P., Franklin, A. and Bock, B. (2008) Examining power struggles as a signifier of successful partnership working: A case study of partnership dynamics. *Journal of Rural Studies*, 24: 458–466. https://doi.org/10.1016/j.jrurstud.2008.03.010 (p. 459).
15. Derkzen, Franklin and Bock (2008) Op. cit. p. 459.
16. White (1996) Op. cit. p. 12.
17. Derkzen, Franklin and Bock (2008) Op. cit. p. 460.

during partnership development. This is described by Cornwall as "*optimum* participation: getting the balance between depth and inclusion right for the purpose at hand."[18]

In her seminal work on citizen participation, Sherry Arnstein classifies "optimal" participation as a state in which citizens are "empowered" to lead and shape decision-making.[19] Dismissing more passive participation processes such as consultation and information provision as "tokenism," she suggests that partnership should enable citizens to negotiate and engage in trade-offs with traditional "power holders" in order to promote change. This view sits well with the idea that partnership should directly involve all relevant stakeholders in decision-making processes so that they take ownership of collaborative outcomes.[20] From a historical perspective, these views also resonate with calls for "participatory" and "people-centred" development in which engagement with "the poor" is promoted as central to ensuring that initiatives are more effective and sustainable.[21]

In order to support a more nuanced view of partnership participation[22] and provide the basis for a practical assessment of engagement avenues for *particular* stakeholders, both internal and external stakeholders can be positioned as actors who might participate in processes that range from a limited or passive association to a more dynamic connection in which the lead is taken in decision-making or the development of an activity (see Table 5.1).[23]

In this scenario, internal stakeholders or partners would be expected to engage in the more active levels of the scale (3 and 4). External stakeholders, meanwhile, might participate at different levels depending on their connection to a partnership initiative, their interest in it and the extent to which their involvement is sought.[24] However, although every effort should be made to ensure that they are not contrived as a substitute for authentic participation, it can also be argued that the passive levels of the scale (1 and 2) are not necessarily less worthy and may sometimes be

18. Cornwall (2008) Op. cit. p. 276.
19. Arnstein, S. (1969) A ladder of citizen participation. *Journal of the American Institute of Planners*, 35: 216–224. https://doi.org/10.1080/01944366908977225
20. Ansell, C. and Gash, A. (2007) Collaborative governance in theory and practice. *Journal of Public Administration Research and Theory*, 18 (4): 543–571. doi: 10.1093/jopart/mum032 (p. 546).
21. See, for example, Freire, P. (1970) *Pedagogy of the Oppressed*, New York, NY, USA: Continuum International Publishing Group; Chambers, R. (1983) *Rural Development: Putting the Last First*, New York, NY, USA: Longman; Korten, D.C. and Klauss, R. *People Centered Development: Contributions toward Theory and Planning Frameworks*, West Hartford, CT, USA: Kumarian Press.
22. Beyond what Cornwall (2008) Op. cit. p. 270 describes as an axis of "good" to "bad" forms of participation.
23. Stott, L. (2008) *How European Social Fund Managing Authorities and Intermediate Bodies Support Partnership*, Brussels, Belgium: European Commission (p. 29); Stott (2009) Op. cit. p. 7.
24. Stott (2009) Op. cit. pp. 7–8.

Table 5.1 Levels of stakeholder participation in partnership

Stakeholders . . .			
4	**Steer**	Lead particular steps or partnership activities	**Active**
3	**Influence**	Participate directly in partnership decision-making, have a vote	↑
2	**Are consulted**	Are involved in partnership discussions, able to express opinions and give feedback	↑
1	**Are informed**	Receive information and are made aware of partnership work/activities	**Passive**

Source: Adapted from Stott (2019)[25]

more appropriate for particular groups, contexts or phases of partnership development.[26]

Further exploration of differentiations in partner (or internal stakeholder) participation, and how this compares to that of external stakeholders can be gleaned from a comparison between the Chamba Valley Partnership in Zambia and Small-scale Sugar Farming Communities Partnership in South Africa.[27] These initiatives have been used to assess how far the different stakeholders involved might be classified as active or passive partnership players (see Table 5.2).

This exercise reinforces the perception expressed by some community partners that they had been "left out" of the Chamba Valley Partnership.[28] It also confirms that the partnership was led and managed by an external player, the Partnership Forum, and that the business partners, Shoprite and Freshmark, assumed greater weight in decision-making. In the Small-scale Sugar Farming Communities Partnership, meanwhile, SASA clearly steered the partnership process and the small-scale cane growers at the centre of the initiative assumed a mainly passive role. In addition, although traditional leaders were described as "influential" stakeholders (and central to promoting community participation), an external stakeholder, the Institute

25. Stott, L. (2019) *How European Social Fund Managing Authorities and Intermediate Bodies Support Partnership*, Brussels, Belgium: European Commission (p. 17).
26. Stott (2008) Op. cit. p. 29.
27. Rein, M., Stott, L., Yambayamba, K., Hardman, S. and Reid, S. (2005) *Working Together: A Critical Analysis of Cross-Sector Partnerships in Southern Africa*, Cambridge, UK: University of Cambridge Programme for Industry (pp. 35–55).
28. Rein, M. and Stott, L. (2009) Working together: Critical perspectives on six cross-sector partnerships in Southern Africa. *Journal of Business Ethics*, 90 (1): 79–89. https://doi.org/10.1007/s10551-008-9915-9 (p. 84).

Table 5.2 Stakeholder participation in the Chamba Valley and Small-scale Sugarcane Farming Communities Partnerships

Stakeholders . . .		***Chamba Valley Partnership***	***Small-scale Sugarcane Farming Communities Partnership***
4	**Steer**	*Partnership Forum*	South African Sugar Association
3	**Influence**	Shoprite/Freshmark	- *Institute of Natural Resources* - Large-scale Cane Growers
2	**Are consulted**	- Chamba Valley Cooperative Society - Ministry of Agriculture and Cooperatives - Zamseed	- Small Cane Growers Cooperatives - Department of Agriculture and Environmental Affairs - District Municipalities
1	**Are informed**	*Other communities*	- *Traditional leaders*
	P Partner (internal stakeholder) *ES External stakeholder*		

Source: Stott (2017)[29]

of Natural Resources (INR), was tasked with articulating SASA's community dialogue processes.[30]

These power dynamics suggest that resources such as money and influence do have an important impact on partner participation. However, some caveats are necessary. The stakeholder relationships in Table 5.1 need to be viewed in relation to particular phases of partnership development. At the time of the research, SASA was completing an extensive community scoping process with support from INR, the long-term aim of which was for small-scale cane growers to take ownership of the partnership process.[31] Although at a later stage in its development, in the Chamba Valley Partnership, the Partnership Forum was also involved in capacity-building community members to assume a greater role in activities.[32] It is also worth noting that, even though the "community" was generally

29. Stott, L. (2017) *Partnership and Social Progress: Multi-Stakeholder Collaboration in Context.* Ph.D. Thesis, University of Edinburgh, UK (p. 75) and see also Rein et al. (2005) Op. cit.
30. Ibid., p. 54. This contrasts with the Mthashana Further Education and Training College Partnership where traditional leaders were 'primary' stakeholders (Ibid., p. 101).
31. Rein et al. (2005) Op. cit. p. 54.
32. Rein and Stott (2009) Op. cit. p. 84.

referred to as a homogenous entity in both cases, it contained a variety of different voices within it. In the Chamba Valley Partnership, for example, women farmers complained about being less well informed than their male counterparts.[33] Finally, although Shoprite and Freshmark appeared to have more power than other partners in the decision-making processes of the Chamba Valley Partnership, the reality was that they did not participate as actively as they might. This was partly due to the weak business case for working with small-scale farmers and a prevailing sense that it was the Partnership Forum that "managed and ran operations."[34] Time factors also impeded greater participation of business and government partners in both the Chamba Valley and Small-scale Sugar Farming Communities Partnerships.[35]

Contextual factors that limit stakeholder inclusion, including the time needed to build relationships, have also been cited as challenges to participation in ESF partnership initiatives.[36] A number of studies further indicate that appropriate stakeholder representation in ESIF partnership arrangements is not always guaranteed and that weak participation channels limit opportunities for genuine stakeholder engagement and local-policy level connections (see Box 5.1).

Box 5.1 Challenges to implementation of the European Code of Conduct on Partnership (ECCP)

The ECCP is an EC delegated act that was passed in 2014 to provide common standards for partner involvement in ESIF Partnership Agreements and programme cycles. Reiterating the need for wider stakeholder involvement across national, regional and local levels to maximise the impact of funds, the key provisions of the ECCP include adequate and appropriate representation of partners; accessible and timely consultation processes; assessment of partner roles in partnership performance and effectiveness; strengthening the institutional capacity of relevant partners; dissemination of good practice examples and exchanges of experience in order to promote learning about partnership across the ESIF.

Findings from a review of the ECCP in 2018 showed that while a number of Managing Authorities had managed to embed the Code's standards in their work, others faced a range of problems in applying

33. Ibid.
34. Rein et al. (2005) Op. cit. p. 44.
35. Ibid., p. 11.
36. Stott (2008) Op. cit. p. 32.

them.[37] Most of these challenges were related to the absence of adequate participation channels for genuine stakeholder engagement in programme design, implementation, monitoring and evaluation. Particular concern was expressed about the lack of diversity in the selection of partners and the involvement of "usual suspects" rather than "non-traditional partners." In this regard, mention was made of the need to more deeply involve actors such as SMMEs and social economy enterprises; academic, research and other educational institutions; civil society organisations working on environmental issues and with groups such as youth, people with disabilities and migrants, as well as non-traditional actors representing the most vulnerable and marginalised; gender equality and non-discrimination bodies, and other networks and partnerships, including end users and local level stakeholders who might add new resources and perspectives to programmes and projects.[38]

Respondents also noted that more attention needed to be paid to the factors that impeded full and appropriate participation of partners and stakeholders in programmes and projects. Many felt that meaningful stakeholder involvement was limited by weak information channels, lack of opportunities for involvement during programme implementation and fragmented institutional strengthening and capacity-building efforts. Effective systems for assessing and checking on the implementation of the partnership principle were also largely absent. To address this, access to appropriate methodologies and enhanced review systems were called for alongside the cultivation of more dynamic exchanges of learning about working in partnership across multiple levels.

The partnership arrangements promoted by the ESF raise additional questions about the power of funding organisations and how donors such as international and regional development agencies, corporations and "northern NGOs" determine the nature of partnership participation. A number of writers find that although attention has been drawn to the role played by such actors in transcribing local partner priorities and unilaterally establishing governance arrangements, more subtle forms of power asymmetry such as size, organisational capacity and institutional contexts may also influence partnership participation.[39] Here the remarks of representatives from ESF

37. Stott, L. (2018) Review of the European Code of Conduct on Partnership (ECCP). *Technical Dossier No.* 7, Brussels, Belgium: DG Employment, Social Affairs and Inclusion, EU.
38. Ibid., p. 20.
39. Fowler, A. ed. (2000a) Questioning partnership: The reality of aid and NGO relations. *IDS Bulletin*, 31 (3); Ashman, D. (2001) Strengthening North-South partnerships for

Managing Authorities that their direction heightened levels of ambition as "top-down approaches go further in setting cooperation conditions than partners would voluntarily do"[40] need to be contrasted with disquiet from those who complained about partnership participation becoming "a formal procedure" rather than a dynamic and innovative means of contributing to social progress.[41] It is also true that many ESF Managing Authorities have found it hard to encourage creativity, local ownership and respect for the autonomy of different partners.[42]

Understanding incentives for participation

Richard Sennett asserts that "the challenge of participation is to make it worth people's time."[43] This suggests that the involvement of stakeholders in partnership processes necessarily requires understanding their drivers for participation. As outlined in Chapter 3, the hypothesis here is that if individuals and groups are motivated to work collaboratively because their incentives or obligations for doing so are clear, they are likely to participate in partnership more enthusiastically.[44] If, however, disincentives outnumber incentives, stakeholders may remain detached and, in some cases, even seek to obstruct partnership activities.[45]

To explore the importance of incentives in determining levels of partnership participation, different "points of power" need to be further unpacked. For this, it is useful to look at the visibility (and invisibility) of individuals, groups and organisations in partnership decision-making processes and activities, with the recognition that these categories are multi-faceted.[46] As noted earlier, the term "community," for example, embraces a range of different voices and levels of power and it is often necessary to look beyond

sustainable development. *Nonprofit and Voluntary Sector Quarterly*, 30: 74–98. https://doi.org/10.1177%2F0899764001301004; Crawford, G. (2003) Partnership or power? Deconstructing the 'partnership for governance reform' in Indonesia. *Third World Quarterly*, 24 (1): 139–159. https://doi.org/10.1080/713701365 and Elbers, W. and Schulpen, L. (2011) Decision making in partnerships for development: Explaining the influence of local partners. *Nonprofit and Voluntary Sector Quarterly*, 40 (5): 795–812. https://doi.org/10.1177%2F0899764010366304

40. Stott, L. and Scoppetta, A. (2013) Promoting local economic development through partnerships in Europe. *Skills@Work: Theory and Practice Journal*, 6: 2–12 (p. 6).
41. Stott (2008) Op. cit. p. 24.
42. Stott and Scoppetta (2013) Op. cit. pp. 9–10.
43. Sennett, R. (2013) *Together: The Rituals, Pleasures and Politics of Cooperation*, London, UK: Penguin Books (p. 234).
44. Caplan, K., Gomme, J., Mugabi, J. and Stott, L. (2007) *Assessing Partnership Performance: Understanding the Drivers for Success*, London, UK: Building Partnerships for Development (pp. 8–10).
45. Stott (2009) Op. cit. p. 9.
46. Stott (2008) Op. cit. p. 30; Stott (2009) Op. cit. pp. 9–10.

those who "speak" on behalf of particular stakeholders, especially when they are vulnerable or marginalised community members.[47]

As both the Chamba Valley Partnership and the Niger Delta example at the start of this chapter confirm, some of the voices that may be difficult to hear are those of women and youth. These groups are, of course, composed of individuals whose identities may be crosscut by issues such as "age, class, cultural beliefs, ethnicity, gender, rural/urban background, political affiliation and health status"[48] which may also change over time. Sarah Lister additionally observes that similar considerations need to be taken into account with regard to partner organisations as they embrace different individuals and personal relationships.[49]

Table 5.3 provides examples of some of the (often overlapping) reasons for low or non-participation of different individuals and groups in

Table 5.3 Limitations to partnership participation

	Individuals/groups are . . .	***Examples***	***Partners may need to . . .***
IMPOSED	**Unrecognised** Invisible and unacknowledged/Not considered as stakeholders	Environmental/ youth organisations, SMMEs/user groups, etc. (ESF Partnerships)	• Reassess partnership context • Review structures, channels and levels of engagement • Examine operational culture, e.g. timing of activities
	Disenfranchised Have no say/not been asked to participate in the right way	People living with HIV/AIDS (Amangwe Village)	
	Intimidated Feel unwelcome/lack confidence	Women farmers (Chamba Valley Partnership)	
	Under-resourced Lack time, money, seniority, etc.	Government officials (Chamba Valley Partnership)	
	Distracted Preoccupied with other concerns	Shoprite Manager (Chamba Valley Partnership) Principal (Mthashana College Partnership)	

(*Continued*)

47. Stott, L. and Keatman, T. (2005) Tools for measuring community engagement in partnerships. *BPD Practitioner Note*, London, UK: Building Partnerships for Development (p. 5).
48. Ibid.
49. Lister, S. (2000) Power in partnership? An analysis of an NGO's relationships with its partners. *Journal of International Development*, 12: 327–239. https://doi.org/10.1002/(SICI)1099-1328(200003)12:2%3C227::AID-JID637%3E3.0.CO;2-U (p. 237).

Table 5.3 (Continued)

	Individuals/groups are . . .	***Examples***	***Partners may need to . . .***
SELF-IMPOSED	**Indifferent** Benefits unclear/uncertain about whether efforts will yield results	Freshmark (Chamba Valley Partnership)	• Identify, clarify and review incentives for participation • Show early tangible results that might trigger participation
	Waiting Need to be convinced participation is worthwhile	Small-scale Sugarcane Farmers (South Africa)	
	Hostile Seen as too risky/ Threatening to particular interests	Ex-Principal (Mthashana College Partnership)	
	Weary Tired of development initiatives that have little or no impact	Community representatives (Amangwe Village)	

Source: Adapted from Stott (2009)[50]

partnership processes. These have been roughly grouped into positions that are "imposed" by external actors and those that are "self-imposed" because stakeholders have made a deliberate choice to exclude themselves.[51] Each stance has been illustrated with examples from the Case Study Map (see Table 1.1) with the addition of some general pointers for how they might be addressed. It should be noted that the positions adopted in Table 5.3 are not static. Conflicting and changing loyalties and demands, and the contextual issues that cut across them will exert further influence on both the manner and depth of partnership participation.[52] What the positions do show, however, is that "the partnership context cannot be removed from its processes" and that participation is often limited by "pressing needs."[53]

Capacity-building

Efforts to increase stakeholder participation in partnership processes often focus on providing capacity-building to organisations that face financial, administrative and operational constraints. In the EU, for example, investment in

50. Stott (2009) Op. cit. p. 10.
51. Many of these positions are also outlined by Cornwall (2008) Op. cit. pp. 279–280.
52. Stott (2009) Op. cit. p. 10.
53. Netshandama, V. (2010) Quality partnerships, the community stakeholders' view. *Gateways: International Journal of Community Research and Engagement*, 3: 70–87. https://doi.org/10.5130/ijcre.v3i0.154 (p. 80).

improving social partner (trade unions and employer organisations) and NGO capacity so that their members can more deeply engage in partnership processes has been supported at national, regional and local levels.[54] In Southern Africa, as noted earlier, both SASA and the Partnership Forum worked to capacity-build community groups so that they could assume more active partnership roles.[55] In the access to basic service case studies, WFP carried out activities to support the growth of small local businesses by capacity-building entrepreneurs in Cochabamba, Bolivia; in Cajamarca, Peru, as well as training a network of local technicians to maintain the SHS, AMP made efforts to ensure community users understood SHS systems and to involve them in local Photovoltaic Electrification Committees. In Guatemala, meanwhile, *TulaSalud* engaged in capacity-building local community facilitators and young female leaders in Alta Verapaz with careful consideration of cultural factors and community acceptance. These latter examples are instructive because they show that capacity-building was carefully integrated into the development of the models (see Boxes 4.1 and 4.4).

In the ESF, some capacity-building initiatives were hampered by constraints in dealing with different levels of capacity, political interference and changes in policy agendas.[56] Both here, and in the Southern African case studies, the time and resources needed for capacity-building, and how far this work might side-track attention from the main partnership agenda, were also highlighted.[57] At a deeper level, questions have been raised about who does the capacity-building and why. It has been noted, for example, that while the partnership discourse centres on equality, capacity-building is mostly led by international agencies and northern NGOs who contribute short-term funding for small-scale efforts that focus on narrow thematic functions, thus limiting possibilities for lasting change.[58] The need to widen this focus is noted by Thorsten Benner et al., who stress that "A significant part of capacity-building is also training and learning – training to operate in a partnership environment and learning how to interact with actors from other sectors."[59] Enhancing the "capacity to participate"[60] of all stakeholders will necessarily involve the sharing of different experiences of collaboration

54. Stott (2008) Op. cit. p. 18.
55. Rein and Stott (2009) Op. cit. p. 84.
56. Stott (2008) Op. cit. pp. 59–60.
57. Ibid., p. 21.and see also Rein and Stott (2009) Op. cit. p. 84.
58. Lauten, B. (2007) Time to reassess capacity-building partnerships. *Forced Migration Review*, July: pp. 4–6.
59. Benner, T., Ivanova, M.H., Streck, C. and Witte, J.M. (2003) Moving the partnership agenda to the next stage: Key challenges. In: Witte, J.M., Streck, C. and Benner, T. eds. *Progress or Peril? Partnerships in Global Environmental Governance: The Post-Johannesburg Agenda*, Washington, DC, USA: Global Public Policy Institute (p. 87).
60. El Ansari, W., and Phillips, C.J. (2001) Empowering healthcare workers in Africa: partnerships in health-beyond the rhetoric towards a model. *Critical Public Health*, 11 (3): 231–225 http://dx.doi.org/10.1080/09581590110066676 (p. 234).

and demand deeper attention to individual (as well as organisational) knowledge of partnering.

Partnership participation in context

In a research visit to Mthashana Further Education College in the South African province of KwaZulu-Natal, the Principal explained that, prior to colonialism, rural livelihood issues were managed by adherence to the notion of Ubuntu.[61] He believed that this form of "Indigenous partnership," in which both tacit and explicit strategies informed value-driven social cohesion could be drawn upon to encourage rural community participation in government-driven partnership arrangements (see Box 5.2). A similar story comes from the Ballyfermot Chapelizod Partnership that supports community development in Dublin.[62] Here "restorative practice" has been used to build social capital through participatory learning and decision-making. This way of working is derived from the concept of "restorative justice" which has its roots in Irish historical traditions and uses cooperative processes to repair the harm caused by crime.[63]

These experiences suggest that, rather than replicating "imposed" or project-based models of stakeholder participation, partnership arrangements might draw upon relevant sociohistoric forms of collaboration. In this way, a "radical transformative agenda" for socio-ecological change may be viewed as relying upon locally based alternatives that pay close attention to place-based factors while connecting to wider transformations.[64] Other examples from the research work used in this book include *izimbizo*,[65] public consultation forums in South Africa[66] and the use of local, cultural and political structures for promoting and managing basic services in Bolivia, Guatemala and Peru.[67] Traditions of collaboration and social dialogue have also been

61. Rein et al. (2005) Op. cit. p. 99.
62. The Ballyfermot/Chapelizod Partnership, see www.ballyfermotpartnership.ie/ (accessed December 4, 2021) is an implementer of the Social Inclusion and Community Activation Programme (SICAP) funded by the Irish Government and European Social Fund.
63. Leonard, L. and Kenny, P. (2010) The restorative justice movement in Ireland: Building bridges to social justice through civil society. *Irish Journal of Sociology*, 18 (2): 38–58. http://dx.doi.org/10.7227/IJS.18.2.4 (p. 40). For more on this concept, see http://restorativejustice.org/ (accessed December 4, 2021).
64. Temper, L., Walter, M., Rodriguez, I., Kothari, A. and Turhan, E. (2018) A perspective on radical transformations to sustainability: Resistances, movements and alternatives. *Sustainability Science*, 13: 747–764. https://doi.org/10.1007/s11625-018-0543-8 (p. 752).
65. *Izimbizo* forums aim to provide a platform for the public to raise concerns with those in authority, see Kondlo, K. (2010) Making participatory governance work: Re-inventing *izimbizo* forums in South Africa. *Journal of Public Administration*, 45 (2): 384–395.
66. Stott (2009) Op. cit. p. 9.
67. Stott (2014) Op. cit. p. 14 and p. 18. See also use of the indigenous concept of *Dadirri* in Australia in Evans, M. and Stott, L. (2008) *Partnership Inclusivity: Whose Are the Unheard Voices?* In:

Box 5.2 Mthashana Further Education and Training College Partnership Programme

Located in a rural part of KwaZulu-Natal, Mthashana Further Education and Training College was established in 2002 as one of a number of new-generation further education institutions in South Africa developed to respond to post-apartheid legislative shifts. These institutions aimed to integrate municipal-level development planning with opportunities and skills that would enhance local work competency, equity and growth. Mthashana Further Education and Training College thus adopted a partnership approach as a means of working more effectively with both employers and the wider community in order to support the livelihoods and earning capacity of the local population. The new College Principal, whose predecessor had been hostile to these changes, believed that local economic activity could be promoted through the development of cooperatives and small businesses that built on the social capital of poorer rural communities. His argument was that prior to the deliberate disruption of rural economies by the migrant labour system, livelihood issues had been managed in a structured way by drawing upon the traditional notion of Ubuntu which he described as "humaneness." Modern manifestations of this include burial clubs and *stokvels* or credit clubs. The Principal saw these forms of "Indigenous partnership" as promoting value-driven social cohesion which could develop partnership connections with local businesses. His idea was that the College's partnership programme would become a hub for "internal" transformation with a curriculum that was appropriate to the needs and opportunities of the area, as well as "external" transformation which would see the College acting as a catalyst for development by stimulating opportunities through training that would add value for current workers and create new opportunities for the unemployed.

drawn upon in ESF partnership processes in countries such as Sweden and Ireland, where local actors are encouraged to engage with and assume responsibility for development.[68]

McManus, S. and Tennyson, R. eds. *Talking the Walk: A Communication Manual for Partnership Practitioners*, London, UK: International Business Leaders Forum (pp. 15–16); and Onaolapo, B. (2006) The missing development link? Social capital and partnerships in the Niger Delta. *Partnership Matters, Current Issues in Cross-Sector Collaboration*, 4: 28–30, London, UK: The Partnering Initiative on the use of customary associations as entry points for promoting partnership participation among communities in the Niger Delta (p. 29).

68. Stott and Scoppetta (2013) Op. cit. p. 8, and see also Nelson, J. and Zadek, S. (2000) *Partnership Alchemy, New Social Partnerships in Europe*, Copenhagen, Denmark: The Copenhagen Centre

While attractive, many writers urge caution about "localism" and the fact that it can mask deep-seated issues of power and control.[69] Here, we are warned against romanticising and homogenising "the local" which, as well as decoupling issues at this level from broader economic and political structures, can also underplay community differences and transmit the erroneous impression that grassroots empowerment may be achieved without negative effects upon "the power of the powerful."[70] It has also been noted that the idea of local "participation as empowerment" can quite easily slide into "participation as power" when a drive to achieve "community consensus" may stifle plurality of interests in order to suit bureaucratic or organisational needs, ultimately benefiting vested interest groups, be they external or local.[71]

The participation processes outlined earlier, however, do not imply a return to some illusory golden age of local or Indigenous collaboration. Rather, they have been drawn upon to support new ways of working that combine connections between specific localities and wider national and international contexts, frameworks and ideas. In Peru, for example, positive relationships for the development of the *Luz en Casa* partnership model in the region of Cajamarca rested upon close linkages with the national Ministry of Energy and Mines which ensured clarity around regulatory requirements. In addition, the local Photovoltaic Electrification Committees developed by and with community users operated on similar lines to traditional organisational structures but also promoted equitable gender representation.[72] In Guatemala, the e-Health partnership addressing high maternal and infant mortality rates among Indigenous communities in remote rural areas of the Department of Alta Verapaz worked closely with the public health system and incorporated a powerful teenage education programme that supported young Indigenous female leaders.[73] These partnership initiatives also blended advances in ICT with local knowledge to create appropriate service arrangements for different community groups.[74] In Sweden, meanwhile, multi-actor cooperation projects addressing employment and social

(p. 11) and Andersen, S.K. and Mailand, M. (2002) *The Role of Employers and Trade Unions in Multipartite Social Partnerships*, Copenhagen, Denmark: The Copenhagen Centre (p. 9).

69. See Cooke, B. and Kothari, M. (2001) *Participation: The New Tyranny*, London, UK: Zed Books.
70. Mohan, G. and Stokke, K. (2000) Participatory development and empowerment: The dangers of localism. *Third World Quarterly*, 21 (2): 247–268. www.jstor.org/stable/3993419 (p. 249).
71. Kapoor, I. (2002) The devil's in the theory: A critical assessment of Robert Chamber's work on participatory development. *Third World Quarterly*, 23 (1): 101–117 https://doi.org/10.1080/01436590220108199 and Kapoor, I. (2004) The power of participation, participatory development: A promise revisited. *Current Issues in Comparative Education* [Online], 6 (2). www.tc.columbia.edu/cice/
72. Stott (2014) Op. cit. p. 9.
73. Ibid., p. 13.
74. Ibid., p. 29.

Box 5.3 Partnership for inclusive sanitation markets in Bolivia

In 2014, the American NGO Water For People (WFP) piloted a collaborative initiative to find new ways for small enterprises to generate income from sanitation services throughout the whole sanitation value chain: from disposal to treatment and from the construction of appropriate systems to the management and sale of organic waste. In the peri-urban areas of Cochabamba in Bolivia, WFP centred this programme on the use of Ecological Dry Toilets (*Baños Ecológicos Secos* or BES). The BES is a sustainable and affordable option in situations where conventional sewerage systems are limited or unavailable. BES adoption and use, however, required culturally appropriate familiarisation to ensure acceptance as well as education related to their care and maintenance. In order to stimulate demand for the BES and position them as an acceptable and viable alternative to the traditional flush toilet, WFP engaged in an extensive process of awareness-raising among potential users. As well as presenting the BES as part of a comprehensive domestic hygiene package that included a toilet, shower and laundry area, WFP used social marketing to promote domestic sanitation arrangements that suited the particular requirements of different families.

exclusion have integrated cross-cutting issues such as gender mainstreaming and access for people living with disabilities.[75]

As well as being flexible enough to respond to contextual changes, these collaborative initiatives encourage stakeholders to test new ways of working. This includes an approach in which experimentation and acceptance of "failure" are considered to be part of the learning necessary to promote positive change. In the eThekwini water and sanitation service model in South Africa, for example, partnership arrangements between local government, academia, the private sector, donor agencies and community groups have involved various iterations.[76] In ESF partnership arrangements, meanwhile, creative transnational peer review processes and methodologies in Austria and Germany ensured that learning from both successes *and* failures was shared and fed back into practice.[77]

These approaches imply that we might distinguish between purely "transactional" and more "transformative" forms of partnership participation (Table 5.4). White describes transformative participation as enabling

75. Scott and Scoppetta (2013) Op. cit. p. 8.
76. Scott (2014) Op. cit. p. 27.
77. Scott and Scoppetta (2013) Op. cit. p. 10.

people to decide and act for themselves in a process that is both a means to an end and a "continuing dynamic."[78] This difference is further reflected in the distinction between participation that pushes for symbolic as opposed to structural change.[79] The implication here is that *transformative* participation in partnership is centred upon change within individuals that may lead to wider and deeper transformation within organisations and society at large.

Although transformative participation is firmly linked to particular localities a connection between the micro and the macro is critical for its success. As noted by Tom Wolff et al., "Without changing policies and systems, transformation at scale cannot be achieved. Policy offers the most direct route to measurable progress."[80] This view is endorsed by other writers who believe that while bottom-up approaches can produce transformational partnership, a top-down approach is needed to complement this.[81] Because the public sector plays an important role in setting the policy and regulatory environment for collaboration, for example, ensuring that SDG targets are

Table 5.4 Transactional and transformative participation

Transactional participation	***Transformative participation***
Hierarchical, top-down	Horizontal, integrates top-down and bottom-up
"One size fits all" methodologies	Tailored for specific contexts
Standard application of latest approaches	Combines and adapts sociohistoric processes and structures
Little room for testing beyond pilot projects	Encourages constant experimentation
Clear targets and focus on accountability	Flexible approaches with room to change direction
Avoidance of conflict	Does not shy away from conflict
Ad hoc, time-bound and limited in scope	Open-ended and holistic
Limited use of learning	Actively promotes and shares learning
Facilitators that direct and manage	Facilitators that shape, encourage and support

Source: Stott (2017)[82]

78. White (1996) Op. cit. pp. 8–9.
79. Sparrow, J. (2021) Neoliberalism wrecked our chance to fix the climate crisis: And leftwing statements of faith have changed nothing, Opinion. *The Guardian*, 14 November.
80. Wolff, T., Minkler, M., Wolfe, S.M., Berkowitz, B., Bowen, L., Butterfoss, F.D., Christens, B.D., Francisco, V.T., Himmelman, A.T. and Lee, K.S. (2016) Collaborating for equity and justice: Moving beyond collective impact. *The Nonprofit Quarterly*, Winter: 42–53 (p. 46).
81. Horan, D.A. (2019) New approach to partnerships for SDG transformations. *Sustainability*, 11: 4947. https://doi.org/10.3390/su11184947 (p. 15).
82. Stott (2017) Op. cit. p. 83.

harmonised, monitored and reported within an overarching national policy framework, government is viewed as having primary responsibility for reinforcing these linkages.[83] However, negative perceptions of bureaucracy, slowness, risk-aversion and political expediency also need to be considered here, as well as concerns that government agencies may dominate partnership activities.[84] As a result, calls have been made for a new kind of global governance for partnership arrangements in which different levels of government work closely with other actors.[85] The importance of linking and integrating different administrative levels in processes of transformative participation is endorsed by the writer George Monbiot whose call for global governance further emphasises the important role that individuals can play in addressing challenges common to us all.[86] To encourage dynamic multi-level collaborative connections between actors and citizens that might enhance the potential for transformation, it seems that there is a need for a new kind of meso space that can cement horizontal links between stakeholders as well as vertical links between local and global levels, and between policy and practice. This space is one that is increasingly being facilitated by partnership brokers.

The role of partnership brokers

In order to assist partnership initiatives operating at the global level to achieve transformational change,[87] recent attention has been given to "a multi-layered backbone structure" able to integrate and mutually reinforce participation at local, regional and international levels. The concept of "collective impact", for example, endorses the presence of an "independent backbone organisation" to enhance collaborative connections.[88] There has, however, been criticism of these kinds of formation from those who believe that they reinforce a top-down hierarchical model of working which is the antithesis of what a collaborative model should offer.[89]

83. Mazzucato, M. (2021) *Mission Economy: A Moonshot Guide to Changing Capitalism*, London, UK: Allen Lane. Mazzucato believes that "only government has the capacity to bring about transformation on the scale needed" (p. 205).
84. Stott (2010) *The Partnering With Governments Navigator, Building Effective Collaboration With the Public Sector in Africa*, London, UK: International Business Leaders Forum and Berlin, Germany: Deutsche Gesellschaft für Technische Zusammenarbeit.
85. Mohan and Stokke (2000) Op. cit. p. 263.
86. Monbiot, G. (2004) *The Age of Consent: A Manifesto for a New World Order*, London, UK: Harper Perennial (p. 11).
87. Patscheke, S., Barmettler, A., Herman, L., Overdyke, S. and Pfitzer, M. (2014) Shaping global partnerships for a post-2015 world. *Stanford Social Innovation Review*, Spring: 2–9.
88. Kania, J. and Kramer, M. (2011) Collective impact. *Stanford Social Innovation Review*, Winter: 36–41 and Hanleybrown, F., Kania, J. and Kramer, M. (2012) Channeling change: Making collective impact work. *Stanford Social Innovation Review*, January: 1–8.
89. Wolff et al. (2016) Op. cit. p. 49.

While power dynamics are always likely to be present, collaborative relationships rely upon concerted efforts to ensure the full participation of all their members in decision-making processes and the equitable valuing of resources that each partner may bring to the table.[90] It is thus important to ensure the espousal of horizontal processes in which decision-making and outcomes are shared by partners. Collaborative initiatives will also, where appropriate, need to respond adequately to the needs of other stakeholders, particularly those who are likely to bear risks as a result of the activities of a partnership arrangement. In this regard, as well as convening structures that promote "coordination, communication, and facilitation,"[91] the positioning of co-creative processes in which the individuals and organisations involved may assume the role of partnership broker is of interest.[92] Partnership brokering has been described as providing the "connective tissue" that enables those engaged in collaborative alliances to work together optimally and augment their ability to achieve positive societal transformation.[93] An increased interest in this intermediary function is demonstrated in some of the different expressions that have been used in its portrayal (see Table 5.5).

Table 5.5 Different terms for partnership broker

Term
Boundary spanner[94]
Bridging agent[95]
Bridge builder[96]
Catalyst[97]

90. Huxham and Vangen (2004) Op. cit. p. 193.
91. Wolff et al. (2016) Op. cit. p. 48.
92. Moreno-Serna, J., Purcell, W.M., Sánchez-Chaparro, T., Soberón, M., Lumbreras, J. and Mataix, C. (2020) Catalyzing transformational partnerships for the SDGs: Effectiveness and impact of the multi-stakeholder initiative *El día después*. *Sustainability*, 12: 7189. https://doi.org/10.3390/su12177189
93. Tennyson, R. and Wilde, L. (2000) *The Guiding Hand: Brokering Partnerships for Sustainable Development*, Turin, Italy: United Nations Staff College and London, UK: Prince of Wales Business Leaders Forum.
94. Williams, P. (2010) Special agents: The nature and role of boundary spanners. *Paper to the ESRC Research Seminar Series-Collaborative Futures: New Insights from Intra and Inter-Sectoral Collaborations*, University of Birmingham, UK.
95. Manning, S. and Roessler, D. (2014) The formation of cross-sector development partnerships: How bridging agents shape project agendas and longer-term alliances. *Journal of Business Ethics*, 123 (3): 527–547. https://doi.org/10.1007/s10551-013-1853-5
96. Brown, D.L. (2015) Bridge-building for social transformation. *Stanford Social Innovation Review*, Winter: 34–39.
97. Hussein, T., Plummer, M. and Breen, B. (2018) How field catalysts galvanize social change. In: *Stanford Social Innovation Review* Winter, Stanford, CA, USA: Stanford University, pp. 48–54; and see also Lee, J.Y. and Waddock, S. (2021) How transformation catalysts take catalytic action. *Sustainability*, 13: 9813. https://doi.org/10.3390/su13179813

Term
Change agent[98]
Convener[99]
Enabler[100]
Engager[101]
Facilitator[102]
Innovation broker[103]
Intermediary[104]
Intervener[105]
Orchestrator[106]
Partnership broker[107]
Scripter[108]
System leader[109]

Working from within partnership arrangements (as partners) or from outside them, the partnership broker role may be assumed by an individual, a team or an organisation (see Table 5.6). While those undertaking this function are often central in bringing different partners together and managing and supporting

98. Russ, C. (2014) The humanitarian partnership broker as change agent. *Humanitarian Practice Network*, 8 October. https://odihpn.org/publication/the-humanitarian-partnership-broker-as-change-agent/ (accessed March 23, 2022).
99. van Hille, I., de Bakker, F.G.A., Ferguson, J.E. and Groenewegen, P. (2020) Cross-sector partnerships for sustainability: How mission-driven conveners drive change in national coffee platforms. *Sustainability*, 12: 2846. https://doi.org/10.3390/su12072846
100. Bolden, R., Gulati, A. and Edwards, G. (2019) Mobilizing change in public services: Insights from a systems leadership development intervention. *International Journal of Public Administration*, 43 (1): 26–36. doi: 10.1080/01900692.2019.1604748
101. Escobar, O. (2015) Scripting deliberative policy-making: Dramaturgic policy analysis and engagement know-how. *Journal of Comparative Policy Analysis: Research and Practice*, 17 (3): 269–285. https://doi.org/10.1080/13876988.2014.946663
102. Moreno-Serna et al. (2020) Op. cit.
103. See www.beyondresults.co.nz/support/innovation-brokering/Agresearch (accessed March 9, 2022).
104. Mignon, I. and Kanda, W. (2018) A typology of intermediary organizations and their impact on sustainability transition policies. *Environmental Innovation and Societal Transitions*. https://doi.org/10.1016/j.eist.2018.07.001
105. Gray, B. and Purdy J. (2018) *Collaborating for Our Future: Multistakeholder Partnerships for Solving Complex Problems*, Oxford, UK: Oxford University Press (p. 914).
106. Horan, D.A. (2019) New approach to partnerships for SDG transformations. *Sustainability*, 11: 4947. https://doi.org/10.3390/su11184947 (p. 15).
107. Tennyson, R. (2005) *The Brokering Guidebook, Navigating Effective Sustainable Development Partnerships*, London, UK: The Partnering Initiative, International Business Leaders Forum; Stott, L. ed. (2018) *Shaping Sustainable Change: The Role of Partnership Brokering in Optimising Collaborative Action*, London, UK: Greenleaf Publishing, Routledge: Taylor and Francis Group.
108. Escobar (2015) Op. cit.
109. Senge, P., Hamilton, H. and Kania, J. (2015) The dawn of system leadership. *Stanford Social Innovation Review*, Winter: 27–33.

Table 5.6 Partnership broker roles in practice

Partnership broker role	***Individual***	***Organisation***	***Specialist unit/team within an organisation***
Internal	- Principal, Mthashana College (South Africa) - Director, eThekwini Water and Sanitation Unit (South Africa) - Founder, *Ciudad Saludable*, (Peru)	- South African Sugar Association (Small-scale Sugar Cane Farming Communities Partnership) - eThekwini Metropolitan Municipality (South Africa) - *TulaSalud* (Guatemala) - *Acciona Microenergía Perú* (Peru)	- eThekwini Water and Sanitation Unit (South Africa)
Internal/ external	- Director, Partnership Forum (Zambia)	- Managing Authorities (ESF Partnerships) - Pobal (Ireland) - gsub (Germany) - Kooo (Austria) - Thematic Groups (Sweden) (ESF Partnerships) - Partnership Forum (Zambia) - *Ciudad Saludable* (Peru)	
External	- Lecturer at University of KwaZulu Natal (South Africa)	- UNAIDS (Zambia Business Coalition on HIV/AIDS) - Institute of Natural Resources (Small-scale Sugar Cane Farming Communities Partnership)	- Staff team from UN Development Programme (UNDP) and Voluntary Service Overseas (VSO) (Zambia Business Coalition on HIV/AIDS)

Source: Adapted from Stott (2017)[110]

partnership initiatives, partnership brokering is fundamentally about providing and nurturing an enabling space for the development of successful collaborative interactions.[111] This requires attention to power dynamics and an understanding that those who act as intermediaries in partnership initiatives must "have the capacity to identify and name practices and processes that intentionally or unintentionally contribute to power imbalances."[112] In so doing, partnership brokers will seek to nurture the connections needed for transformative

110. Stott (2017) Op. cit. p. 85.
111. Tennyson (2005) Op. cit. p. 12.
112. Wolff et al. (2016) Op. cit. p. 49.

participation and ensure that their work is directed towards structural rather than symbolic change.[113] Some of the approaches used for this are increasingly innovative and incorporate methodologies that test and challenge standard ways of doing things. In this sense partnership brokers can play a role that moves collaboration beyond simple exchanges and transactions that are ad hoc or short term in nature to connections that support lasting systems change. This work inevitably requires a delicate balance between being pragmatic and reflective, or what has been described as "the ideology of collaborative working and the pragmatism needed to get things done."[114]

Although not all the partnership brokers listed in Table 5.6 made connections that promoted transformative participation, some were able to do so. Pobal in Ireland, gsub in Germany, Kooo in Austria and the Thematic Groups in Sweden, for example, developed and reinforced ongoing linkages between policy and practice in ESF partnership initiatives (see Box 5.4).[115] The eThekwini Water and Sanitation Unit (EWS) in South Africa, Tula-Salud in Guatemala and *Acciona Microenergía Perú* (AMP), and the individuals working within these organisations also initiated the local, national, regional and international ties that supported collaborative efforts to improve access to basic services.[116] Their efforts suggest that partnership brokers can support transformation in a number of important ways; by reinforcing contextual links, promoting inclusion and facilitating space for productive conflict.

Box 5.4 Partnership brokers in Europe

The programme management body – Pobal, Ireland[117]

Pobal was founded in 1992 and has worked on behalf of the Irish Government with communities and local agencies to support local and community development. Pobal's main strength lies in its extensive knowledge and experience in working with partnership. The organisation has supported collaborative activities through a liaison system that offers information, feedback, training inputs and discussion, all of which serve to ensure that the voice of target groups is clearly positioned in planning and practice. Great emphasis is also placed on learning from partnership experiences through ongoing exchange and the sharing of examples from practice.

113. Sparrow (2021) Op. cit.
114. Huxham, C. and Vangen, S. (2004) Doing things collaboratively: Realizing the advantage or succumbing to inertia? *Organizational Dynamics*, 33 (2): 199. http://dx.doi.org/10.1109/EMR.2004.25132
115. Stott and Scoppetta (2013) Op. cit.
116. Stott (2014) Op. cit. p. 30.
117. www.pobal.ie

The service organisation – gsub, Germany[118]

In Germany, the partnership programme *Perspective 50plus* was managed by gsub via a contractual arrangement with the Federal Ministry of Labour and Social Affairs (BMAS). This involved supporting welfare offices and other labour market participants to come together in 78 regional employment pacts for older workers across Germany. Gsub put great effort into building a tightly woven collaborative network where participants could share their knowledge and experience and disseminate new approaches and examples from practice. Both BMAS and gsub worked hard to ensure that the *Perspective 50plus* programme was focused, flexible and non-bureaucratic. Indicators that measured results were kept to a minimum and dialogue and peer exchanges were consistently practiced. Participative methodologies facilitated ongoing learning processes and the incorporation of innovative elements such as "idea competitions" and the use of "pact ambassadors" to change public perceptions of older people.

The innovation hub – Kooo, Austria[119]

When the Austrian Territorial Employment Pacts (TEPs) were launched at the end of the 1990s, a "neutral" coordination body, Kooo, was set up by the Austrian Federal Ministry for Labour, Social Affairs and Consumer Protection (BMASK) to assist regional partners in developing TEPs. Kooo was established as an independent organisation with a base outside the Ministry to offer networking, coordination, policy advice, evaluation and public relations support to the TEPS. The Austria-wide TEP network developed over time, starting with joint dialogue on how to best set up partnerships at the regional level and moving towards assisting the development of innovative active labour market policy measures for those in need, all steered with hands-off facilitation by Kooo. Kooo's perceived impartiality assisted the creation of a fruitful learning environment among TEP partners through initiatives such as the TEP Open Reflection Cycle which shared learning from successes and failures, and promoted trust-building between actors.

The learning agency – Thematic Groups, Sweden

The Structural Fund Partnerships in the eight regions of Sweden have supported multi-actor cooperation projects addressing employment and exclusion issues that ensure the integration of cross-cutting issues

118. www.gsub.de
119. www.zsi.at/en/object/project/1025 (accessed March 30, 2022).

in their work. To do this, during the 2007–13 programming period, five national Thematic Groups provided support by gathering project experiences, knowledge and results in order to promote improvements and share lessons from the fields of youth, workplace learning and labour market transition, inclusion of disadvantaged individuals and groups in working life, equal rights and opportunities at work, and entrepreneurship. The Groups engaged with projects through telephone contact, meetings, networks, seminars, training and written guidance. Their focus was on ensuring that results had a long-term impact and that lessons were shared proactively between projects and regions, as well as transnationally.

Strengthening contextual links

The ability to assess how collaborative efforts that address systemic issues might be developed within specific operational contexts is central to partnership brokering. This liaison role involves making linkages between policy and practice, and between geographical, sociohistoric, sectoral, organisational and individual contexts. Charles Leadbeater's notion of the "rooted cosmopolitan" who "creates new combinations of ideas drawn from a mix of the local and the cosmopolitan" is a useful analogy here and one that is reflected in many of the examples provided earlier.[120] In Zambia, for example, the Partnership Forum was composed of a team of professionals with connections to international development trends and organisations that they drew upon to develop their local activities. The individuals promoting the innovation partnership models in Latin America and South Africa also had strong international ties and access to relevant examples and resources. In Europe, the intermediary organisations mentioned in Box 5.4 provided partnership stakeholders with an understanding of "the bigger picture" and clarity around the links between policy and practice in relation to European Structural and Investment Funds (ESIF) and made useful connections to existing initiatives covering similar themes.

Partnership brokering can thus offer what might be described as a translation service in which both top-down and bottom-up connections are enhanced as international or national requirements are made sense of at regional and local levels.[121] Such mediation can also assist in ensuring that partnership initiatives work within relevant policy and regulatory environments, particularly when partnership goals relate to the achievement of national development goals and country targets. Among the partnership

120. Leadbeater, C. (2014) *The Frugal Innovator, Creating Change on a Shoestring Budget*, London, UK: Palgrave Macmillan (pp. 144–145).
121. Stott and Scoppetta (2013) Op. cit.

arrangements that addressed access to basic services in Latin America and South Africa, for example, partnership brokers played a crucial role in ensuring that linkages were developed with national, regional and local levels of government.[122] By engaging with the public sector in this way, an enabling environment was promoted in which partnership was favoured by more progressive legislation for collaborative endeavours tackling access to services such as energy, waste management, maternal health and water and sanitation.

Effective partnership brokering also involves keeping abreast of contextual developments and variations, and anticipating, diagnosing and responding to situations rapidly. In this way those exercising the intermediary role are able to assist prospective partners to "read" different environments, make decisions about whether or not to work in partnership and adapt collaborative efforts to changing circumstances so that they become more sustainable.[123] Wolff et al. have also noted the importance of advocacy and political skills that are circumscribed in a strategic plan for achieving policy impact.[124]

Reinforcing inclusion

Vhonani Netshandama observes that a commitment by partnership facilitators to working "with" rather than "for" people is enhanced by long-term presence and a rigorous appreciation of ethics and responsibilities.[125] This is endorsed by partnership practitioners such as those working with the Ballyfermot Chapelizod Partnership in Dublin where principles such as respect, dignity and equality were highlighted in their work with communities. Other partnership broker skills that are frequently mentioned as critical include active listening and reflection.[126] As noted in Chapter 4, these values and dialogic exchange processes are core elements of transformational partnership arrangements.

As well as being perceived as fair by the parties involved, the impression that partnership systems are clear and functional is important in endorsing a commitment to inclusivity.[127] Such clarity can do much to assist in "shifting us from a *self-interest frame* of thinking to a *common-interest frame*, where our underlying mode of thought is structured by a concern for both ourselves

122. Stott, L. (2014) *Partnerships for Innovation in Access to Basic Services*, Madrid, Spain: itdUPM and Washington, DC, USA: MIF, IaDB (p. 32).
123. Stott and Scoppetta (2013) Op. cit.
124. Wolff et al. (2016) Op. cit. p. 47.
125. Netshandama (2010) Op. cit.
126. Tennyson (2005) Op. cit. p. 35 and pp. 77–78.
127. Tennyson, R. and Mundy, J. (2017) *Partnership Brokers in Action, Skills, Tools, Approaches, Partnership Brokers Training, Course Workbook*, 2nd edition, London, UK: Partnership Brokers Association (p. 22).

and others."[128] In this way, we can begin what Otto Scharmer and Katrin Kaufer describe as a journey "from ego-system to eco-system awareness, or from *me* to *we*."[129] This notion is reinforced by an acceptance that partnership brokering is a collective process that may be assumed by different individuals, teams and organisations from both inside and outside a partnership initiative over time.[130] The ability to let go of "self" and embrace the fluidity of this role further indicates that partnership brokers should be willing to hand over to others when necessary.[131] Such an idea is captured well in the conceptualisation of effective "system leaders" who "learn to 'follow the energy' and set aside their strategy when unexpected paths and opportunities emerge."[132]

In the examples of partnership brokers in Europe (Box 5.4), emphasis on dialogic communication is shown in the opportunities for participatory review and open reflection cycles offered by Kooo and gsub which incorporated continuous dialogue on what had worked and what had not.[133] These illustrations further endorse the need for a blend of pragmatic and reflective skills so that a push for action is balanced with opportunities for debate and discussion with the stakeholders involved. This way of working has been described as a way of helping people to see the larger system and build a shared understanding of complex problems, foster reflection and "more generative conversations" and move away from "reactive problem-solving to co-creating the future."[134]

Scharmer and Kaufer suggest that transforming society depends upon leaders capable of understanding systems from the perspective of others, particularly the most marginalised, and working to co-create a system that promotes communal well-being.[135] Viewed in this way, partnership brokering may be positioned as a form of "integrative leadership"[136] that promotes collective thinking and bridge-building[137] across individual, group, organisational

128. Krznaric, R. (2015) The empathy effect, how empathy drives common values, social justice and environmental action. *Paper for Friends of the Earth*: 4. empathy-effect.pdf (friendsoftheearth.uk) (accessed December 5, 2021).
129. Scharmer, O., and Kaufer, K. (2013) *Leading From the Emerging Future: From Ego-System to Eco-System Economics*, San Francisco, CA, USA: Berret Koehler Publisher (p. 16).
130. Manning and Roessler (2014) Op. cit. p. 528.
131. Tennyson and Mundy (2017) Op. cit. p. 22.
132. Senge et al. (2015) Op. cit. p. 32.
133. Stott and Scoppetta (2013) Op. cit.
134. Senge et al. (2015) Op. cit. pp. 28–29.
135. Scharmer, O. and Kaufer, K. (2013) *Leading From the Emerging Future: From Ego-System to Eco-System Economics*, San Francisco, CA, USA: Berret Koehler Publisher (p. 12).
136. Brown, D.L. (2015) Bridge-building for social transformation. *Stanford Social Innovation Review*, Winter: 34–39 (p. 3) describes this as "cross-boundary leadership" that promotes collective thinking and bridge-building while Crosby, B.C. and Bryson, J.B. (2010) Integrative leadership and the creation and maintenance of cross-sector collaborations. *The Leadership Quarterly*, 21: 211–230 https://doi.org/10.1016/j.leaqua.2010.01.003 (p. 228) refer to it as "integrative leadership" across individual, group, organisational and inter-organisational levels.
137. Brown (2015) Op. cit.

and inter-organisational levels.[138] These attributes are inherent in the idea of "servant leadership" developed by Robert Greenleaf in the late 1970s in which a conscious choice is made to serve rather than rule people.[139] This does not mean that a firm and pragmatic hand is not needed. Partnership brokering is also about shaping and steering, or "scripting" in which there is "a structuring force intended to foster certain forum dynamics and an overall narrative for participants to take away."[140]

Facets of partnership brokering also appear to be reflected in a growing number of concepts that are helping to challenge and reframe more traditional views of leadership, including "collective leadership," "distributed leadership" and "adaptive leadership."[141] Perhaps, however, the notion of "transformative leadership" in which leadership is regarded as an "everyday, everyone, everywhere" relational process is most relevant here. Positioned as a process of collaboration, participation and creativity which encourages "transformation for mutual benefit,"[142] transformative leadership combines both personal and social transformation by incorporating "the psychological and spiritual as well as the social world and the quest for social justice."[143] This form of leadership resonates with Sandra Waddock's description of "intellectual shamans" who promote long-term system change by acting as sense-makers, connectors and healers with "the notion of creating a better world, discipline, theory, or set of practices."[144]

The elements of a new kind of collaborative and transformative leadership sit well with the calls made in this book for greater attention to the personal and relational connections that inform partnership, and to the added value that collaboration may bring for individuals, organisations and society as a whole. While acknowledging the need for reflective debate around issues

138. Crosby and Bryson (2010) Op. cit. p. 228.
139. Greenleaf, R. K. (1977) *The Servant as Leader*, Servant Leadership – A Journey into the Nature of Legitimate Power and Greatness, New York, NY, USA: Paulist Press (p. 6).
140. Escobar (2015) Op. cit. p. 278.
141. For Collective Leadership, see Cullen, K., Willburn, P., Chrobot-Mason, D. and Palus, C. (2014) *Networks: How Collective Leadership Really Works*, Cincinnati, NC, USA: University of Cincinnati: Center for Creative Leadership; for "Connective Leadership," see Lipman-Blumen, J. (2000) *Connective Leadership, Managing in a Changing World*, Oxford, UK: Oxford University Press; for "Distributed Leadership," see Spillane, J. (2006) *Distributed Leadership*, San Francisco, CA, USA: Jossey-Bass; for "Shared Leadership," see Pearce, C.L. and Conger, J.A. (2002) *Shared Leadership: Reframing the Hows and Whys of Leadership*, London, UK: Sage Publications and for "Stewardship," see Block, P. (1996) *Stewardship: Choosing Service over Self-Interest*, San Francisco, CA, USA: Berrett-Koehler Publishers.
142. Montuori, A. and Donnelly, G. (2018) Transformative leadership. In: Neal, J. ed. *Handbook of Personal and Organizational Transformation*, New York, NY, USA: Springer International Publishing AG. doi: 10.1007/978-3-319-29587-9_59-1 (p. 3).
143. Ibid., p. 4.
144. Waddock, S. (2015) Reflections: Intellectual shamans, sensemaking, and memes in large system change. *Journal of Change Management*, 15 (4): 259–273. doi: 10.1080/14697017.2015.1031954 (p. 269).

that may be difficult or uncomfortable, this kind of leadership is also about being brave enough to contest existing power relations and present more imaginative and ambitious ways of doing things that challenge "business as usual" models.[145]

Facilitating space for productive conflict

If we accept that transformative participation involves challenging power relations, it is likely that it will generate tension and conflict.[146] This, according to White, is a test of its worth: "The absence of conflict in many supposedly 'participatory' programmes is something that should raise our suspicions. Change hurts."[147] Sennett further notes that disruption can encourage bonding as relationships are often strengthened after being tested,[148] a finding that has been observed in other studies where the expression of negative emotions after a critical incident appeared to cement relationships and enhance partnership participation.[149] Rather than avoiding or delegitimising confrontation,[150] the implication here is that "productive conflict" enables differences to surface and assumptions to be tested and challenged, and can thus establish the basis for transformational change.[151]

Bulbul Baksi believes that partnership brokers can allow productive conflict to surface by creating a "brave space"[152] where people can express their emotions, work through them and find creative ways of handling their differences so that their diversities contribute to the richness of working together.[153] Among the factors that contribute to the creation of a brave space, Baksi emphasises the importance of helping partners to explore underlying interests, needs and concerns and the ability to be empathetic by listening

145. See Mazzucato (2021) Op. cit. p. 206.
146. According to White (1996) Op. cit. p. 12, these might include co-option from "below" or a particular group using participation for leverage or empowerment. See also Kapoor, I. (2004) Op. cit. p. 129.
147. White (1996) Op. cit. p. 15.
148. Sennett (2013) Op. cit. p. 155.
149. This is endorsed by Sloan, P. and Oliver, D. (2013) Building trust in multi-stakeholder partnerships: Critical emotional incidents and practices of engagement. *Organization Studies*, 34 (12): 1835–1868. https://doi.org/10.1177%2F0170840613495018 who find that expressing negative emotions after a critical incident can cement relationships and enhance partnership participation.
150. Poncelet, E.C. (2001) A kiss here and a kiss there: Conflict and collaboration in environmental partnerships. *Environmental Management*, 27 (1): 13–25. https://doi.org/10.1007/s002670010130
151. Derkzen et al. (2008) Op. cit. p. 459. The authors view power struggles as a manifestation of low levels of inequality among partners and, in consequence, as a sign of a "healthy" partnership.
152. Shapiro, D. (2016) *Negotiating the Nonnegotiable, How to Resolve Your Most Emotionally Charged Conflicts*, New York, NY, USA: Viking.
153. Baksi (2018) in Stott. ed. Op. cit. p. 57.

well and asking meaningful questions.[154] In his book on empathy, Roman Krznaric tells us that, more than active listening, we need "radical listening" which relies on "presence" and suspension of judgment, a focus on identifying the feelings of "the other" and a determination to understand their needs.[155] These views are endorsed by Richard Sennett, who notes that empathy involves curiosity about others.[156] He also suggests that, rather than assuming an assertive stance, empathy can be assisted by what he calls "the subjunctive mood" or tentativeness in communication which allows people to explore ambiguities and create the space for cooperation to emerge.[157] Meaningful cooperation, then, demands a process of communication that places emphasis on *understanding* rather than *convincing* those who have different viewpoints from one's own.[158]

As we have noted, the transversality of partnership means that learning from a vast range of different disciplines can provide new insights into collaboration. In this regard, as well as materials from the leadership field, the concept of "conflict transformation" which has emerged from the disciplines of conflict resolution, management and prevention is of relevance. Unlike conflict management, which is focused on mitigating conflict through the use of relevant tools, or conflict resolution, which centres on offering creative solutions for addressing conflict, conflict transformation works to understand the systems and structures that promote conflict and use the energy generated by conflict in a constructive manner to foster transformation.[159] By working with different personal, relational, cultural and structural facets of human experience, conflict is seen as an opportunity "to develop capacities to engage in change processes at the interpersonal, intergroup, and social-structural level" and to understand different perceptions of power.[160] Conflict transformation is presented as a comprehensive and multidimensional approach that addresses and links different stakeholders, contextual levels and timescales.[161] These dimensions are mirrored in the nuanced relational layers that inform multi-stakeholder collaboration which, in embracing and integrating interpersonal aspects, reinforce the centrality of people in promoting transformative processes of change.

154. Ibid.
155. Krznaric, R. (2014) *Empathy, Why It Matters and How to Get It*, London, UK: Rider, Random House Group (pp. 112–113).
156. Sennett (2013) Op. cit. pp. 20–22.
157. Ibid., p. 18.
158. Ibid., pp. 78–83.
159. Lederach, J. and Maiese, M. (2003) *Conflict Transformation*. www.beyondintractability.org/essay/transformation (accessed December 5, 2021).
160. Ibid.
161. Miall, H. (2004) *Conflict Transformation: A Multi-Dimensional Task*, Berlin, Germany: Berghof Foundation (p. 17).

6 Partnership – where next?

While use of the term "partnership" is widespread, an increase in alternative expressions to describe this way of working has been noted in recent years. In a study conducted by Marianne Beisheim and Nils Simon in 2015 to explore how the UN might improve governance services for partnerships, some of the interviewees appeared to be uncomfortable with the term partnership, preferring instead to use labels such as cooperation and collaboration.[1] The authors surmised that this was "due to the unclear definition of partnerships, their contested role, and their mixed track record in the past."[2] However, although this change could be interpreted as a reflection of negative perceptions of partnership, it might also signal, "evidence of a paradigm shift away from arm's length, atomistic and transactional notions of exchange between organisational actors, towards an approach which foregrounds intense interaction, relationships and networks."[3] Such a shift is perceptible in the movement of some of these new forms of collaboration towards transformational partnership connections; greater acknowledgement of the interplay between individuals, organisations and society as a whole and the embracing of some of the more reflective elements of collaboration. This chapter explores where, why and how a selection of these new collaborative forms is taking place, and what they might mean for the future of partnership.

New collaborative arrangements

A large number of emerging forms of "boundary-spanning collaboration"[4] that have been developed among diverse actors and citizens over the last

1. Beisheim, M. and Simon, N. (2015) Multistakeholder partnerships for the SDGs: Actors' view on UN metagovernance. *Global Governance*, 24: 497–515. http://dx.doi.org/10.1163/19426720-02404003 (p. 20).
2. Ibid.
3. Seitanidi, M.M. and Ryan, A. (2007) A critical review of forms of corporate community involvement: From philanthropy to partnerships. *International Journal of Nonprofit and Voluntary Sector Marketing*, 12: 247–266. https://doi.org/10.1002/nvsm.306 (p. 256).
4. Carter, B. (2017) Effectiveness of working in consortia. *K4D Helpdesk Report*, Sussex, UK: Institute of Development Studies.

DOI: 10.4324/9781003199434-7

10–15 years include multi-stakeholder arrangements such as dialogues, networks, consortia, hubs, platforms, coalitions, partnerships and even new institutions. To these, we may add processes of social innovation, collective impact and "co-working" arrangements such as co-creation, co-production and co-responsibility. It is also worth noting that similar trends can be found in collaborative processes involving citizens including, for example, citizens' assemblies, juries and panels.[5]

Because they share common features and intersect with one another, these collaborative initiatives are difficult to categorise systematically. Moreover, the terms employed to describe them are often used interchangeably. While some of these tendencies have been criticised as being simplistic or in need of deeper analysis,[6] and there have also been calls for a return to "single-handed" approaches,[7] they indicate that partnership is being reappraised and reformulated in terms of form, process and values with, in some cases, the blending of all three becoming an emerging trend.

The reasons for the development of so many new multi-stakeholder initiatives are varied and overlapping. Evidence from a selection of examples suggests that among the drivers for this expansion are a desire to achieve better focus and coordination; exploitation of digital communication; interest in innovation and testing; working with diversity and the promotion of knowledge exchange and learning.

Focus and coordination

As well as access to diverse resources, some new forms of collaboration have emerged with the express remit of ensuring better focus and coordination, often by adapting, combining and building upon existing approaches and constructs. A good example here is the **cluster**, a concept developed by Michael E. Porter to describe a grouping of interrelated companies, suppliers and service providers working in the same

5. For more examples, see OECD (2020) *Innovative Citizen Participation and New Democratic Institutions, Catching the Deliberative Wave*, Paris, France: OECD Publishing, https://doi.org/10.1787/339306da-en
6. Voorberg, W.H., Bekkers, V.J.J.M. and Tummers, L. G. (2014) A systematic review of co-creation and co-production: Embarking on the social innovation journey. *Public Management Review*, 17 (9): 1333–1357. http://dx.doi.org/10.1080/14719037.2014.930505 and Wolff, T., Minkler, M., Wolfe, S.M., Berkowitz, B., Bowen, L., Butterfoss, F.D., Christens, B.D., Francisco, V.T., Himmelman, A.T. and Lee, K.S. (2017) Collaborating for equity and justice: Moving beyond collective impact. *The Nonprofit Quarterly*, Winter: 42–53.
7. Egels-Zandén, N. and Wahlqvist, E. (2007) Post-partnership strategies for defining corporate responsibility: The business social compliance initiative. *Journal of Business Ethics*, 70: 175–189. http://dx.doi.org/10.1007/s10551-006-9104-7 They have used the term "post-partnerships" to indicate a move by business away from "inefficient and unproductive collaboration" to "single-handed" corporate responsibility approaches.

geographic locality.[8] The collective benefits of creating "industrial clusters" are presented as increased productivity and enhanced capacity to innovate.[9] This notion has been expanded by the United Nations Industrial Development Organisation (UNIDO) in their positioning of industrial clusters as central to a sustainable development centred upon "private sector based inclusive growth" that involves and sustains local communities.[10] However, the cluster concept has now transcended the realm of private sector growth and industrial development with, for example, its adoption in the field of humanitarian action where it seeks to bring different organisations in the sector together to strengthen system-wide preparedness in emergency contexts (see Box 6.1).[11]

Box 6.1 Humanitarian clusters

Following the 2005 earthquake in Pakistan, 11 clusters of humanitarian organisations, including the United Nations as well as others, were established in sectors such as water, health, shelter and logistics. Their aim was to strengthen system-wide preparedness by ensuring the availability of critical materials and expertise through co-leadership, joint planning and clarity around resource allocation, roles and responsibilities with single contact points for settling issues, addressing enquiries and working more closely with affected communities.[12] One of the clusters, the UN's global Food Security Cluster (gFSC), was formed in 2010 to ensure appropriate, efficient and well-resourced food security responses in major emergencies. The cluster, which now provides support in 27 countries, is co-led by the World Food Programme (WFP) and the UN's Food and Agriculture Organisation (FAO) and has over 40 partners including NGOs, donors and UN agencies. The International Committee of the Red Cross (ICRC) also participates as an observer. The work of the cluster is governed by a Strategic Advisory Group that includes members of the co-lead agencies and NGOs with a focus on ensuring that country-level operations are well-staffed and equipped to respond to food security crises.[13]

8. Porter, M.E. (2000) Location, competition, and economic development: Local clusters in a global economy. *Economic Development Quarterly*, 14 (1): 15–34. doi:10.1177/089124240001400105
9. Ibid., p. 23.
10. UNIDO (2020) The UNIDO approach to cluster development. *Technical Paper*, Vienna, Austria: UNIDO. www.unido.org/sites/default/files/files/2020-09/Clusters_Brochure.pdf (accessed February 25, 2022).
11. UNHCR *Cluster Approach in Emergency Handbook*, Geneva, Switzerland: UNHCR. https://emergency.unhcr.org/entry/41813/cluster-approach-iasc (accessed February 25, 2022).
12. Ibid.
13. See www.wfp.org/food-security-cluster (accessed February 25, 2022).

In a similar manner, **consortia,** which have traditionally involved actors from specific sectors, such as business or NGOs coming together to address a development interest or focus area, are now expanding with a more diverse membership. The prevalence of so many new consortia has been attributed to the complexity and level of challenge posed by the targets of the UN SDGs which necessitate new and larger alliances that combine broad and complementary knowledge, skills and resources.[14] The consortium model is also increasingly proposed by donor organisations and cooperation agencies to ensure a more strategic approach to obtaining funds by encouraging different development actors to work together under a single umbrella and joint logo.

Box 6.2 Development consortia

The START Network (formerly the Consortium of British Humanitarian Agencies) was developed in 2010 in response to a call for proposals by the UK government's Department for International Development (DFID) to strengthen the capacity of NGOs for disaster response. Although the founding members stressed that they did not constitute a partnership, they agreed to work in the "spirit of partnership" which was defined as cooperation, mutual support and a commitment to strengthen and complement each other while respecting each member's specific identity.[15] The Consortium has since expanded to include 50 members from national NGOs and international agencies with support from a variety of governments and foundations. Its work includes long-term projects and START Labs to promote new ideas and experiments that seek to transform humanitarian response through innovation, fast funding, early action and localisation.[16]

In 2017, a Consortium was established by WASH Alliance International (WAI),[17] SNV and Plan International Netherlands to develop the Netherlands Water, Sanitation and Hygiene (WASH) SDG Programme. Led by Simavi, in partnership with the Dutch Ministry of Foreign Affairs (DGIS/IGG), the Consortium sought to contribute to the SDGs, particularly SDG 6, in order to achieve an improved WASH situation in seven countries: Bangladesh, Ethiopia, Indonesia, Nepal, Tanzania, Uganda and Zambia. The WASH SDG Consortium has worked to ensure that WASH facilities and services are sustainable,

14. BOND and TPI (2020) *Trends in Cross-Sector Partnering for INGOs*, London, UK: BOND and Oxford, UK: The Partnering Initiative (pp. 8–9).
15. PBA (2016) *START Network, Dealing with Paradox; Stories and Lessons from the First Three Years of Consortium-Building*, London, UK: Partnership Brokers Association. https://partnershipbrokers.org/w/2559/dealing-with-paradox/ (accessed February 25, 2022).
16. See https://startnetwork.org/about-us (accessed February 25, 2022).
17. Consisting of Simavi (lead), Amref, Akvo, IRC, Wetlands, PRACTICA, RAIN (now a brand of Aidenvironment), WASTE (via Nedworc-STIP), IRC, Wetlands, PRACTICA and RUAF (now Hivos).

climate resilient, gender sensitive and socially inclusive by working with households, businesses, financial institutions and governments.[18]

The complexity of development challenges and a growing focus on sustainability have also led to a growing number of **multi-stakeholder dialogues** (widely known as MSDs). MSDs have emerged as important spaces for different actors to come together to build consensus around complex, multifaceted, and in some cases, divisive issues.[19] Building upon social and civic dialogue processes, MSDs have been organised at local, national, regional or international levels with small groups of individuals representing different experiences and areas of expertise, constituencies and communities.[20] A key objective of an MSD is to enhance levels of trust between different actors, to share information and institutional knowledge, and to generate solutions and relevant good practices.[21] Frequent interactions and professional facilitation are also viewed as enabling those involved to develop closer relationships.[22]

Box 6.3 Multi-stakeholder dialogues for the SDGs

At global and national levels, MSDs are often facilitated by international agencies such as the UN, World Bank and national development agencies. The development of the Sustainable Development 2030 Agenda, for example, emerged from dialogue processes facilitated by the United Nations involving stakeholders from government, the private sector and civil society over a three-year period. These dialogues resulted in the development of the 17 SDGs, proposals on sustainable development financing, General Assembly dialogues on technology facilitation, as well as others.[23] The Action Dialogues for Effective Development Cooperation that have been established under the auspices of the Global Partnership for Effective Development Cooperation (GPEDC) also provide an example of an MSD process linked to sustainable development. Led by partner country governments, these dialogues bring stakeholders together at the country level to reinforce partnerships that maximise development impact through the implementation of the SDGs. In addition to making

18. See https://wash-alliance.org/washsdg-programme/ (accessed February 25, 2022).
19. Dodds, F. and Benson, E. (2013) *Multi-Stakeholder Dialogue: Stakeholder Forum for a Sustainable Future*, Johannesburg, South Africa: Civicus (p. 1).
20. Ibid., p. 2.
21. Ibid., pp. 1–2.
22. Veldhuizen, M., Blok, V. and Dentoni, D. (2013) Organisational drivers of capabilities for multi-stakeholder dialogue and knowledge integration. *Journal on Chain and Network Science*, 13 (2): 107–117. DOI:10.3920/JCNS2013.1002 10 (p. 108).
23. See https://sustainabledevelopment.un.org/post2015/negotiations (accessed February 25, 2022).

development cooperation more effective at the country level, these Dialogues also seek to build momentum toward the Global Partnership's High-Level Meetings.[24]

Digital communication

The use of technology, particularly digital communication, has clearly enhanced many new collaborative trends. Indeed, a **collaborative network** (CN) has been defined as a multi-entity alliance composed of people and organisations that collaborate to achieve common and compatible goals, whose interactions are supported by a computer network.[25] The language of ICT is also integrated into descriptions of CNs as involving actors or "nodes" whose relationships or "ties" dominate their work.[26] CNs may assume a variety of different forms, including "service-oriented virtual organizations, virtual enterprises, dynamic supply chains, professional associations, industry clusters, professional virtual communities, collaborative virtual laboratories, etc."[27] Here we may also find initiatives such as crowdfunding and crowdsourcing in which money, information and skills are sourced from groups of people through social media platforms. Virtual forms of collaboration and "remote partnering" also appear to be expanding as partners operating across different geographical and time zones experiment with digital methodologies and tools in order to build and reinforce their connections.[28] During the COVID-19 pandemic, ambitious multi-stakeholder initiatives such as *El Día Después* (EDD) further demonstrated that virtual collaboration can be built quickly and deliver societal impact (see Box 6.5).[29]

Box 6.4 Collaboration hubs

A form of collaboration that combines digital connections and innovation is the **collaboration hub**; a type of workspace, often in

24. See www.effectivecooperation.org/content/action-dialogues-2021-effective-development-co-operation-briefs (accessed February 25, 2022).
25. Camarinha-Matos, L.M. and Afsarmanesh, H. (2006) Collaborative networks, value creation in a knowledge society. In: Wang, K., Kovacs, G., Wozny, M. and Fang M. eds. *International Federation for Information Processing (IFIP)*, Vol. 207, Knowledge enterprise: Intelligent strategies. In *Product Design, Manufacturing, and Management*, Boston, USA: Springer, pp. 26–40. http://dx.doi.org/10.1007/0-387-34403-9_4 (p. 30).
26. Long, J., Cunningham, F. and Braithwaite, J. (2013) Bridges, brokers and boundary spanners in collaborative networks: A systematic review. *BMC Health Services Research*, 13: 158. https://doi.org/10.1186/1472-6963-13-158 (p. 2).
27. Camarinha-Matos and Afsarmanesh (2006) Op. cit. p. 26.
28. See, for example, www.remotepartnering.org/ (accessed March 11, 2022).
29. Moreno-Serna, J., Purcell, W.M., Sánchez-Chaparro, T., Soberón, M., Lumbreras, J. and Mataix, C. (2020) Catalyzing transformational partnerships for the SDGs: Effectiveness and impact of the multi-stakeholder initiative El día después. *Sustainability*, 12 (17): 7189.

a metropolitan area, that is designed to promote interaction, community and teamwork. Hubs have a strong link to entrepreneurial activity and are often built around start-ups. Tuukka Toivonen and Nicolas Friederici position hubs as part of a "global social entrepreneurship movement" operating in countries as diverse as Kenya, Japan and the UK with shared values and purpose. According to the authors, collaboration hubs operate on an equitable basis in which participants have an equal say in the formulation of shared goals and decision-making processes.[30] Each member is also expected to show strong individual agency and contribute to the overall energy of the group as a whole: "Hubs thus view individuality, leadership, collaboration, and community participation as complementary rather than opposing characteristics."[31] Innovation that cultivates "creative clashes" between people from different backgrounds, networks and domains is also highlighted.

Innovation and experimentation

A variety of new collaborative trends incorporate the concept of **social innovation** which has been defined as any new and useful solution to a social need or problem. Such solutions may build on existing approaches to address a social need or problem in the form of a new product, service or model "that is better than existing approaches (i.e. more effective, efficient, sustainable, or just) and for which the value created (benefits) accrues primarily to society as a whole rather than private individuals."[32] In developing innovative ideas, new social relationships and collaborations are created which, in turn, improve the lives of those involved.[33] The ability to test innovative solutions in their particular environments and ensure that the changes they promote are sustainable is a central element of many new collaborative initiatives. These arrangements thus encourage space for experimentation so that opportunities can be explored, reviewed and reflected upon. This kind of "testing" often includes acceptance that learning from what has not worked can be used to develop, refine and improve ideas and solutions. Space for innovation is further strengthened by constant and direct exchanges of both knowledge and experience

30. Toivonen, T. and Friederici, N. (2015) Time to define what a "hub" really is. *Stanford Social Innovation Review*. https://doi.org/10.48558/N1BD-8S82
31. Ibid.
32. Dax, T., Strahl, W., Kirwan, J. and Maye, D. (2016) The leader programme 2007–2013: Enabling or disabling social innovation and neo-endogenous development? Insights from Austria and Ireland. *European Urban and Regional Studies*, 23 (1): 56–68. doi:10.1177/0969776413490425
33. Ibid.

through feedback loops and cycles that involve different actors and levels, including links between practice and policy.[34]

Working with diversity

New and emergent forms of collaboration have a strong focus on the participation of different actors, often through the use of processes such as co-creation and participatory decision-making. In addition to impact and results, attention is paid to relationships between actors and the process of working together, and how these aspects influence the achievement of results. **Collective impact,** for example, is described as a structured form of collaboration that brings together different actors around a common agenda for solving a specific problem.[35]

Multi-stakeholder platforms or MSPs are another example of arrangements that are centred upon the involvement of a wide variety of actors. Among the MSPs that have been developed to support the SDGs, a report by TPI includes global and national dialogue platforms; knowledge exchange platforms organised around thematic issues; reporting and standard-setting platforms that build on dialogue and knowledge exchange in order to create new norms and standards via multi-stakeholder processes and transformative partnership platforms that support the development of partnerships for the SDGs.[36] Jodie Thorpe et al. believe that MSPs are a recognition that addressing complex, systemic problems requires forms of governance which bring stakeholders together to plan and act in new ways.[37] This view is shared by those who view platforms as joining organisations and projects on the basis of shared objectives, methodologies and evaluation systems that align disconnected initiatives and generate greater impact.[38] By combing their different goals, perceptions, priorities and capacities, platform members can deepen their knowledge about the nature of complex problems, create potential solutions to them and gain a better and more holistic understanding of the context in which these solutions will be implemented.

34. Moreno-Serna, J., Sánchez-Chaparro, T., Stott, L., Mazorra, J., Carrasco-Gallego, R. and Mataix, C. (2021) Feedback loops and facilitation: Catalyzing transformational multi-stakeholder refugee response partnerships. *Sustainability*, 13: 11705. https://doi.org/10.3390/su132111705
35. See Kania, J. and Kramer, M. (2011) Collective impact. *Stanford Social Innovation Review*, Winter: 36–41.
36. Prescott, D. and Stibbe, D. (2020) *Partnership Support Platforms for the SDGs: Learning from Practice*, London, UK: The Partnering Initiative and New York, NY, USA: UN DESA, pp. 10–12.
37. Thorpe, J., Guijt, J., Sprenger, T. and Stibbe, D. (2021) *Multi Stakeholder Platforms as System Change Agents: A Guide for Assessing Effectiveness*, Sussex, UK: IDS Institute of Development Studies and Wageningen, the Netherlands: Wageningen University and Research (p. 4)
38. Espiau, G. (2018) *Social Innovation Platforms for International Development in La Caixa Foundation Work 4Progress: Platforms That Trigger Innovation*, Barcelona, Spain: La Caixa Foundation.

Box 6.5 Multi-stakeholder platforms (MSPs)

One of the many MSPs developed to support the implementation of the SDGs is the 2030 Agenda Partnership Accelerator, a collaborative initiative developed by the United Nations Department of Economic and Social Affairs (UN DESA) and The Partnering Initiative (TPI), in collaboration with the United Nations Office for Partnerships (UNOP), the UN Global Compact and the UN Development Coordination Office, which aims to significantly accelerate effective partnerships in support of the SDGs.[39] Another example is GIZ's Partnerships 2030 Platform, supported by the German Federal Ministry for Economic Cooperation and Development (BMZ) with the involvement of *Deutsche Gesellschaft für Internationale Zusammenarbeit* (GIZ) GmbH and Engagement Global – bengo, to strengthen and support multi-stakeholder partnerships and share information and guidance on partnership-related issues.[40] More recently, the *El Día Después* Initiative (EDD) promoted by the energy company, Iberdrola, the Innovation and Technology for Development Centre at the *Universidad Politécnica de Madrid* (itdUPM), ISGlobal, a global health research centre, and SDSN Spain, the Spanish node of the Sustainable Development Solutions Network, has established itself as an important collaborative platform to support the achievement of the SDGs. Set up in 2020 in response to the COVID-19 crisis, EDD has developed four multi-stakeholder communities that combine scientific and practical knowledge with linkages to public policy frameworks in order to generate collaborative solutions to sustainability challenges.[41]

Knowledge exchange and learning

Many new collaborative ventures are built around knowledge exchange and learning. These include **communities of practice** and networks that promote peer-to-peer learning on collaboration and partnership (see Box 6.6). Etienne Wenger describes a community of practice (CoP) as a group of people who have a common interest in a problem and interact with one other by sharing knowledge and skills in order to address it over time.[42] This connection is essentially about learning and

39. See https://sustainabledevelopment.un.org/PartnershipAccelerator (accessed February 25, 2022).
40. See www.partnerschaften2030.de/en/
41. See https://diadespues.org/ (accessed February 25, 2022) and Moreno-Serna et al. (2020) Op. cit.
42. Wenger, E. (2000) Communities of practice and social learning systems. *Organization*, 7 (2): 225–246. https://doi.org/10.1177%2F135050840072002

the co-generation of knowledge which develops organically rather than being imposed by organisational structures or directives.[43]

Box 6.6 Communities of Practice on Partnership in the European Social Fund

Transnational learning networks linked to the European Social Fund (ESF) have worked to support the implementation of the partnership principle. They have included two iterations of the Community of Practice on Partnership (2007–11) which informed the development of the European Code of Conduct on Partnership (ECCP), and the Thematic Network on Partnership (PTN) (2015–19), one of nine networks that made up the ESF's Transnational Cooperation Platform.[44] PTN members included ESF managing authorities, intermediate bodies, NGOs and social partners who engaged in a series of peer reviews, physical and virtual meetings and exchanges in different Member States and worked together to review the ECCP, explore how partnership was being applied in other EU funds and programmes and provide guidance on how ESF Managing Authorities promote and manage partnership. More recently, the European Community of Practice on Partnership (ECoPP) has been created with the intention of working across different funds in order to assist managing authorities and wider stakeholders to improve their partnership practice and update and reinvigorate the ECCP.

The co-trends

In parallel to the developments outlined earlier, the phenomenon of what might be described as "co-trends" that offer a new and more inclusive way of developing and delivering public goods and services is of interest. These movements, which embrace practices such as co-production, co-creation, co-innovation, co-design, co-construction and co-responsibility, have different origins and focus areas (see Table 6.3).

43. McGregor, J. (2003) Collaboration in communities of practice. In Bennett, N. and Anderson, L. eds. *Rethinking Educational Leadership, Challenging the Conventions*, London, UK: Sage Publications (p. 113).
44. Toland, J. ed. (2019) *Lessons Learned From Transnational Cooperation*, Brussels, Belgium: European Commission, Directorate-General for Employment, Social Affairs and Inclusion. https://data.europa.eu/doi/10.2767/327475

Table 6.1 The co-trends

	Co-production	***Co-creation***	***Co-design***	***Co-responsibility***	***Co-construction***
Origins	Emerged from the work of Elinor Ostrom and Edgar S. Cahn and their interest in community management of resources[45]	Popularised by C.K. Pralahad and Venkat Ramaswamy to describe a business management model seeking better engagement with customers[46]	Also known as participatory or cooperative design, this movement emerged in the 1960s and 70s with the aim of involving community stakeholders in architectural processes[47]	Proposes stakeholder involvement in the living environment with access to basic services and citizen engagement in new governance models[48]	Developed to involve students more deeply in educational decision-making[49]
Focus	Greater citizen participation in the development of communal products and public services	Focus on added value for business through better customer connections and co-innovation that creates shared value and ecosystems of interdependence between individual and organisational actors from different sectors	All relevant stakeholders valued as partners in decision-making processes related to the development of products and services	Approach in which councils, civic associations and citizens as parents, service users, patients, tenants, residents, passengers co-operate and work together to achieve social well-being	Students seen as active partners in the design, implementation and evaluation of their education

Source: Adapted from Stott (2018)[50]

45. Ostrom, E. (1990) *Governing the Commons, the Evolution of Institutions for Collective Action*, Cambridge, UK: Cambridge University Press. Cahn, E.S. (2004) *No More Throw-away People: The Co-Production Imperative*, Washington, DC, USA: Essential Books; Griffiths, M. (2016) Co-production. *Presentation at ESF Transnational Platform Thematic Network on Partnership Meeting*, Dublin, Ireland, November 27, 2016.
46. Prahalad, C. and Ramaswamy, V. (2000) Co-opting customer competence. *Harvard Business Review*, 78 (1): 79–89. https://hbsp.harvard.edu/product/R00108-PDF-ENG Prahalad, C. and Ramaswamy, V. (2004) Co-creating unique value with customers. *Strategy & Leadership*, 32 (3): 4–9. https://doi.org/10.1108/10878570410699249
47. Szebeko, D. and Tan, L. (2010) Co-designing for society. *Australasian Medical Journal*, 3 (9): 580–590. http://dx.doi.org/10.4066/AMJ.2010.378
48. Bloomfield, J. (2012) *TOGETHER Final Report*, EU: Urbact. www.forumdascidades.pt/sites/default/files/Projetos/together_final_report_rev.pdf
49. Hargreaves, D. (2006) A new shape for schooling? *SSAT, the Schools, Students and Teachers Network*. www.ssatuk.co.uk and Osborne, S., Radnor, Z. and Strokosch, K. (2016) Co-production and the co-creation of value in public services: A suitable case for treatment? *Public Management Review*, 18 (5): 639–653. https://doi.org/10.1080/14719037.2015.1111927
50. Stott, L. (2018) Co-production, enhancing the role of citizens in governance and service delivery. *Technical Dossier* No.4., ESF Transnational Platform, Luxembourg: Publications Office of the European Union.

Box 6.7 Co-production and co-creation in the European Union

In the European Union, integrated and participatory service models that incorporate stronger connections between the public sector and civil society actors such as NGOs, community-based organisations and associations, and citizens themselves have emerged in response to disaffection with both public and private systems for providing public goods or public services.[51] The search for more innovative public service models was reinforced by the socio-economic crisis of 2007–8 which precipitated interest in social innovation, multi-level and cross-sector approaches to support those most affected by austerity measures such as lower income groups, women, youth and migrants.[52] In this sense, multi-stakeholder collaborative efforts to generate and deliver services that *appropriately* met the *different* needs of these and other groups were viewed as integral to co-production and co-creation processes that strengthened citizen engagement through more inclusive, bottom-up and participatory connections.

The collaborative local government initiative in Amersfoort, the Netherlands, provides an example of how co-production works in relation to governance. Here, administrative changes in the Netherlands after the 2007–8 crisis involved the transferring of competences from the national to city level while at the same time reducing their budgets. Annual surveys showed that citizens were becoming increasingly dissatisfied with the city council's performance and that, as the social situation declined, many were becoming involved in self-organised bottom-up initiatives. City leaders in Amersfoort therefore began to look at the possibility of re-engaging with citizens by delivering public services in collaboration with them. From 2013 onwards, multiple experiments took place with pilot projects such as collective innovation forums, exchange initiatives and new participative processes. The success of these initiatives led to the implementation of a new model of collaboration between the city's population and its administration in which citizens claim that their voices have become more audible and inequalities better addressed.[53]

Beginning in 2017, a series of social innovation and co-creation processes was developed in European cities under the auspices of the Social Innovation Community (SIC). The aim of this project was to

51. European Commission (2011) *Empowering People, Driving Change: Social Innovation in the European Union*, Luxembourg: Publications of the European Union (p. 19).
52. Ibid., p. 22.
53. Jégou, F. (2015) Amersfoort: Designing a collaborative city administration. *Case Study*, Social Innovation in Cities, URBACT II Capitalisation and Wingelaar, M. (2016) Social innovation, Amersfoort. *Presentation at ESF Transnational*, Seminar, Brussels, 21 June 2016.

collectively define and co-create solutions to challenges in cities in Croatia, Estonia, Italy and Norway. To do this, staff at host centres in each city facilitated processes through which local stakeholders such as public employees, civil servants, young professionals, private businesses and refugees co-defined specific local challenges for which they wished to find solutions, including refugee integration, urban revitalisation, families at risk of eviction, holistic public services and job opportunities for young people. In Zagreb (Croatia), public servants, representatives of creative industries such as start-ups and museums, and stakeholders from academia worked together to promote sports and active recreation in the city, language training for asylum seekers and the use of empty spaces for new cultural projects, services and products. In Turin (Italy), the Municipality, Torino Social Innovation (TSI) and the University of Bologna organised an experimental process to improve the efficiency and coordination of social service delivery, while in Pärnu (Estonia) networks of community leaders and local NGOs, freelancers and entrepreneurs worked with young residents, community organisations and policy makers to address the lack of housing and work opportunities for young people. In Oslo (Norway), meanwhile, a large and diverse group of participants from the public sector, businesses and civil society joined social entrepreneurs to promote the inclusion of refugees in the workforce.[54]

Towards transformation?

While many of the collaborative trends outlined earlier overlap in their intention to bring together the resources and skills of different actors to address problems, there are also important differences between them. These differences ultimately relate to the depth of change that they seek and whether they have the potential to be a "game-changer."[55] Some of the differential factors worth noting here include the extent to which these initiatives are focused on "whole" systems or parts of systems; participation or empowerment; facilitation or management, and learning or scaling.

Systems or parts of systems?

An increasing number of collaborative initiatives make an explicit link to systems transformation and the need to work at multiple "scales."[56] Among

54. See www.siceurope.eu/ (accessed February 25, 2022).
55. Voorberg et al. (2014) Op. cit. p. 16.
56. Ratner, B.D. and Stafford Smith, M. 2020. *Multi-Stakeholder Dialogue for Transformational Change.* Scientific and Technical Advisory Panel to the Global Environment Facility. Washington, DC, USA: STAP (p. 1).

the co-trends, for example, attention has been drawn to the fact that "the focus is not upon the service alone but upon how it is produced within the holistic service system and upon novel combinatory means to improve such service delivery."[57] This approach can clearly be seen in Amersfoort's multi-disciplinary and cross-departmental work and the transversal use of social innovation in the city experiments in Zagreb, Turin, Pärnu and Oslo (see Box 6.7). Addressing systemic inequalities has also been a focus in the facilitation of multi-stakeholder dialogues to manage natural resource competition in Uganda, Zambia and Cambodia. Here, the Strengthening Aquatic Resource Governance (STARGO) project has noted the importance of analysing different understandings of historical patterns of conflict and collaboration; integrating gender equity in dialogue processes; creating linkages between actors to strengthen accountability and "learning to adapt, tap new support, and scale through structured reflection and joint learning."[58]

A focus on systems change is also notable in new multi-stakeholder platforms that focus on the facilitation of innovative collaborative approaches.[59] In addition to bringing key stakeholders from different sectors together around issues of common interest, the emphasis here is on building an enabling environment for collaborative working through capacity and trust building alongside coordinated commitment to SDG action.[60] Jaime Moreno-Serna et al. further note the existence of "systemic multi-stakeholder platforms" that seek to catalyse structural changes and align the activities of different stakeholders over longer time horizons.[61] These kinds of platforms are a recognition that transformation in complex systems cannot be achieved through simple or technical fixes.[62] As well as adopting working principles such as community listening and co-design of interventions, a growing number of "innovative" platforms also place emphasis on supporting **collaborative ecosystems** in which spaces for experimentation encompass different forms and processes while embracing values such as solidarity and mutual benefit.[63]

57. Osborne, S., Radnor, Z. and Strokosch, K. (2016) Co-production and the co-creation of value in public services: A suitable case for treatment? *Public Management Review*, 18 (5): 639–653 https://doi.org/10.1080/14719037.2015.1111927 (p. 648).
58. Ratner, B.D., Burnley, C., Mugisha, S., Madzudzo, E., Kosal Mam, I.O., Rüttinger, L., Chilufya, L. and Adriázola, P. (2017) Facilitating multistakeholder dialogue to manage natural resource competition: A synthesis of lessons from Uganda, Zambia, and Cambodia. *International Journal of the Commons*, 11 (2): 733–753. DOI: 10.18352/ijc (p. 748).
59. Prescott and Stibbe (2020) Op. cit. p. 13.
60. Ibid.
61. Moreno-Serna et al. (2020) Op. cit.
62. Thorpe et al. (2020) Op. cit. p. 4.
63. Espiau (2018) Op. cit.

Participation or empowerment?

Acknowledgement that stakeholder involvement may assume distinct forms in different contexts appears to be a feature of various new collaborative arrangements. However, attention to how far this involvement includes stakeholders, citizens and end users as key decision-makers varies. Among the co-trends, for example, while closer engagement with users is widely promoted, there are distinctions with regard to how far collaboration is understood as a process that works *with* or *for* end users. The role played by "lead" organisations such as public administration bodies, and the extent of their control of collaborative processes, is notable here. A further manifestation of this difference can be found in the ambiguous use of collaborative terms to describe models that promote heightened citizen participation in developing new forms of service delivery as well as a process by which government bodies relinquish social and regulatory "control" to the market. It has been noted, for example, that in Scandinavia, co-design has been promoted as a way of working with trade unions to promote worker participation in decision-making processes with the "user as partner," while in the United States, its focus is on customer involvement in product design processes with the "user as subject."[64] This differentiation can also be seen in a vision of the end user as a citizen and another in which they are a customer or client who is "an interesting source of product and service innovation."[65]

As well as perceptions of "controlled" engagement, the issue of ongoing stakeholder participation also merits attention. The engagement processes of Collective Impact, for example, have been questioned by critics who contrast the intentionality of engaging community representatives as equal partners with the reality of their occasional involvement, noting that failure to engage with those most directly affected is likely to reinforce "the dominance of those with privilege."[66]

As evidence suggests that systems change relies upon a continuous process of stakeholder engagement and the constant renewal of connections between diverse social actors,[67] questions about the nature and depth of participation are important to address here. This will involve examining the extent to which participation is ad hoc or ongoing, short or long term and how far it encourages the development of differentiated approaches and models. In co-production processes, for example, the ESF stresses the need

64. Sanders, E.B.N. and Stappers, P.J. (2008) Co-creation and the new landscapes of design. *CoDesign*, 4 (1): 5–18. https://doi.org/10.1080/15710880701875068 (p. 4).
65. Voorberg et al. 2014 Op. cit. p. 2.
66. Wolff et al. (2016) Op. cit. p. 45.
67. Stott, L. (2018) Co-production, enhancing the role of citizens in governance and service delivery. *Technical Dossier* No.4., ESF Transnational Platform, Luxembourg: Publications Office of the European Union (p. 22).

for flexibility in developing high-quality public services with recognition of contextual differences and the tailoring of initiatives for and with different groups of citizens.[68] Transformative participation, as we have seen in Chapter 5, also relies upon the ability to embrace dialogic and deliberative elements with the creation of spaces in which "people can speak openly, and on their own terms, about what is meaningful to them."[69] Within this approach, there is acknowldegment of the "power of awareness" in which attention is given to operational contexts, the perspectives of others and new possibilities.[70]

Facilitation or management?

In many new collaborative initiatives, the importance of a facilitator function is highlighted. Although this role resonates with that of partnership broker and a shift away from a directive to a collective form of leadership (see Chapter 5), this form of facilitation has been presented as primarily one of coordination and administration. The tasks of a facilitator in **collaborative networked organisations** (CNOs), for example, have been described as working "to support the controlled transfer of specialised knowledge between groups, increase cooperation by liaising with people from both sides of the gap, and improve efficiency by introducing 'good ideas' from one isolated setting into another."[71] Collective Impact initiatives, meanwhile, document the need for a "backbone organisation" or centralised infrastructure with dedicated staff who attend to planning, management and support through a structured process that includes shared measurement, ongoing communication and mutually reinforcing activities.[72] An important question here is how far these structures are truly collective and whether endowing these responsibilities to a backbone organisation "creates a top-down organization versus a truly collaborative one where leadership and responsibility are dispersed."[73]

In transformational arrangements, the partnership brokering role involves much more than simply coordinating or managing relationships. It is about providing space for partners to connect, develop and take collective responsibility for their work; the building of equitable and open partner relationships which promote shared ownership and horizontal accountability; overcoming challenges and ensuring results and impact. More crucially, it is about moving beyond "business as usual" approaches so that partnership adds real value for

68. Ibid., p. 10.
69. Escobar, O. (2011) *Public Dialogue and Deliberation: A Communication Perspective for Public Engagement Practitioners*. Edinburgh, UK: Beacons for Public Engagement (p. 22).
70. Ratner et al. (2017) Op. cit. p. 739.
71. Long et al. (2013) Op. cit. p. 12.
72. Kania and Kramer (2011) Op. cit. p. 40.
73. Wolff et al. (2016) Op. cit. p. 49.

individuals, partner organisations and wider society.[74] As the building of trust between partners is an important part of this process, jointly clarifying interests and assumptions and establishing mutually defined systems of accountability are important tasks for partnership brokers. It has also been observed that it is useful to make trust an explicit discussion topic with, for example, reflection on how trust can be constructed as part of the partnership-building process and assessment of the consequences of breaking it.[75]

Learning or scaling?

Although much emphasis has been placed on the need to replicate and scale up collaborative initiatives so that they have a wider impact, it is important to remember that these arrangements are intimately linked to specific locations and circumstances. Here we return to the argument that when examining collaboration, partnership and joint working schemes, the relevance of context cannot be underestimated.[76] The emphasis then should be less on the *transfer of models and approaches* and more on the *transfer of learning* regarding how they work in specific and dynamic contexts.[77]

Using a learning focus in relation to the idea of "scaling" is helpful in assisting assessment of how far a partnership arrangement, or elements of it, might be used to inspire the development of transformational collaborative initiatives elsewhere. Here "scaling" is positioned in relation to change within individuals and organisations that can also contribute to societal transformation through processes of learning across three interconnected levels:[78]

- **Scaling out** to spread and replicate the learning acquired from partnering across different spatial levels
- **Scaling up** so that the learning and engagement between partners affect policies and institutional norms, and promote changes in the "rules of the game"

74. Stott, L. ed. (2018) *Shaping Sustainable Change: The Role of Partnership Brokering in Optimising Collaborative Action*, London, UK: Greenleaf Publication, Routledge: Taylor and Francis Group.
75. Ratner et al. (2017) Op. cit. p. 738.
76. El Ansari, W., Phillips, C.J. and Hammick, M. (2001) Collaboration and partnerships: Developing the evidence base. *Health and Social Care in the Community*, 9 (4): 215–227. https://doi.org/10.1046/j.0966-0410.2001.00299.x (p. 223).
77. Rein, M., Stott, L., Yambayamba, K., Hardman, S. and Reid, S. (2005) *Working Together, A Critical Analysis of Cross-Sector Partnerships in Southern Africa*, Cambridge, UK: University of Cambridge Programme for Industry (p. 125).
78. Moore, M.L., Riddell, D., Vocisano, D. (2015) Scaling out, scaling up, scaling deep: Strategies of non-profits in advancing systemic social innovation. *Journal of Corporate Citizenship*, 58: 67–84. doi:10.9774/GLEAF.4700.2015.ju.00009 and McLean, R. and Gargani, J. (2020) *Scaling Impact: Innovation for the Public Good*, Vancouver, Canada: IRDC and Abingdon, UK: Routledge, Taylor and Francis.

- **Scaling deep** to promote durable change through the learning and process of partnering that influences values, cultural practices and the quality of relationships

Acknowledging that "one size does not fit all," particular emphasis here is placed on the learning derived from "scaling deep." Here, attention is paid to changes among people and organisations in terms of narrative, values, beliefs and identities so that a systems approach is supported and embedded in societal culture.[79] The embedding of the learning derived from working collaboratively may be reinforced by frank and ongoing exchanges of knowledge and experience that explore what works and what does not, with emphasis on internal reflection and feedback loops that promote exchange between partners, partnership arrangements and sectors, as well as between practice and policy.[80] Figure 6.1 presents this learning and scaling process as one in which engagement in collaborative initiatives can add value to individuals, organisations and society. At the base of the pyramid, a majority of collaborative arrangements are likely to engage in project-related activities, particularly at the start of their work. Some, however, will make concerted efforts

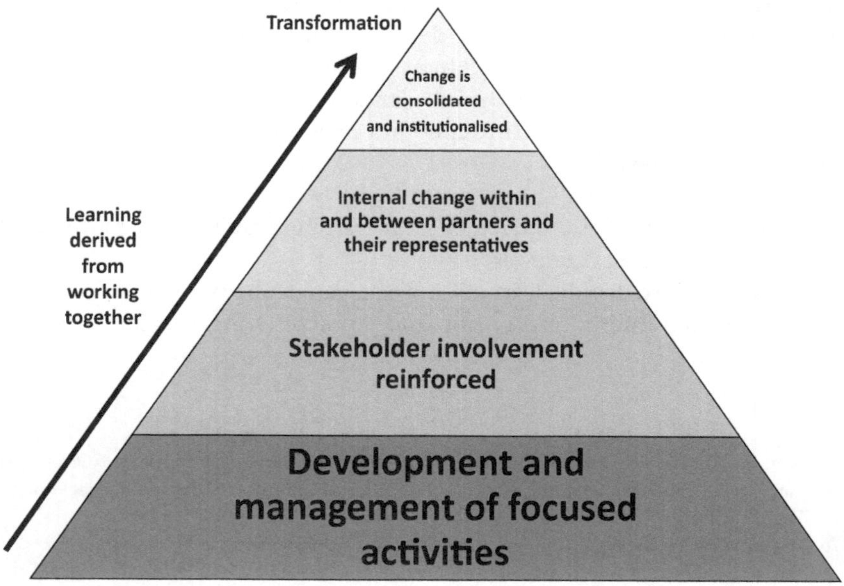

Figure 6.1 Learning and scaling through multi-stakeholder collaboration

79. McLean and Gargani (2020) Op. cit. pp. 17–18.
80. Moreno-Serna et al. (2021) Op. cit. believe that constant feedback loops within, between and across organisations working in collaboration can assist consolidation of internal learning and should thus be considered as essential practices for the effective management of complex multi-stakeholder partnerships.

to engage in a manner that reinforces the worth of working collectively and enhances stakeholder involvement. As well as heightening commitment, the knowledge and experience gained from working together can encourage learning within and between the organisations involved so that they begin to make adjustments in the way they operate. This, in turn, may precipitate a knock-on effect as collaborative learning is mainstreamed with the institutionalisation of changes in both policy and practice. According to Tennyson, such transformation takes place when working in partnership has challenged "entrenched institutional/sectoral behaviour" and its impacts are more than "transitory or superficial."[81]

The innovative partnership models for basic services in Latin America and some of the co-production efforts in Europe offer examples of this process in action. In these cases, following the demonstration of tangible change for stakeholders through their activities in the short term, partners internalised the learning from working with others over the medium term so that new routines, behaviours and norms became part and parcel of their organisational cultures. The long-term impact derived from this has been manifested in the institutionalisation of learning and reinforcement of changes that have become accepted practice.[82]

The depth of learning derived from working in multi-stakeholder collaboration is intimately related to the promotion of reflective practice, in which reflections are encouraged, captured and collated in a systematic manner so that connections and patterns are identified.[83] Linda Finlay's four principles are useful to bear in mind when seeking to integrate reflective practice in the process of partnering or collaborating. They include presenting reflective practice carefully so that partners and stakeholders understand its purpose and are motivated to use it; providing adequate support, time, resources, opportunities and methods for reflection; encouraging and developing skills of critical analysis and questioning; and taking proper account of factors that promote or inhibit reflection at institutional and professional levels, and in the broader context.[84]

Like partnership, the new and emerging collaborative trends outlined in this chapter reflect tensions between pragmatic and reflective dimensions and show variances in the nature and depth of the change they seek.

81. Tennyson, R. (2011) *The Partnering Toolbook*, London, UK: The Partnering Initiative (IBLF) (p. 33).

82. Stott, L. (2014) *Partnerships for Innovation in Access to Basic Services*, Washington, USA: Multilateral Investment Fund/Inter-American Development Bank (MIF/IDB) and Madrid, Spain: Innovation and Technology for Development Centre/*Universidad Politécnica de Madrid* (itdUPM) (pp. 39–40).

83. See https://beta.cipduat.co.uk/Images/reflective-practice-guide_tcm18-12524.pdf (accessed March 16, 2022).

84. Finlay, L. (2008) Reflecting on "reflective practice". In: *Practice-Based Professional Learning Paper* 52, Milton Keynes, UK: The Open University (pp. 16–20).

However, although these forms are constantly changing and reshaping, there does seem to be an incipient movement away from instrumental and managerial forms of cooperation to more ambitious collaborative models that seek transformation through flexible, fluid and dynamic multi-actor connections. At the heart of this shift is a recognition that "people's capacities for cooperation are far greater and more complex than institutions allow them to be."[85] A deeper appreciation of the enormous capacity of humankind to work together across geographical, sectoral, organisational and personal boundaries in creative and meaningful ways is, then, central to the future of partnership.

85. Sennett, R. (2013) *Together: The Rituals, Pleasures and Politics of Cooperation*, London, UK: Penguin (p. 29).

7 Some reflections on partnership, sustainability and citizenship

As this book is part of a series on Citizenship and Sustainability in Organisations, it seems appropriate to dedicate this final chapter to looking more deeply at where partnership sits in relation to this topic, particularly with regard to how citizens can contribute to collaborative initiatives that promote the transformations needed for sustainable development. Noting that the complexity of current human and organisational relationships has reached a point that may be difficult for future generations to make sense of, the series editors, Alison Marshall and David F. Murphy, ask what this might mean for current commitments to citizenship, sustainability and partnerships.[1] This question provides a good starting point for exploring the connections between the three concepts, the individual and collective efforts that inform them and how they might contribute to imagining, inventing and co-creating a more hopeful planetary future.[2] The reflections that follow are derived from different perspectives on these themes in the literature, all of which reinforce the importance of collaboration as fundamental to transformation.

Understandings of sustainability and citizenship

Like partnership, the expressions "sustainability" and "citizenship" are "fuzzwords" that can be stretched to meet the agendas and needs of almost any audience. Noting that "the word 'sustainable' has been flogged for everything from 'environmentally sensitive' to 'respect for indigenous ways of doing things' to 'affordable over the long term,'" Maggie Black reminds us that the global appeal of sustainability derives from its ability to integrate

1. Marshall, A. and Murphy, D.F. (2020) Introduction. In *Citizenship and Sustainability in Organizations: Exploring and Spanning the Boundaries*. New York, NY, USA: Routledge.
2. Mazzucato, M. (2021) *Mission Economy: A Moonshot Guide to Changing Capitalism*, London, UK: Allen Lane (p. 201); Senge, P., Hamilton, H. and Kania, J. (2015) The dawn of system leadership. In *Stanford Social Innovation Review*, Palo Alto, CA, USA: Stanford University, Stanford Center on Philanthropy and Civil Society, pp. 27–33.

DOI: 10.4324/9781003199434-8

a range of different perspectives under a single umbrella.[3] Conflation of the expression sustainability with sustainable development has further reinforced this sensation with both terms used interchangeably and, according to the economist, Robert Solow, imprecisely.[4]

More than 30 years after its publication, and in a much-changed global context, the 1987 Brundtland report's definition of sustainable development as "development that meets the needs of the present without compromising the ability of future generations to meet their own needs" is still the most widely known and used.[5] The report positions sustainable development as resting upon the harmonisation of economic growth, social inclusion and environmental protection with special attention given to the eradication of poverty, the reduction of inequalities and improved management of natural resources and ecosystems.[6] In current times, however, the possibility of harmonising a model of economic growth based on consumer capitalism with social and environmental sustainability has been increasingly questioned. Dennis Meadows, co-author of the celebrated study *Limits to Growth*,[7] for example, describes sustainability as an oxymoron, the intention of which is belied by its links to a pattern of development that depletes resources and pollutes on a large scale.[8] This contradiction has been explored by writers such as Tim Jackson and Serge Latouche who believe that economic growth should be decoupled from sustainability with emphasis placed instead on the well-being that may be attained from sharing work, consuming less and devoting more time to art, music, family, culture and community.[9]

Citizenship is also a slippery term. Generally defined as the condition of being a member of a particular country or nation-state and having rights and duties because of this,[10] citizenship is also presented as a collective connection based on membership of a community. The OECD notes that a citizen may

3. Black, M. (2007) *The No-Nonsense Guide to International Development*, Oxford, UK: New Internationalist Publications (p. 99).
4. Solow, R. (1993) Sustainability: An economist's perspective. In: Dorfman, R. and Dorman, N. eds. *Economics of the Environment*, New York, NY, USA: Norton (p. 1002).
5. United Nations (1987) *Report of the World Commission on Environment and Development: Our Common Future*. New York, NY, USA: United Nations (p. 37).
6. Ibid.
7. Meadows, D.H., Meadows, D.L., Randers, J. and Behrens III, W.W. (1972) *The Limits to Growth, A Report for the Club of Rome's Project on the Predicament of Mankind*. New York, NY, USA: Universe Books.
8. Meadows, D.H. (2010) Is Sustainable Development an Oxymoron? In: *Pictures of the Future*. Munich, Germany: Siemens, Spring.
9. Jackson, T. (2009) *Prosperity Without Growth? The Transition to a Sustainable Economy*, UK: Sustainable Development Commission; Latouche, S. (2010) *Farewell to Growth*, London, UK: Polity Press.
10. Heater, D. (1999) *What Is Citizenship?* Cambridge, UK: Polity Press (p. 53). and Karlberg, M. (2008) Discourse, identity and global citizenship. *Peace Review: A Journal of Social Justice*, 20 (3): 310–320. http://dx.doi.org/10.1080/10402650802330139 (p. 310).

be "an inhabitant of a particular place," which, depending on the context, could mean a village, town, city, region, state or country.[11] As well as a specific locality, however, a broader view of citizenship can be construed as one of people throughout the world belonging to a single human community.

The idea of a global citizenship that transcends political and geographic borders has received much attention of late.[12] A 2016 report by the Global Citizenship Commission positions this concept as complementary to notions of local and national citizenship, all of which imply moral connections that focus on "a duty to care."[13] Citizenship is here embedded in respect for human rights and treating people with dignity.[14] Derek Heater takes this conceptualisation further in his description of "world citizenship" as "a cosmopolitan mentality in which individual citizens have a moral responsibility for the condition of the planet and its people (and non-humans too)."[15] This view links global citizenship to sustainability and a focus on how humans, collectively, address common and interrelated social and ecological problems.[16] A link between global citizenship and sustainable development is also propounded by the UN in their portrayal of socially responsible individuals acting for the benefit of society as a whole.[17]

Connecting partnership, sustainability and citizenship

Acknowledging that the term sustainability is broad and evolving, Barbara Gray and Jenna Stites propose a definition for those working in partnership as "improvements to the total quality of life, both now and in the future, in a way that maintains the ecological processes on which life depends while satisfying the needs of all stakeholders."[18] This description is of interest here because it positions the importance of discussion and debate with regard to understandings of sustainability and the diverse requirements of different societal actors. Indeed, the authors believe that how partners choose to define sustainability will have an impact on the manner and direction in which they address problems, their motivations for choosing to work in partnership and the extent to which they are able to find common ground.[19]

11. OECD (2020) *Innovative Citizen Participation and New Democratic Institutions, Catching the Deliberative Wave*, Paris, France: OECD Publishing. https://doi.org/10.1787/339306da-en
12. Karlberg (2008) Op. cit.
13. Brown, G. ed. (2016) *The Universal Declaration of Human Rights in the 21st Century: A Living Document in a Changing World*, Cambridge, UK: Open Book Publishers. http://dx.doi.org/10.11647/OBP.0091 (pp. 26–27).
14. Ibid., p. 27.
15. Heater (1999) Op. cit. p. 134.
16. Karlberg (2008) Op. cit. p. 311.
17. See www.un.org/en/academic-impact/global-citizenship (accessed January 28, 2022).
18. Gray, B. and Stites, J. (2012) *Sustainability through Partnerships: Capitalizing on Collaboration*, Canada: Network for Business Sustainability (p. 14).
19. Ibid.

An emphasis on finding common ground is integral to a view of citizenship that centres on the securing of commitment to shared ideals and principles among diverse actors. Such an understanding resonates with calls for multi-level, networked or collaborative governance and positions citizens as members of a political community with the right to participate in public decision-making.[20] Jocelyne Bourgon builds upon this idea with the observation that, beyond simply making decisions and implementing them, governance is about collective problem-solving, adapting to changing circumstances and "co-creating a new future."[21]

The concepts of sustainability, citizenship and partnership may thus be combined in a view of people working together in a collective effort to promote human well-being and stewardship of the planet.[22] This notion of "shared activity in the spirit of mutual good will"[23] may further be understood as resting upon relational values that encompass connections between people and nature.[24] To promote relational values and safeguard the planet, Otto Scharmer and Katrin Kaufer have argued that humanity must move away from an "an ego-system" in which human beings are focused on individual well-being to an "eco-system" that places emphasis on the well-being of all.[25] This transformation, they believe, ultimately rests upon the quality of the individual and collective attention that people apply to their actions within these systems.[26] Bourgon complements this view with the suggestion that, in view of the complex problems faced by societies globally, governments should seek to blend and balance their traditional authority by facilitating *collective power* and working with citizens to debate *alternative* futures, how to get there and the challenges that this may involve.[27] The transformational focus of these perceptions implies that to "co-create the future," we will need to transcend purely instrumental views of sustainability, citizenship and partnership.

In the field of environmental sustainability, it has been noted that as well as an instrumental view of nature that sees "the value of living

20. Bellamy, R. (2015) Citizenship, historical development of. In: Wright, J.D. ed. *International Encyclopedia of the Social and Behavioral Sciences*, 2nd edition, Vol. 3, Oxford, UK: Elsevier (p. 647).
21. Bourgon, J. (2011) *A New Synthesis of Public Administration: Serving in the 21st Century*. Canada: Queen's Policy Studies: McGill-Queen's University Press, and Civil Service College Singapore (2017) Interview: The new synthesis in the field: Conversation with Jocelyne Bourgon. www.csc.gov.sg/articles/the-new-synthesis-in-the-field-conversation-with-jocelyne-bourgon (accessed November 10, 2021).
22. Ibid., p. 127.
23. Heater (1999) Op. cit. p. 56.
24. Chan, K., Gould, R. and Pascual, U. (2018) Editorial overview: Relational values: What are they, and what's the fuss about? *Current Opinion in Environmental Sustainability*, 35. 10.1016/j.cosust.2018.11.003.
25. Scharmer, O. and Kaufer, K. (2013) *Leading From the Emerging Future: From Ego-System to Eco-System Economics*, San Francisco, CA, USA: Berret Koehler Publisher.
26. Scharmer and Kaufer (2013) Op. cit. p. 3 and p. 9.
27. Ibid.

entities as means to achieve human ends," a more intrinsic understanding of nature embraces its inherent value which is "independent of human judgement."[28] In parallel, the economist and philosopher, Amartya Sen, has suggested that beyond the "purely instrumental," effective citizenship should be part of what we should seek to nurture and sustain.[29] This view is endorsed by Jon Alexander in his depiction of an empowered citizenry that is more complex and multidimensional than standard portrayals of citizens as "subjects" or "consumers."[30] Meanwhile, as we have seen in this book, a generalised tendency to see partnership as an instrument may be counterbalanced by a perception of partnership as having intrinsic value and relational qualities.

To explore this further, Table 7.1 provides a preliminary overview of some of the pragmatic (instrumental) and reflective (intrinsic) dimensions encompassed by the terms sustainability, citizenship and partnership.

Table 7.1 Pragmatic and reflective dimensions of sustainability, citizenship and partnership

	Pragmatic	***Reflective***
Sustainability	• Focus on the SDG 2030 Agenda • Emphasis on results and impact • Metagovernance that steers • "Fit for purpose" mechanisms	• Focus beyond the SDGs • Emphasis on process and change • Metagovernance that facilitates • Emphasis on values and mindsets
Citizenship	• Place-based citizenship • Public sector lead • Emphasis on accountability • Participatory decision-making • Stakeholder engagement • Acknowledgement of agency	• Global citizenship and stewardship • Emphasis on collective responsibility • Attention to relational values • Deliberative decision-making • Tailored stakeholder engagement • Deep recognition of agency and capacity to act
Partnership	• Viewed as a means to an end • Results and outcomes focus • Emphasis on robust structures • Evaluation and measurement	• Viewed as an end in itself • Relational and values focus • Emphasis on embedding results and processes • Reviewing and learning

A pragmatic view of sustainability highlights the need for joint action by countries, organisations and citizens in order to achieve the targets of the UN 2030 Sustainable Development Agenda, often through structured

28. Pascual, U., Balvanera, P., Díaz, S., et al. (2017) Valuing nature's contributions to people: the IPBES approach. *Current Opinion in Environmental Sustainability*, 26, pp. 7–16. http://dx.doi.org/10.1016/j.cosust.2016.12.006 (p. 9).
29. Sen, A. (2004) Why we should preserve the spotted owl. *London Review of Books*, 26 (3): 5).
30. Alexander, J. and Conrad, A. (2022) *Citizens*, Kingston-upon-Thames, UK: Canbury Press.

collaborative arrangements. The focus here is primarily on ensuring that "fit for purpose" constructs are in place that demonstrate results and impact, often in quantitative terms. A "steering" type of "metagovernance" or "higher-level decision-making"[31] that oversees sustainability in a systematic manner also sits within this categorisation. At a more reflective level, meanwhile, and beyond the 2030 Agenda, consideration of "alternative futures" and diverse "ideals of sustainable development"[32] is prevalent. The nature and depth of change are also of concern, particularly in the face of natural resource constraints that conflict with the continuation of a development model based on economic growth and consumerism. Metagovernance here is about providing an overarching framework that facilitates and nurtures sustainable approaches. Attention is also given to process and relationship-building elements, including ethical principles and values.

Box 7.1 Transformation, the SDG Agenda and Goal 17

Interest in sustainability, citizenship and partnership has undoubtedly been given a boost by the United Nations (UN) Agenda for 2030 and its 17 Sustainable Development Goals (SDGs). Building upon the perceived success of the global development framework adopted by the Millennium Development Goals (MDGs) between 2000 and 2015, the SDG Agenda provides a global framework for transforming our planet through collective action that is committed to the fostering of "intercultural understanding, tolerance, mutual respect and an ethic of global citizenship and shared responsibility."[33] The Agenda also addresses the three pillars of sustainable development; social, environmental and economic, in a "profound," "interconnected" and cohesive manner with a call for urgent and transformational action by all countries and stakeholders to ensure that "no one will be left behind."[34]

In view of this focus, SDG 17, which has a special focus on "Partnerships for the Goals," might have been expected to provide a strong steer on how collaborative action and stakeholder participation, including citizen

31. See, for example, Beisheim, M. and Simon, N. (2015) Meta-governance of partnerships for sustainable development, actors' perspectives on how the UN could improve partnerships' governance services in areas of limited statehood. *SFB-Governance Working Paper Series*, No.69, Berlin: Collaborative Research Center (SFB); Beisheim, M. and Simon, N. (2016) Multi-stakeholder partnerships for implementing the 2030 agenda improving accountability and transparency. *Paper prepared for the 2016 ECOSOC Partnership Forum*. http://dx.doi.org/10.2139/ssrn.2767464, and Horan, D. (2019) A new approach to partnerships for SDG transformations. *Sustainability*, 11: 4947. doi:10.3390/su11184947
32. Sneddon, C., Howarth, R.B. and Norgaard, R.B. (2006) Sustainable development in a post-Brundtland world. *Ecological Economics*, 57: 253–268. https://doi.org/10.1016/j.ecolecon.2005.04.013 (p. 265).
33. UN (2015) *Transforming Our World: The 2030 Agenda for Sustainable Development*. Resolution 70/1 Adopted by the United Nations General Assembly on 25 September 2015. 2015.
34. Ibid., p. 1.

engagement, could promote transformation.[35] However, the goal focuses primarily on improving international development cooperation in the areas of finance, technology, trade, capacity-building, policy coherence, partnerships and data. A government-led Global Partnership for Sustainable Development is proposed for strengthening international cooperation and development assistance with support from richer "developed" countries to "developing" and "least developed" countries through increased aid; assistance with long-term debt; technology transfer and support for a universal, fair and open trading system under the World Trade Organisation. Meanwhile, multi-stakeholder partnerships working at global, regional, national and sub-national levels are positioned in a cluster of systemic issues such as policy and institutional coherence and data, monitoring and accountability that need to be "enhanced" to support the achievement of the SDGs, particularly in "developing countries," in order to mobilise and share knowledge, expertise, technology and financial resources to support the implementation of the SDGs.[36]

As well as marginalising the role that partnership can play in supporting a multi-dimensional view of sustainability, SDG 17 has been criticised for endorsing a much-contested "neoliberal capitalist approach to development" that is likely to deepen rather than reduce social and environmental problems.[37] The promotion of Official Development Assistance (ODA) from "providers" to "recipients"[38] and inadequate mechanisms for holding rich and powerful actors such as governments, large corporations and financial institutions to account for the delivery of the targets are also viewed as demonstrating an unwillingness to challenge "status quo politics and existing power relations."[39] Within this framework, multi-stakeholder partnerships are depicted as instrumental mechanisms at the service of donor relationships. Moreover, the inclusion of public-private partnership within the category of multi-stakeholder partnerships does not reflect the broad and inclusive collaborative approach that ostensibly underpins the 2030 Agenda.[40]

35. Stott, L. and Scoppetta, A. (2020) Partnerships for the goals: Beyond SDG17, *Revista Diecisiete: Investigación interdisciplinar para los Objetivos de Desarrollo*, 2, 29–38. http://dx.doi.org/10.36852/2695-4427_2020_02.02
36. UN (2015) Op. cit. p. 27.
37. Schleicher, J., Schaafsma, M. and Vira, B. (2018) Will the sustainable development goals address the links between poverty and the natural environment? *Current Opinion in Environmental Sustainability*, 34: 43–47. https://doi.org/10.1016/J.COSUST.2018.09.004 (p. 46).
38. Mahn, T. C. (2017) Accountability for development cooperation under the 2030 Agenda. *Discussion Paper*, No. 10, Deutsches Institut für Entwicklungspolitik (DIE), Bonn (pp. 12–13).
39. Gupta, J. and Vegelin, C. (2016) Sustainable development goals and inclusive development. *International Environmental Agreements*, 16: 433–448. https://doi.org/10.1007/s10784-016-9323-z (p. 444).
40. Meuleman, L., Strandenaes, J.G. and Niestroy, I. (2016) From PPP to ABC: A new partnership approach for the SDGs. *IISD, SDG Knowledge Hub*. http://sdg.iisd.org/commentary/guest-articles/from-ppp-to-abc-a-new-partnership-approach-for-the-sdgs/ (accessed November 1, 2021).

The idea of citizenship as focused principally on governance and openings for citizens to participate in decision-making processes alongside the state is pragmatic in outlook and reinforced by calls for participatory democracy and the empowerment of citizens. At a more reflective level, however, a view of global citizenship that embraces humankind's stewardship of the planet may be proposed, alongside an understanding of citizen engagement as contributing to human well-being and improved quality of life.[41] Elinor Ostrom's arguments for the inclusion of affected individuals in the making of rules about resources as critical for sustainable human-environment systems sit well here.[42] Rather than relying solely upon a government lead, this view encompasses the idea that accountability should be collective, with all stakeholders assuming responsibility for improving society and contributing to the welfare of the planet. Beyond simple acknowledgement of agency, this involves deep recognition of the capacity that citizens have to take an active role in shaping their lives. In this regard, the idea of *participatory democracy* is enhanced by the concept of *deliberative democracy* in which citizens are encouraged to engage in processes of meaningful deliberation to enable improved decision-making that, in turn, informs action and change.[43]

Partnership may also be construed in both pragmatic and reflective terms. At a pragmatic level, the multi-stakeholder collaboration that it embraces is based on structures involving different groupings of organisations that have a strong focus on results and impact. A more reflective understanding, meanwhile, recognises partnership as an ongoing relationship between individuals and organisations that can add value at different levels. A richer appreciation of the intrinsic and relational value of working in partnership may be viewed as promoting a deeper understanding of the transformations required for sustainability, thus assisting a movement away from "linear one-way relationships of pure extraction" to "systems that are circular and reciprocal."[44]

Catalysing transformation across the three spheres

While pragmatic views of the concepts of partnership, sustainability and citizenship are clearly important, particularly in providing strong directives for action, lasting change to structures, systems and mindsets requires a more radical *transformative* "push." Among the writers and thinkers who have called for such a boost is Mariana Mazzucato, whose recipe for "rethinking capitalism" includes reconsideration of the role and capacities of government and

41. GCPSE and UNDP (2016) *Citizen Engagement in Public Service Delivery: The Critical Role of Public Officials*, Singapore: UNDP Global Centre for Public Service Excellence (p. 4).
42. Ostrom, E. (1990) *Governing the Commons, The Evolution of Institutions for Collective Action*, Cambridge UK: Cambridge University Press.
43. OECD (2020) Op. cit.
44. Klein, N. (2014) *This Changes Everything: Capitalism vs the Climate*, London, UK: Allen Lane (p. 446).

engagement in more ambitious partnership arrangements.[45] Naomi Klein takes this a step further in her book *This Changes Everything, Capitalism vs Climate*, where she calls for "an alternative worldview" that is "embedded in interdependence rather than hyper-individualism, reciprocity rather than dominance, and cooperation rather than hierarchy."[46] These sentiments are echoed by Riane Eisler in her call for a more caring economics that embraces "the life-supporting activities of households, communities and nature."[47]

In order to promote this "rethinking" and the co-creation of a bolder vision of what the future might be, concerted endeavours need to be made to integrate the more reflective elements that sustainability, citizenship and partnership embrace at individual, organisational and societal levels. In this way, efforts to promote systems change are more likely to be consolidated.[48] To do this, it is useful, for example, to think beyond the SDGs and the limitations of Goal 17 to a more rounded view of the potential that multidimensional and multilevel relationships offer with regard to sustainability. An understanding that the *process* of building collaborative relationships may offer lasting benefits is central to this.

The wide range of individual and collective shifts required to promote transformation and "lead from the emerging future"[49] may be located under the banner of what Frank Biermann has described as "earth system governance"; a system that aims to achieve Brundtland's vision of sustainable development by involving actors from different sectors of society in decision-making processes "in order to influence the co-evolution of human and natural systems in a way that secures the sustainable development of human society."[50] Within the vision for this overarching system, three overlapping collaborative tendencies are of interest; the adoption of nexus approaches to sustainability; an overarching "metagovernance" that facilitates as well as steers partnership arrangements promoting sustainability, and the promotion of forms of deliberative decision-making that involve different groups of citizens.

Nexus approaches to sustainability

An integrated and holistic approach to sustainable development requires cohesion across the social, economic and environmental pillars of sustainability.

45. Mazzucato (2021) Op. cit.
46. Klein (2014) Op. cit. p. 262.
47. Eisler, R. (2008) *The Real Wealth of Nations, Creating a Caring Economics*, Oakland, CA, USA: Berrett-Koehler Publishers, Ind (p. 3).
48. Seitanidi, M.M. and Crane, A. (2009) Implementing CSR through partnerships: Understanding the selection, design and institutionalisation of nonprofit-business partnerships. *Journal of Business Ethics*, 85: 413–429. https://doi.org/10.1007/s10551-008-9743-y (pp. 421–422).
49. Scharmer and Kaufer (2013) Op. cit.
50. Biermann, F. (2007) Earth system governance as a crosscutting theme of global change research. *Global Environmental Change*, 17: 326–337. https://doi.org/10.1016/j.gloenvcha.2006.11.010 (p. 329).

Rather than silo approaches, arrangements working to support sustainability thus require a "nexus approach" in which multiple problems and policy domains connect.[51] Greater attention to these bonds has been recommended for the implementation of the SDG 2030 Agenda with calls for new forms of "cross-sectoral institutionalisation" to support the sectoral focus of the goals.[52] SDG interconnections have also been called for across fields such as finance, agriculture, energy, technology and transport; among societal actors such as local authorities, government agencies, the private sector and civil society, and between and among low-, medium- and high-income countries.[53] A nexus approach for sustainability, both for the SDGs and beyond, will further require the joining up of initiatives operating at organisational and administrative levels (global, regional, national and local). The promotion of more robust linkages between policy and practice so that projects, programmes and policies mutually inform one another is also crucial.

Joyeeta Gupta and Courtney Vegelin believe that a nexus approach to the SDGs must incorporate principles that support social, environmental and relational inclusiveness in order to address the "multi-level drivers of inequality, exclusion and vulnerability."[54] In order to enhance possibilities for inclusive development, the authors underscore the importance of engaging with different actors to question and confront "business as usual" approaches and address the power relations inherent in these. Here we return to the integration of a reflective element in interactions between stakeholders and citizens which allows spaces for contesting, debating and reflecting upon options for the future of the planet. The interplay between individual, organisational and societal contexts is crucial to this as, when they incorporate a strong reflective element, these mutually reinforcing linkages may enable new ways of working to emerge, develop and become consolidated.

Flexible partnership metagovernance

A central premise of the more "radical transformation" proposed earlier is that sustainability, citizenship and partnership do not operate in a vacuum, and that an overarching global framework is needed for their interrelationship to work well and have a lasting impact. In response to this, a number of authors have proposed some form of metagovernance for partnership arrangements working

51. Boas, I., Biermann, F. and Kanie, N. (2016) Cross-sectoral strategies in global sustainability governance: Towards a nexus approach. *International Environmental Agreements*, 16: 449–464. https://doi.org/10.1007/s10784-016-9321-1 (p. 455).
52. Ibid.
53. Stafford-Smith, M., Griggs, D., Gaffney, O., Ullah, F., Reyers, B., Kanie, N., Stigson, B., Shrivastava, P., Leach, M. and O'Connell, D. (2017) Integration: The key to implementing the sustainable development goals. *Sustainability Science and Implementing the Sustainable Development Goals*, 12: 911–919. https://doi.org/10.1007/s11625-016-0383-3 (p. 212).
54. Gupta and Vegelin (2016) Op. cit. p. 433.

to meet the targets of the SDGs.[55] Metagovernance, which has been described as "the governance of governance,"[56] is used here to refer to "higher-level rules" such as principles and norms, as well as institutions, that might collectively guide, steer and coordinate "the partnership system"[57] so that partnership arrangements are more effective, inclusive and transformative.[58]

In line with Bourgon's argument that an overarching framework for collective decision-making to address "wicked" problems must be provided by the state, there appears to be general agreement that metagovernance for SDG partnership arrangements should be overseen by government either under the auspices of the UN[59] or through different state mechanisms. The premise here is that "only governments have the resources, decision tools and legitimacy to mobilize stakeholders at a scale necessary for transformation."[60] This, as Bourgon argues, is not an authoritarian function, but rather one that is based on encouraging an enabling environment in which different societal actors are able to participate and engage in promoting changes to goods, services and policies.[61]

While a state-supported framework that involves other actors in efforts to meet sustainability goals such as the SDGs[62] may sound attractive, there are some caveats to this. First, a government lead raises questions about how far the public sector is likely to operate in a networked manner, particularly in strongly hierarchical or non-democratic states. Second, as mentioned earlier, concerted efforts are needed to manage the integration of collaborative sustainability efforts within and between different spatial, administrative and institutional levels in different contexts. Third, and in line with Ostrom's reflections on "governing the commons," careful attention needs to be paid to solutions for protecting natural resource systems that have been developed and managed by communities in situ.[63] A key question, then, is how to ensure a partnership metagovernance that promotes common principles while also acknowledging the existence of distinct pathways to achieve them at different levels in diverse locations.[64]

55. See Beisheim and Simon (2015); Beisheim and Simon (2016) and Horan (2019) Op. cit.
56. Jessop, B. (2003) Governance, governance failure, and meta-governance. *Paper Presented at Policies, Governance and Innovation for Rural Areas. International Seminar*, 21–23 November, Sicily: Università della Calabria, Arcavacata di Rende (p. 13).
57. See Beisheim and Simon (2015); Beisheim and Simon (2016) and Horan (2019) Op. cit.
58. Beisheim, M. and Simon, N. (2018) Multistakeholder partnerships for the SDGs: Actors' view on UN metagovernance. *Global Governance*, 24, 497–515. http://dx.doi.org/10.1163/19426720-02404003 (p. 500).
59. Ibid.
60. Horan (2019) Op. cit. p. 13.
61. Civil Service College Singapore (2017) Op. cit.
62. GCPSE and UNDP (2016) Op. cit.
63. Ostrom. E. (1990) Op. cit.
64. Meuleman, L. and Niestroy, I. (2015) Common but differentiated governance: A metagovernance approach to make the SDGs work. *Sustainability*, 7: 12295–12321. doi:10.3390/su70912295

To address these concerns, it is helpful to look again at the idea of partnership as integrating both pragmatic and reflective elements and the assumption that, for the achievement of transformation, more attention to the latter is required. Thus, while metagovernance clearly encompasses a "technocratic" and instrumental approach in its adherence to meeting concrete goals and principles, it will also require the deliberate cultivation of what Bob Jessop describes as "reflexive self-organization," flexible responses involving ongoing processes of dialogue among different actors that develop and refine goals, planned outcomes and the processes by which to achieve them.[65]

Beisheim and Simon mirror this need for both pragmatic and reflective dimensions in their call for a partnership metagovernance that is both ensuring and enabling.[66] Ensuring metagovernance, they assert, implies systematic oversight of partnership arrangements so that they are formalised and accountable with "binding rules of conduct." Enabling metagovernance, on the other hand, involves supporting and encouraging the development of partnership initiatives through knowledge-sharing, capacity-building and access to different resources, including funding and networks. These two approaches may be described as one that "steers" and one that "facilitates" different partnership schemes.

Although "common but differentiated governance"[67] for partnership arrangements that focus on sustainability will require some form of steering or shaping, the nature of collaboration and the links between different actors and levels indicate that more dedicated attention to nurturing and facilitating collaborative approaches and processes is essential. This enabling function has been mentioned most particularly in relation to connecting local collaborative initiatives with global frameworks.[68] For some, this implies the need for a bottom-up partnership governance system using, for example, national platforms or community committees.[69] Others, while acknowledging that a bottom-up approach is vital to the development of partnership arrangements for the SDGs, believe that the achievement of transformation will depend on complementing this with a top-down governance approach.[70] David Horan, for example, suggests that a coalition of governments and other stakeholders promoting the SDGs could provide a multi-level framework for transformational partnership arrangements.[71] Transformation will thus depend upon different social actors working together to assume "collective and interlinked accountability" for the SDG Agenda as well as future

65. Jessop, B. (2011) Metagovernance. In: Bevir, M. ed. *The Sage Handbook of Governance*. London, UK: Sage, pp. 106–124.
66. Beisheim and Simon (2015) Op. cit. pp. 10–11.
67. Meuleman and Niestroy (2015) Op. cit.
68. Ibid., p. 6.
69. Beisheim and Simon (2015) Op. cit. p. 23.
70. Horan (2019) Op. cit. p. 16.
71. Ibid.

sustainability efforts.[72] In this way, complex challenges will be addressed in a joined-up rather than "incremental or piecemeal" manner.[73] Such concerted collective action, in which all stakeholders involved are fully confident of progress towards a common goal may, it has been argued, also minimise free rider problems and the possibility that, while benefiting from a collaborative initiative some stakeholders will refrain from full or active involvement to support them.[74]

Beyond a "whole of government" approach that promotes policy coherence for the achievement of sustainability targets, a multi-level metagovernance framework for partnership will rest upon a "whole of society" approach that fosters and enables the active engagement of diverse stakeholders so that they form an integral part of both the SDG agenda and sustainability approaches going forwards.[75] Within this scenario, creative and tailor-made approaches in different contexts may include a role for NGOs and CSOs as well as broader collaborative networks, communities of practice and social movements in holding governments to account for the delivery of sustainable development targets.[76]

Deliberative decision-making

Although efforts to foster collaborative governance often minimise a role for citizens,[77] it is clear that they are central to both addressing complex problems and promoting collective accountability for sustainable development.[78] Here, as Sen again reminds us, the relevance of citizenship is not

72. Mahn, T.C. (2017) Accountability for development cooperation under the 2030 Agenda. *Discussion Paper*, No. 10, Deutsches Institut für Entwicklungspolitik (DIE), Bonn, Germany (pp. 27–28).
73. Lee, J.Y. and Waddock, S. (2021) How transformation catalysts take catalytic action. *Sustainability*, 13: 9813. https://doi.org/10.3390/su13179813
74. Bowen, K.J., Cradock-Henry, N.A., Koch, F., Patterson, J., Häyhä, T., Vogt, J. and Barbi, F. (2017) Implementing the "Sustainable Development Goals": towards addressing three key governance challenges – collective action, trade-offs, and accountability, *Current Opinion in Environmental Sustainability* 26–27:90–96. https://doi.org/10.1016/j.cosust.2017.05.002 (p. 93)
75. Gornitzka, C.P. and Pipa, A.F. (2018) *A New Type of Leadership From National Governments Is Essential for Success of the SDGs*. Washington, DC, USA: The Brookings Institution.
76. Bowen et al. (2017) Op. cit. and Gupta and Vegelin (2016) Op. cit. p. 445.
77. Gupta and Vegelin (2016) Op. cit.
78. See Fong, A. (2015) putting the public back into governance: The challenges of citizen participation and its future. *Public Administration Review*, 75 (4): 513–522. www.jstor.org/stable/24757808 Fong argues that "Citizens can make several important contributions to solving wicked problems. First, citizens can help frame the particular problem in more accurate and viable ways than professionals acting alone. Second, when decisions involve important ethical or material trade-offs, citizens may be best placed to adjudicate those trade-offs. Third, citizens, who are often most affected by efforts to address public problems, are well placed to provide information relevant to devising solutions and evaluating implementation. Finally, citizens can sometimes become directly engaged in solving public problems and thus contribute additional resources through coproduction" (p. 5).

just instrumental but forms an important part of the notion of sustainability promoted by Brundtland; "one that sees them as agents whose freedoms matter, not just as patients who are no more than their living standards."[79]

Sen's words are endorsed by those who insist that integrated development strategies rely upon local level, place-based participative approaches that include formal and informal groupings of local actors and citizens.[80] Thus, as well as ensuring collective problem-solving and reinforcing the "leave no one behind" principle at the heart of the SDG agenda, the engagement of citizens' groups can support the development of new ideas and ways of working.[81] It has also been noted that civil society representatives may assist in addressing entrenched power relations and integrating the economic, social and environmental pillars of Agenda 2030 and sustainable development more broadly.[82] In this regard, Biermann notes that "earth systems governance" will depend upon finding ways to ensure that civil society participation is encouraged at all levels and that a new kind of "democratic governance beyond the nation state" is able to demonstrate accountability, legitimacy and fairness to all.[83]

While civil society involvement in grassroots activity is broad and may include initiatives such as large-scale network engagement, digital democracy and adjustments to political parties,[84] the growth of citizen-based initiatives is of particular interest here. Arrangements such as citizens' assemblies, citizens juries and panels, civic dialogues, advisory councils, stakeholder meetings, public hearings, participatory budgeting, focus groups and citizens surveys, among others[85] appear to indicate that a "deliberative wave" is taking place in which citizens are engaging with public authorities through "facilitated collaboration."[86] As these initiatives are numerous and varied caution has been expressed about trying to group and classify them, particularly as so many of them are experimental and take place at the local or micro level.[87] However, central to the "deliberative wave" is the notion of "informed participation"[88] in which diverse actors are encouraged to participate in decision-making through well-planned "deliberative systems."[89] Beyond simply

79. Sen (2002) Op. cit. p. 5.
80. Stott, L. (2018) Review of the European Code of Conduct on Partnership (ECCP). *Technical Dossier No.* 7, Brussels, Belgium: DG Employment, Social Affairs and Inclusion (pp. 20–21).
81. Gornitzka and Pipa (2018) Op. cit.
82. Gupta and Vegelin (2016) Op. cit. pp. 444–445.
83. Biermann (2007) Op. cit. p. 335.
84. Youngs, R. (2021) It's not all about populism: Grassroots democracy is thriving across Europe. *The Guardian*, September 16. www.theguardian.com/world/commentisfree/2021/sep/16/populism-grassroots-democracy-thriving-europe (accessed March 23, 20202).
85. Papadopoulos, Y. (2012) On the embeddedness of deliberative systems: Why elitist innovations matter more. In: Parkison, J. and Mansbridge, J. eds. *Deliberative Systems: Deliberative Democracy at the Large Scale*, Cambridge, UK: Cambridge University Press (p. 125).
86. OECD (2020) Op. cit.
87. Papadopoulos (2012) Op. cit. p. 125.
88. Sen (2002) Op. cit. p. 4.
89. Horan (2019) Op. cit. p. 15.

being empowered to participate, deliberative democracy is centred upon carefully managed processes of discussion and debate between citizens and other stakeholders which may serve as the basis for changing policies, norms and practices.[90]

As well as the effort required to break silos and involve citizens as key decision-makers, questions about the ability of public agencies to relinquish "control" by granting greater rights to citizens in the development of new models[91] imply that deeper coalescence among the broad and disparate range of "small-scale democracy initiatives" is needed to ensure a stronger and more transformational political agenda.[92] Alexander's reminder that democracy is supposed to be "government by Citizens not government of Citizens" and his exhortation that citizens should step up and shape the world is also of relevance here.[93]

A belief that citizens can reshape society by collectively drawing upon their capacities for collaboration, capability and creativity[94] is complemented by the philosopher Martha Nussbaum's affirmation that citizenship in a pluralistic, democratic society enmeshed in a globalised world is dependent upon "the ability to see oneself as a member of a heterogeneous nation and world."[95] She links this to the need for an education that cultivates the capacity for self-criticism, critical thinking and reasoning, and the ability to empathise by being an intelligent reader of the story of others. This brings us back, once again, to Ryszard Kapuściński's conviction that how we relate to others is what defines our humanity. Human interchange, Kapuściński insists, demands recognition that "the other" is not fixed or still but, instead, moveable and dynamic in relation to context, time, expectation, mood and stage of life. As a result, every encounter with another person is an "enigma."[96] The courage to engage with the "unknown" and discover common aims and values is at the heart of sustainability, citizenship and partnership, and essential for co-creating the future.

90. Ercan, S.A. and Dryzek, J.S. (2015) The reach of deliberative democracy. *Policy Studies*, 36 (3): 241–248. https://doi.org/10.1080/01442872.2015.1065969
91. See Kleinhans, R. (2017) False Promises of co-production in neighbourhood regeneration: The case of Dutch community enterprises. *Public Management Review*, 19 (10): 1500–1518. https://doi.org/10.1080/14719037.2017.1287941 (p. 1514).
92. Youngs (2020) Op. cit.
93. See https://medium.com/new-citizenship-project/subject-consumer-or-citizen-three-post-covid-futures-8c3cc469a984 and see also www.jonalexander.net/the-idea (both accessed March 23, 2020).
94. Ibid.
95. Nussbaum, M. (2007) Cultivating humanity and world citizenship. Excerpted from *Forum Futures* 2007, Cambridge, MA, USA: Forum for the Future of Higher Education (pp. 38–39).
96. Kapuściński, R. (2018) *The Other*, London, UK: Verso (pp. 14–15).

Afterword

This book has sought to refresh standard views of partnership and its potential for transformation in several ways: first, by endorsing a stronger blending of academic and practitioner perspectives; second, by encouraging a deeper exploration of how partnership is understood and implemented in context; third, by transcending traditional categorisations, particularly those that link partnership exclusively to collaboration with the private sector and a capitalist development model and fourth, by advocating for a balance between pragmatic and reflective dimensions of partnership, with emphasis on deeper integration of the latter in both the theory and practice of partnership.

In the introduction, I noted that although an enormous amount of research has been undertaken on diverse forms of collaboration to address pressing issues and challenges, much of it is difficult to locate because of its dispersed nature. Thus, as well as conducting new research using more diverse tools and methodologies, accessing existing information on partnership experiences through dynamic and imaginative exchanges of learning between academics and practitioners is recommended. Such efforts will do much to assist further exploration of the realities beneath the rhetoric of partnership and contribute to a deeper understanding of how, and under what circumstances, working in this way might promote positive socio-ecological change.

More robust and inventive ways of capturing partnership stories and experiences in different contexts are central to ensuring a deeper appreciation of the transformational prospects for partnership. Explorations that focus on the "chemistry" of collaboration and interaction between different individual and organisational layers in diverse operational settings are an important part of this. These approaches also demand that traditional views of partnership are superseded by a broader appreciation of multi-stakeholder collaboration and what it might offer. Here, while a conceptualisation of partnership that focuses on managerialism and collaboration with the private sector still has traction, the possibility of a more transversal and inclusive kind of partnering that pursues a vision of society that is more ecological, equitable and progressive also needs to be acknowledged. This latter view is evidenced by the emergence of new and innovative collaborative models and tendencies

DOI: 10.4324/9781003199434-9

as well as calls for more meaningful forms of participation and collaboration in discourses relating to sustainability and citizenship. The positioning of a richer view of partnership will, I have argued, depend on efforts to integrate more reflective dimensions into conceptions of partnership, both in theory and in practice. Such an endeavour will also require the courage to challenge and contest standard ways of doing things through processes of deliberation and productive conflict that enhance opportunities for transforming structures, systems, routines and behaviours.

Drawing upon and learning more deeply from the wisdom of both the distant and recent past can do much to stimulate a more profound reflection on the promise of partnership. In writing this book, I have come back repeatedly to the work of well-known writers and thinkers who have provided important insights into perspectives of development, sustainability and the participatory processes that inform different understanding of partnership. The views of individuals such as Robert Chambers, Riane Eisler, Ryszard Kapuściński, Dennis Meadows, Martha Nussbaum, Elinor Ostrom, E.F. Schumacher, Amartya Sen and Richard Sennett, among others, point to the importance of acknowledging that meaningful deliberation and critical thinking are central to the pursuit of positive transformation and the collaborative processes that support this. Of greater significance, however, is the sensitivity of these writers to the human connections that inform the world we live in. The transformational potential of multi-stakeholder collaboration, we are reminded, depends fundamentally upon constructive relationships between people.

Index

Note: Page numbers in italics indicate a figure and page numbers in bold indicate a table on the corresponding page. Page numbers followed by "n" indicate a note.